The Artist in the Machine

Also by Arthur I. Miller

Colliding Worlds: How Cutting-Edge Science Is Redefining Contemporary Art
137: Jung, Pauli, and the Pursuit of a Scientific Obsession
Empire of the Stars: Friendship, Obsession and Betrayal in the Quest for Black Holes
Einstein, Picasso: Space, Time, and the Beauty That Causes Havoc
Insights of Genius: Imagery and Creativity in Science and Art
Imagery in Scientific Thought: Creating 20th-Century Physics

The Artist in the Machine

The World of AI-Powered Creativity

Arthur I. Miller

The MIT Press
Cambridge, Massachusetts
London, England

This book was set in Stone Serif and Stone Sans by Westchester Publishing Services. Printed and bound in the United States of America.

Library of Congress Cataloging-in-Publication Data

Title: The artist in the machine : the world of AI-powered creativity / Arthur I. Miller.
Description: Cambridge, MA : The MIT Press, 2019. | Includes bibliographical references and index.
Identifiers: LCCN 2018059352 | ISBN 9780262042857 (hardcover : alk. paper)
Subjects: LCSH: Art and computers. | Creative ability. | Computer art.
Classification: LCC NX180.C66 M55 2019 | DDC 776--dc23
LC record available at https://lccn.loc.gov/2018059352

ISBN: 978-0-262-04285-7

10   9   8   7   6   5   4   3   2   1

For Lesley, as always

Contents

Illustrations

The best way to predict the future is to invent it.

—Alan Kay

Preface

I've always been fascinated by creativity: what it is, how it works, what happens at the moment of inspiration. The many thrilling developments in AI that we are hearing about have cast creativity in an entirely new light. I feel the time has come to put down my thoughts, bringing together creativity and machines, the culmination of much that I've been thinking about for many years.

My interest in creativity began a long time ago, when I was a boy growing up in the Bronx. I was one of those students who fell through the net of the New York educational system. Raised in a somewhat dysfunctional household, I did poorly in IQ tests when I was eight or nine and suffered for this throughout my entire public school education, assigned to classes with subpar teachers and uninterested students. The only upside for me was that the classwork was so trivial that I had a lot of time for other pursuits.

I escaped through books. I became a voracious reader and frequented the local public library, which in those days was a magisterial building chockfull of books. It also had an ample supply of records. Always interested in drawing, one day I was struck by an album cover that showed an interesting sketch of a man deep in thought. Although I had never heard of the composer, I borrowed it. It was Tchaikovsky's Fifth Symphony. It blew me away. I had never heard anything like it. I began to work my way back in time, and the further back I went the more amazed I was at what I was hearing. Then I discovered Bach. My first thought was, how did these people dream up music like that? I became hooked on creativity.

But at that time, if you were smart, or thought you were, you studied physics. I did so and enjoyed the intellectual challenges. I studied at CCNY and MIT and then began research. But my heart was never really in it. My passion lay elsewhere—in creativity: what it is, where it comes from. I've always refused to believe that it is a mystery.

So I turned my attention to the history and philosophy of science. Reading the original German-language papers on relativity theory and quantum physics, one thing that leapt out was the importance of visual imagery in creativity in science. Along the way it had become clear to me that aesthetics and beauty were also key ingredients in the creative process. These of course are part and parcel of artistic creativity, and this in turn led me to study the relationship between creativity in art and creativity in science. I concluded that at the nascent moment of creativity, the moment of inspiration, boundaries blur between artist and scientist. Both think along the same conceptual lines.

My work on the role visual images play in creative thinking led me to look into cognitive science, to study how images are formed and then stored in the brain. At the time, cognitive scientists were discussing the so-called imagery controversy. The issue was whether images actually affect thought or are merely epiphenomena. I, of course, was and am convinced that images do affect thought. The crucial argument for those of us in the proimagery faction was that if images really do play a role in thinking, then how does the brain store and manipulate them? It helps to compare the brain to a computer, to think of the brain as being akin to an information-processing system. I was fascinated by this idea and thus also by the question of whether computers can help us understand creativity too.

Over the following years, I wrote a great deal on human creativity and also touched on machine creativity. In this book I look at the two creativities together and ask: What is creativity? Can computers be creative? Can computers create art, literature, and music? What will a computer's creativity be like? And, for that matter, what will a creative computer be like?

One topic I do not intend to discuss in any detail is the many dystopian scenarios that surround AI. Every panel on AI that I've sat on or witnessed tends to focus on dystopian scenarios, the downside of AI. It is a theme of many movies and features prominently in newspapers. Shelves in bookstores sag with the weight of doom and gloom tomes. The public loves it.

In this book, I explore the upside of AI: its cultural side, what its creativity holds in store. I hope that this book will show how creativity can amaze, inspire, and open new vistas, as it did for me one day long ago in a New York public library.

Arthur I. Miller

Emeritus Professor
University College London, 2019
http://www.arthurimiller.com
http://www.collidingworlds.org

Where to look and listen

If you'd like to see the art and hear the music discussed in these pages, my website www.artistinthemachine.net brings alive the URLs cited and much more.

Introduction

In principle, because the brain obeys the laws of physics, computers can do anything the brain can do.
—Murray Shanahan[1]

The brain is just a computer like any other. ... Traits previously considered innate to humans—imagination, creativity, even consciousness—may be just the equivalent of software programs.
—Demis Hassabis[2]

The time when humans can have meaningful conversation with an AI has always seemed far off and the stuff of science fiction. But for Go players that day is here.
—Andy Okun[3]

Will computers ever think like us? Could they ever have flashes of inspiration like we do or come up with mad ideas? Could they invent something no one ever thought of before and never thought was needed? Could they dream up the plays of Shakespeare?

Or do they need to? Perhaps they will function in totally other ways than human beings, come up with ideas just as great or solutions just as effective but different from the ones we would come up with.

This book strives to look into such questions. It is about creativity in the age of machines—our creativity and their creativity.

What do we mean when we talk about being creative? Is it that flash of inspiration when we suddenly think up something new—a melody, a poem—that no one has ever thought of before? That eureka moment, like Archimedes in the bath, when we suddenly see the solution to a knotty problem with blinding clarity? Is it the creating of something from nothing,

like a novelist dreaming up a story or some outrageous science fiction scenario? Is this what it means for human beings to be creative?

Today we are rapidly developing ever more sophisticated machines,
computers that can think. Perhaps one day soon machines will be able to
think like us. Or will they evolve in a totally different direction? Will they
think differently from us, function differently from us? Will computers too
be able to be creative? In this day and age, we are going to have to rethink
what we mean by thinking and what we mean by creativity.

Imagine a world in which machines produce bold new works of art and
music, discover scientific theories, write stories, make business decisions,
tell jokes, or function as the brain that operates a robot. Imagine an AI as
the next James Dyson, dreaming up a whole new generation of vacuum
cleaners. What will this mean for the future of our jobs? Perhaps the next
Turner Prize winner might be a machine, or the next Pulitzer Prize winner, or the next Frank Gehry, whose creative projects already rely a great
deal on computing. Imagine if the next Keats was a computer, or the next
Beethoven. Suppose the next legendary chef was a computer, or the next
stand-up comic. In the future, might your lover or your new best friend—or
your therapist—be a robot? And what place will humans occupy in this
brave new world?

Can humans and robots exist side by side? Will machines' intelligence
surpass ours? And what will this mean for the future of the human race?

To find answers to these and many other questions, I've gone to the
experts. I've interviewed scientists working on frontier problems in computer thinking to find out what the latest developments are, what might
be possible in future, and what problems could arise. I have focused on key
players who are developing AI that creates art, literature, and music. All of
them are doing extraordinary work, pushing forward the frontiers. And all
have insights to impart.

Tony Veale of University College Dublin claims that "the question of
whether computers are truly creative will fade away as people value the
results."[4] Ian Goodfellow of Google, inventor of the groundbreaking generative adversarial networks (GANs), asserts that "machines are already
creative."[5] Gerfried Stocker of Ars Electronica suggests that "we might
need machines to create art as a way of communicating with them and
understanding them."[6] But Allison Parish of NYU demurs: "I'm going to

be a hardliner and say that computers cannot be creative."[7] Hod Lipson of
Columbia University says that "the more intelligent AI becomes, the more
sophisticated its art will be."[8] Kevin Warwick of Coventry University studies
cyborgs. He says, "Creativity in machines is there, whether we humans
understand it or not. If we can figure out how memory works, then chips
will go beyond memory, and will improve our creativity enormously."[9]
Douglas Eck of Google tells me, "Technology is special because it gives us
AI, and AI may create things so beautiful that we may care differently about
them."[10] Murray Shanahan of Imperial College in London was the technical
adviser on the film *Ex Machina*. He states emphatically, "In principle, because
the brain obeys the laws of physics, computers can do anything the brain
can do."[11] Blaise Agüera y Arcas of Google says provocatively, "When we do
art with machines I don't think there is a very strict boundary between
what is human and what is machine."[12]

*   *   *

Very often, the greatest discoveries are of things we never realized we needed.
It's not so much a question of solving a problem as of seeing a problem that
no one else had even known was there. Take Chester Carlson, for example.

Chester Carlson was an affable-looking thirty-two-year-old with a degree
in physics and a restless imagination. He had held a series of low-level scientific jobs, but he was bored. So he decided to try law school. But he was
so broke that he couldn't afford books and spent his time sitting in libraries,
copying passages of text. "There should be some way of making copies,"
he thought. There were duplicating machines, but that involved making a
master copy first, a complex and time-consuming process. Working in his
tiny kitchen in New York City, in 1938, Carlson built a device that could
copy a document onto a second piece of paper with no intermediate steps.
The process involved electrostatics and powders that gave off noxious
fumes. His device was primitive, and experimentation was dangerous. If
only he had the funding, he was sure his invention would take off. But by
this time, he had used up his savings and his clothes were threadbare.

Over the next eight years, Carlson tried selling his primitive photocopier
to over twenty companies, including IBM. They all turned him down. None
of them could see any point in the concept. After all, who would want
to make thousands of copies of anything? In addition, the executives he

pitched to were put off by someone who looked more like a mad scientist than a captain of industry. As Carlson later recalled, they couldn't see the point of disseminating information, of spreading around the contents of memos and reports.

Finally in 1946, John Dessauer, chief of research at the Haloid Company in Rochester, New York, a fledgling business that produced photographic paper, heard of Carlson's invention and decided to take a gamble. By 1956 Haloid, with Carlson on board, had produced the famous prototype 914 Paper Copier. Some billions of dollars later, the company changed its name to Xerox Corporation. Nobody had ever needed a copier or even imagined one until Xerox produced one.

A little over a decade later, Xerox set up its own version of Bell Labs, AT&T's think tank. It was called Xerox PARC (Palo Alto Research Center). One of its first inventions was the laser printer. But by then Xerox was after bigger game than photocopiers: the computer revolution had begun.

About this time, a young man named Alan C. Kay arrived for an interview. His interest in computers had been sparked by a stint in the air force, where he programmed the huge IBM 1401. Afterward, Kay obtained a PhD in computer graphics, in the process learning about systems that allowed computers and humans to communicate by moving icons on a screen.

In the course of his interview at Xerox PARC, Kay was asked about his dream project. "A personal computer," he replied.[13] His interviewer was incredulous. This was the age of mainframe computers that filled a large room. What else could one possibly desire? Draw one, he challenged Kay. The resulting sketch looked much like today's laptops. "Yeah, right," the interviewer replied (in other words, "Who needs this?"), just as IBM had replied to Carlson.[14] A few years later, Bill Gates and Steve Jobs took up Kay's idea, and soon everyone needed their own personal computer—their own PC. Kay's invention had quite literally changed the world and changed our concept of what we needed.

Kay's brilliant realization was that trying to guess the future was a waste of time. "The best way to predict the future is to invent it," he said.[15] By the time the twenty-first century rolled around, this mantra had changed the very concept of creativity.

Creativity is the last great mystery. Where do ideas come from? How does a new idea pop into our minds? How can we cultivate it? How can we nurture and encourage our own creativity? I've worked on the study of creativity for decades and have come to the conclusion that it has certain qualities, certain characteristics shared by all thinkers across diverse fields.

Have you ever noticed that the keypad on your phone is laid out in a very specific design—three rows of three numbers starting with 1, ending in 9, and a fourth with a zero in the middle? (On today's twelve-button keypad, the 0 is flanked by star and pound keys.) Has it ever occurred to you that this configuration might have anything in common with Einstein's discovery of relativity theory?

The keypad was the brainchild of John E. Karlin, at Bell Labs, who applied insights from the behavioral sciences to telephone design. At the time, no one had ever thought there was any connection between the two. For Karlin, the dynamics of using a telephone required far more than speaking and hearing. Karlin was a man of many dimensions. In college in South Africa, he cast his net wide, studying philosophy, psychology, and music; he was a violinist in the Cape Town Symphony Orchestra. He then completed a PhD in mathematical psychology at the University of Chicago and went on to study electrical engineering at the Massachusetts Institute of Technology (MIT). He joined Bell Labs in 1945, where he made critical design changes to old-fashioned rotary telephones. He was also instrumental in changing phone numbers to include only numerals, not letters; the large number of telephones coming into use made this change essential.

By the late 1950s, rotary dialing was about to be replaced with touch-tone dialing, touted to be much faster. The problem was what keyboard design— that is, *keypad* design—would be best for speed and accuracy. Several were considered. Based on empirical research on how people use phones, Karlin's turned out to be the most intuitive, the most user-friendly, and hence the quickest way to make a call. It has been with us ever since.

For Karlin, it was a creative leap. Similarly, Einstein hit on a hitherto unrecognized connection between the theory of heat, thermodynamics, and the motion of bodies in space and time. The result was his theory of relativity.

Both these leaps involved someone realizing the relationship between areas that at first sight seemed to have nothing to do with one another.

*   *   *

But could a computer spot these connections and come up with a better keypad design or even a new theory of relativity or a new style in art? Can computers be creative? And if they do start to think, need they think in the same way that we do? Perhaps they will be creative in entirely different ways from us.

Computers are already trespassing on territory traditionally considered to belong only to very brilliant and perhaps rather eccentric individuals. Machines have defeated champions at complex games such as chess, *Jeopardy!*, and Go. They can recognize faces, generate dramatically new and unexpected forms of art and music. Google's Project Magenta aims to have its computer produce compelling art and music without being preprogrammed so that eventually it will be taken seriously as a creative artist. Computers are already being used to develop driverless cars and are having an impact on law and medicine. Today everyone lives surrounded by devices— phones, cars, remote-controlled ovens, heating systems, all connected to the web, via the so-called internet of things. All this is underpinned by computer systems performing tasks that we have always assumed require human intelligence. This is what we call artificial intelligence (AI).

So what is machine creativity? Does it or will it differ from human creativity? If so, in what ways? Will machines ever have consciousness, a trait usually assumed to go hand in hand with creativity? Will computers come to have emotions? Could a computer flying a plane experience an emergency situation and feel fear, bringing about an "adrenaline rush" and providing that extra impetus to think outside the box and avert disaster? Would a robot ever fix its hair in the mirror, as Arnold Schwarzenegger does in *Terminator*? Could machines suffer, and have awareness of themselves and others, like the replicant in *Blade Runner*?

*   *   *

We humans are slowly and imperceptibly merging with machines. Think of the intimate relationship you have with your cell phone, which is actually a tiny computer. Electronic implants are no longer science fiction. There is already a cochlear implant, an electronic device that replaces the function of the damaged inner ear, although this is not connected to our brain. In twenty years, we may have chips implanted in our brains that will give us direct access to the web and thus to all known knowledge and enable us to use that knowledge to create new knowledge. When brain implants become reality, we will no longer ever need to forget a name or face. Scientists with devices in their brains will be able to scan thousands of pages of research material in seconds and use it to make and weigh hypotheses.

There is already at least one computer that can do just this: IBM Watson, which became grand champion of the complex quiz game *Jeopardy!* Its victory was so impressive that for the first time people began to wonder seriously whether it had actually been thinking. As David Ferrucci, team leader of the Watson project, said, in an oft-repeated quote, "Can a submarine swim?"[16] From which we can extrapolate the answer: "Yes. But not like a fish. Better." Similarly, when chess grand master Garry Kasparov played against the computer Deep Blue, he reported that he sensed "a new kind of intelligence." Perhaps soon there will be no limits to our creativity—or to that of machines, either.

People often say that computers cannot be creative because they merely follow the instructions that we, their human creators, have embedded in their algorithms. But surely this is akin to saying that Mozart couldn't have been creative because his father taught him music and should therefore have all the credit for his son's achievements. Today's computers often transcend their algorithms to create new forms of art, literature, and music, just as we transcend what we have learned. This is what we call creativity.

But before we can get to grips with the creativity of machines, we first need to understand exactly what human creativity is and means.

$$* \qquad * \qquad *$$

I will start by focusing on the great thinkers and creators who have radically changed our view of the world. These are people whose extraordinary powers distinguish them from most others and cannot be attributed just to hard work. We can call them geniuses. Although we can probably never equal them, we can learn from and be inspired by their thought processes, by looking into the ways they work. If we can understand what highly creative people and geniuses have in common, that may enable us to increase our own creativity. I have devoted decades to this study and have identified hallmarks of high creativity and of genius, which we will examine in the next chapters.

The great question is whether computers too can develop these qualities, or whether they will develop their own ways of thinking and begin to operate and function autonomously—not as replica people but as an altogether different and independent form of intelligence.

This will involve looking into the "lives" of computers, exploring their creativity, their innermost thoughts, to what extent they may be similar to ours and to what extent different. To do so, I will look in depth at the extraordinary new art, literature, and music that computers are creating today.

In the end, we will probably never be able to grasp how machines understand purely on the basis of how we understand. Writers on AI frequently offer a dystopian view of the future, a view of a world ruled by hostile machines. But this need not be the case. AI may well not be the final link in a chain of technological innovation stretching back to the steam engine and beyond, one engine following another until human beings disappear, to be replaced by machines.

There may well be a happier ending to our story.

I Understanding Creativity

[Émile Zola's] was an intelligence that was willful, conscious, methodical, and seemingly made for mathematical deduction: it gave birth entirely to a romantic world. The other [Henri Poincaré's] was spontaneous, little conscious, more taken to dream than for the rational approach and seemingly throughout apt for works of pure imagination, with subordination to reality: it triumphed in mathematical research. And this is one of the surprises, which calls for direct studies touching on the deepest mechanisms.

—Édouard Toulouse[1]

The French psychiatrist Édouard Toulouse pointed out the extraordinary fact that Zola—a novelist—thought like a scientist yet produced artistic creations, whereas Poincaré—a scientist—thought like an artist yet applied his poetic imagination to mathematical discoveries. For Toulouse, who was deeply interested in creativity, this apparent paradox demanded "direct studies touching on the deepest mechanisms."[2] I will begin my exploration of creativity with mechanisms like these, which are at the very heart of the creative process for us and to some extent for computers, too.

1 What Makes Us Creative?

Over two thousand years ago, Plato, in *Meno*, pondered the origins of new knowledge, how new concepts can emerge from those already established in the brain: How can a system produce results that go far beyond the material it has to work with? This is the problem of creativity.

Let's start with a working definition that I've arrived at from many years' study of creativity: Creativity is the production of new knowledge from already existing knowledge and is accomplished by problem solving.

In the case of scientists, it is obvious that what they are doing is solving problems. Why is the universe as it is? What keeps us on this planet? Why do we not all fly off into space? Where do we come from, and why do we look a lot like apes? These are problems that we have puzzled over for millennia. To work on them, thinkers through the ages have built on the knowledge accumulated by great minds of the past and pushed it forward, extending the boundaries of what we know.

In recent years, the problems have become more focused, more sophisticated: Can we understand how species evolve? Can we identify the building blocks of life? How can we unify quantum physics with gravity? How can we connect computers with each other?

Engineers also solve problems: how to make a bridge or a building or a mighty cathedral in such a way that it will not fall down; what electricity is and how to harness it.

Like scientists, artists, writers, and musicians build on knowledge built up over the centuries. They all begin by working within rules, though they may choose to break them. The knotty problem that Picasso put his mind and genius to was how to reduce the forms we see around us, the natural world of people and places, to geometry. He began by working within the

rules of postimpressionism, then broke those rules to produce images showing all perspectives at once, from which emerged cubism.

Writers need a subject. Dramatists and poets like Shakespeare and Words-
worth confronted problems like how to tell a story or evoke a scene or a
feeling within the constraints of language and of the literary traditions of
their day. The constraints of the sonnet form, for example, or of iambic
pentameter in themselves can spark creativity. Searching for a rhyme can
set the imagination roving in new directions.

In fact, constraints—problems—are what spur the creative act itself. A
writer needs a subject. You don't just decide to write; you need to have
a subject, something to write about, and that itself is the first problem. A
novelist will confront multiple problems: what sort of plot to use, who the
characters are, where the climax is. Writers too may work within the framework of a particular set of rules, then break out, as Apollinaire, Gertrude
Stein, and the Beat poets did.

Composers have to follow the rules of composition and may then break
them, as Beethoven, Eric Satie, Igor Stravinsky, Philip Glass, and Steve Reich
did. They all broke traditional rules and came up with new ones. This is
how artistic forms move forward as one movement supersedes another.

The definition of creativity as the production of new knowledge from
already existing knowledge, accomplished by problem solving, applies
equally to the brain as an information-processing system and to the computer. It takes into account both the final product and the process of producing it.

For us, thinking consists of receiving perceptions that the brain acts on
and uses to create new knowledge. Similarly, the computer is fed data, which
it processes and uses to generate, for example, art, literature, or music.

But what are the means by which the brain and the computer process
information? Neither we nor a computer are born with a completely clean
slate, a tabula rasa. There must be at least the potential to create knowledge.
There have to be concepts of some sort that are innate, hardwired in.

To return to our definition: Every day we come up against situations
that we deal with by turning them into problems, from drawing up a shopping list to studying the Middle East quandary to exploring string theory
in physics to painting, composing, and writing. To start with, we need to
distinguish between everyday creativity, like discovering a different route
to work—little-c creativity—and the big domain-breaking feats of creativity,
such as discovering the theory of relativity—big-C Creativity.

Einstein, Bach, Picasso: What Makes These People Special?

Some people are born with extraordinary creative facilities and have a command of a subject that cannot be obtained merely by hard work. We often call them geniuses. Although we cannot duplicate their creative feats, we can learn from the way they think, thereby increasing our own creativity.

The world of the intellect is not a level playing field. For most of us, no matter how diligently we paint, practice music, ponder science, or write literature, we will never be Picasso, Bach, Einstein, or Shakespeare. Some people are simply smarter than others. And even then, it is a matter of time and place that determines whether budding geniuses will be able to grow and flourish and achieve their potential.

People of such caliber spring up without warning, and it usually has little to do with heredity. Few geniuses had families with extraordinary mental attributes. Einstein's father ran a succession of unsuccessful companies that manufactured electrical apparatuses, and Picasso's father was a low-level artist. Bach came from a family of highly competent musicians, but they produced no notable works. Nor is there any correlation between a high score on an IQ test and genius. Richard Feynman, the suave, eminently quotable, and iconoclastic physics genius who made key contributions to working out how electrons interact with light, was reported to have had an IQ of 125—high but not exceptional—and Poincaré, himself interested in the nature of creativity, scored very low on an early version of the Binet-Simon Intelligence Scale, a forerunner of the modern IQ test.

Over the course of many years' study, I've examined the lives of many geniuses and high achievers in great detail: towering figures such as Einstein, Poincaré, Picasso, Georges Braque, Erik Satie, Philip Glass, Subrahmanyan Chandrasekhar, Arthur Stanley Eddington, Wolfgang Pauli, Werner Heisenberg, Niels Bohr, Carl Jung, Gustav Mahler, and Bach. In the twenty-first century, there is a new sort of genius, too, people who dream up ideas for tech start-ups that dramatically change our view of the world and our relationship to it. These include Jeff Bezos, who created Amazon; Sergey Brin and Larry Page, whose search engine was the basis for Google; Bill Gates and Paul Allen, who standardized personal computers with MS-DOS; Steve Jobs and Steve Wozniak, who began Apple; Demis Hassabis, Shane Legg, and Mustafa Suleyman, whose great idea was DeepMind; Peter Thiel, the venture capitalist who invented PayPal; Elon Musk, who pioneered Tesla and SpaceX; and Mark Zuckerberg, founder of Facebook.

From my studies of these people's lives, seven hallmarks of big-C Creativity emerge:

- The need for introspection
- The need to know your strengths
- The need to focus, persevere, and not be afraid to make mistakes
- The need for collaboration and competition
- The need to beg, borrow, or steal great ideas
- The need to thrive on ambiguity
- The need for experience and suffering

I have also identified two marks of genius that cannot be taught:

- The ability to discover the key problem
- The ability to spot connections

In the next chapter we will look at each of these in detail.

Geniuses, as well as most high-caliber thinkers, can be self-inspired as well as self-starters, always working on something new, always thinking up their own problems. They sometimes accomplish their intellectual achievements under physical conditions that would drive most others to despair: working in unheated ateliers, taking an uninspiring nine-to-five job, working heavy production schedules to make a living, or turning ideas spawned in garages into marketable items.

Einstein worked as a clerk in a patent office—a job he obtained through a friend's father—for eight hours a day, six days a week. Suffering poor reviews and huge losses on his operas, Philip Glass took jobs as a mover, plumber, and taxi driver while continuing to compose. "I have a wonderful gene," he wrote, "the I-don't-care-what-you-think gene."[3] As a young man in Paris, Picasso stole milk from neighbors' doorsteps. Bill Gates and Paul Allen and Steve Jobs and Steve Wozniak gave new meaning to the term "garage workshops." These people turned inward into themselves, doing what they had to do to survive in order to find their Holy Grail: to create. As Picasso put it, "The important thing is to create. Nothing else matters; creation is all."[4]

Their stories are hugely inspirational.

What went on in the brain of a Picasso, a Bach, or an Einstein—or a Steve Jobs? That is the first question this book sets out to explore.

2   Seven Hallmarks of Creativity and Two Marks of Genius

The formulation of a problem is often more essential than its solution, which may be merely a matter of mathematical or experimental skill.

—Albert Einstein[5]

As Einstein observed, creativity is all about problem solving, and the first step is to find the problem. Let's look at the seven hallmarks of big-C Creativity and the two marks of genius in more detail and see how they emerge from the lives of great thinkers.

1.   The Need for Introspection

Introspection is the ability to sit by yourself and think. Looking inside your own mind, you can increase your own creativity and enhance your intellectual strengths. The best way is to sit in silence, with no distractions.

Luis Alvarez, a Nobel Prize–winning physicist, always followed this suggestion made by his father, an eminent medical researcher: "He advised me to sit every few months in my reading chair for an entire evening, close my eyes, and try to think of new problems to solve. I took his advice very seriously and have been glad ever since that I did."[6]

Practitioners of mindfulness and meditation will be well aware that introspection sharpens and clarifies the mind.

2.   Know Your Strengths

To make discoveries and enhance creativity, we need to focus, which means homing in on our strengths.

As a child, Einstein enjoyed mathematics, but at university discovered he had no nose for the fundamental problems in the subject. Realizing this, he chose to focus on physics.

Physicist Werner Heisenberg had to abandon a career as a concert pianist to focus on science. He went on to discover quantum mechanics. At a reception at Cambridge University in 1939, a don, doubting Heisenberg's claims, challenged him to play something. Heisenberg sat down at the piano and, without further ado, played Beethoven's highly complex Piano Sonata no. 32 from memory, flawlessly.

Marcel Duchamp chose art over his true passion, chess, although he sometimes regretted it. In 1919, during a decade when he was deeply engaged in chess, a game that he claimed energized his creativity, he wrote, "I am absolutely ready to become a chess maniac."[7] He continued to be a committed chess player throughout his life.

Steve Wozniak focused on coding and hardware at Apple, while Steve Jobs stuck to the areas of design and business, which were his strengths. "Jobs was awed by Wozniak's engineering wizardry and Wozniak was awed by Jobs' business drive," writes Walter Isaacson, Jobs's biographer.[8]

Investor, cofounder of PayPal, and Silicon Valley provocateur Peter Thiel argues against a multifaceted range of interests if one wants to win in the rough-and-tumble world of start-ups. "Instead of pursuing many-sided mediocrity and calling it 'well-roundedness,' a person determines the one best thing to do and does it," he writes.[9]

The key lesson is to realize through self-examination where our strengths lie and not to fritter away our talents on hopeless pursuits.

3. Focus, Persevere, and Don't Be Afraid to Make Mistakes

Focus and perseverance involve the single-minded pursuit of a problem. Highly creative thinkers shut down and exclude everyone around them. There is no creation out of nothing. Artists and scientists work long hours. They encounter dead ends and make endless mistakes. The key lesson is not to be afraid of failure.

As the Danish physicist Niels Bohr said, "An expert is a person who has found out from his own painful experience all the mistakes we can make in a very narrow field."[10] At Bell Labs, AT&T's premier research laboratory, the number of mistakes a scientist made was taken as a sign of the progress of his research—provided, of course, that he eventually came up with a viable result.

When he was developing rockets for his SpaceX program, Elon Musk bore in mind the many failures of the American and Russian space programs. "I have a lot of respect for those that persevered to produce the vehicles that are mainstays of space launch today," he says.[11] He recommends attempts that will fail quickly so that you can go on to new ones straightaway.[12]

As Steve Jobs put it, "If you want to live your life in a creative way, as an artist, you have to not look back too much. You have to be willing to take whatever you've done and whoever you were and throw them away."[13]

4. Collaborate and Compete

"Real technologists wear T-shirts and jeans," writes Peter Thiel.[14] Today's high-tech geniuses cultivate the casual look. People like Steve Jobs and Mark Zuckerberg, the founder of Facebook, operate in teams, in workplaces purpose-designed with large open areas. Coffee machines, essential to provide fuel, are strategically placed so that teams working on different problems make contact. Milling around the coffee machine, people talk about what they are working on. A member of another team may overhear and chime in that they've been thinking about a similar problem and are close to a solution, and the result is a collaboration.

Even so-called lone geniuses such as Einstein and Picasso had think tanks that kept them au courant with what was going on in art, literature, philosophy, and science. Einstein's was an informal study group made up of close friends with a keen interest in philosophy and science who called themselves the Olympia Academy; Picasso's was a group of mainly young literati who went under the name *la bande à Picasso*.

In Einstein's most creative period, his days at the patent office between 1902 and 1909, he sat in an open-plan office, did his work, and daydreamed. He could think wherever he was, he said.

A pioneering example of the move toward open-plan environments was Theo van Doesburg's studio in 1920s' Weimar, Germany, where several artists worked together on a common project.

Pixar's immense success as an animation studio is predicated on close collaboration in an open-plan environment. As Ed Catmull, one of Pixar's founders, recalled upon seeing a traditional closed office setup, "To put it simply, it struck me as a lousy work environment."[15]

There's considerable controversy over whether open-plan offices are conducive to collaboration or whether in fact they hinder it. A recent study by Harvard University suggested that workers in large open-plan offices talk less and email more.[16] But it seems that the Harvard report related mainly to extreme open-plan offices.[17] Those that offer a degree of privacy—meeting rooms, breakout spaces, telephone booths—work much better. The debate is ongoing.

In the sciences, collaborative modes of thought came into vogue in the 1920s when the German atomic physicist Max Born in Göttingen and the Danish physicist Niels Bohr in Copenhagen formed groups to work together. But the real breakthroughs were made by individuals sitting alone at their desks. This was how Werner Heisenberg discovered quantum mechanics and his uncertainty principle, and how Erwin Schrödinger nailed his famous equation and later his sometimes alive, sometimes dead cat—though the creative juices that helped with the discovery of Schrödinger's equation were stirred by an illicit weekend.[18]

Then there was the Manhattan Project, based in Los Alamos, New Mexico, put together to develop the atomic bomb—a supreme example of a vast, top-level collaborative project. Many of the scientists involved were alumni of the group think sessions in Göttingen and Copenhagen. The periodic get-togethers have become the stuff of legend. Groups working on different parts of the project met to discuss their own work and comment on the work of others. The sessions were entirely democratic—and so was the general atmosphere, which was one of no-holds-barred exchanges. For example, the brash young physicist Richard Feynman felt free to call a suggestion put forth by the great Niels Bohr "a crazy idea."[19]

There are many other forms of collaboration in the sciences and the arts: husband-and-wife teams such as Marie and Pierre Curie or Ted Hughes and Sylvia Plath; lovers such as Anaïs Nin and Henry Miller; artists such as Picasso and Georges Braque; writers such as T. S. Eliot and Ezra Pound; musicians such as Aaron Copeland and Leonard Bernstein; string quartets; theater troupes; and the huge number of international collaborators on modern-day, high-energy physics projects such as that at CERN. Successful collaborators bootstrap each other's creativity.[20]

In addition to collaboration, competition is often a crucial catalyst. A team at Sussex University searching for the structure of carbon 60 (C_{60}), which occurs on Earth and in the atmospheres of stars, had become bogged down. The team's work was languishing until its members heard of a group in Germany that claimed to be close to finding the elusive carbon 60 structure. The Sussex group members immediately sprang to life, looked at their data afresh, and realized that the structure of C_{60} was much like the Buckminster Fuller dome, made famous at the 1967 Montreal Expo. They called it the buckminsterfullerene or buckyball. Harry Kroto, the group's leader, brought to bear his experience as a graphic artist to deduce a three-dimensional shape from two-dimensional data—to "see" the deep meaning. The discovery of this highly symmetrical molecule opened new areas in chemistry, ranging from phenomena in space to materials on Earth.

5. Beg, Borrow, or Steal Great Ideas

Bach borrowed heavily from the Italian and French baroque, often weaving their melodies into his works, overshadowing composers such as Corelli and Scarlatti for three centuries. Some contend that the scores of his remarkable Prelude 1 in G Major for the keyboard and the melody for his Christmas Cantata 142, *Uns ist ein Kind geboren*, were lifted from the German composer Johann Kuhnau, a practice that was not unusual in those days when there were no copyright laws.[21] It is said that Shostakovich too often lifted from the works of other composers without attribution. He incorporated themes of the fourth movement of Beethoven's Seventh Symphony into his own Fifth Symphony, for a start.[22]

Similarly, in the 1920s, Diego Rivera warned young artists in Paris not to let Picasso into their studios because he would steal their ideas—and he probably did.

But such "theft" is never mere plagiarism. The likes of a Bach or a Picasso use the ideas of others to stimulate their ever-fertile minds. What they see or hear soon becomes theirs, woven into their own pattern of ideas and elevated to a level far beyond the original. We are constantly absorbing the ideas of others. They are stored in our memory banks and over time become our own.

In principle, of course, no one is wholly original. Accumulation—building upon what you and others have accomplished—is part and parcel of creative activity. But some people see the world in an entirely new way. Galileo saw the motion of a pendulum not as a swinging back and forth but as a falling and rising, which gave him a way to test his revolutionary theory of falling bodies, based on falling through a vacuum, a concept that went against the scientific and religious doctrines of his day—the horror vacui, the fear of empty space, devoid of God. Thus he confirmed his theory that the speed of a falling body is independent of its weight and that the distance through which a body falls is directly proportional to the time it takes, squared.

Einstein saw the physics of 1905 in a dramatically different way from just about everyone else, as a subject riddled with asymmetries that, in his opinion, did not appear in nature. The spectacular result was his discovery of the theory of relativity.

Bach often plagiarized himself, recycling parts of scores. So did Mozart, some of whose pieces for clarinet or flute are almost identical.

In the 1970s, the early days of Microsoft, Bill Gates offered to find a program that would manage all of a computer's hardware and software—in other words, an operating system that would be standard for IBM computers. At the time, IBM was falling behind in producing mainframes and feared it would soon be overtaken in the fledgling business of personal computers, too. Gates realized that whatever operating system IBM chose would become the standard system and would dominate the computer industry. He began preliminary discussions with a company that was producing one possible system, but negotiations soon fell through—so he decided to have a go at finding a system by himself.

Gates and his partner, Paul Allen, turned to a struggling start-up company that had built an operating system called QDOS—Quick and Dirty Operating System. They convinced the developer to sell it to them for $50,000, free and clear, to be used however they wanted. They did not, however, tell the owner what they had in mind. They made a few changes and turned it into MS-DOS, which would dominate the software industry for three decades.

Microsoft is now among the world's largest software companies. As Gates recalled, "An innovator is probably a fanatic, somebody who loves what they do, works day and night, may ignore normal things to some degree and therefore may be viewed as a bit unbalanced. Certainly in my teens and 20s I fit that model."[23] He certainly did. In fact, based on this quote alone, Gates ticks many of the boxes of my hallmarks of big-C Creativity, such as focus, perseverance, and not being afraid to make mistakes.

Steve Jobs famously "borrowed" a revolutionary graphical interface developed at Xerox PARC. As Jobs put it, "We have always been shameless about stealing great ideas."[24] He liked to quote Picasso as saying, "Good artists copy, great artists steal."[25] Perhaps he considered Picasso a buccaneer like himself.

Jobs said of Xerox, "They were copier-heads who had no clue about what a computer could do."[26] So Jobs's action was no mere theft. He saw the possible uses of the interface—and Apple went on to improve the initial concept enormously.

A legendary story is that of the origins of Facebook. From an early age, Mark Zuckerberg, its founder, was a wunderkind at programming. As an interviewer writes, "Some kids played computer games. Mark created them."[27] Friends who were artistically inclined came over to his house with pictures they had drawn, and he would create games about them. Zuckerberg had long been interested in linking computers to transmit messages. At Harvard, he developed various social networking sites, which brought him to the attention of Divya Narenda and twins Cameron and Tyler Winklevoss, who asked him to help them develop their site.

At this point, the stories differ. Zuckerberg's is that he tired of assisting them and created his own site, which went on to become Facebook. It took off almost immediately, and he dropped out of Harvard to run it. He claims that whereas Narenda and the Winklevosses's website emphasized dating, his focused on networking.

Narenda and the Winklevosses, however, claimed that Zuckerberg stole their idea. They eventually reached a settlement, but litigation continues. So there may well be a grain of truth on both sides.

The point is that art and science are Darwinian enterprises: only the fittest survive. There is no copyright on ideas. One must fight for one's place in the sun.

6. Thrive on Ambiguity

In periods of ambiguity, geniuses thrive while others go quiet.

By mid-1925, all the viable theories of atomic physics had been demolished, and it seemed as if the subject lay in ruins. Bohr himself tried to rework the foundations of his original theory, which postulated that the atom was like a miniscule solar system, but he got nowhere. Then he and his coworkers tried abandoning the laws of conservation of energy and momentum—cornerstones of physics—as being inexact. This too was refuted by experiments. One major physicist, Wolfgang Pauli, wanted to disappear into Hamburg café society, perhaps even produce movies. Others, having tried everything and failed, were on the verge of nervous breakdowns. It seemed that atomic physics had hit a dead end. Ambiguity reigned.

But Pauli's colleague, Werner Heisenberg, an unassuming young German physicist, thrived in such situations. That June, after salvaging parts of past attempts, he hit on the solution: the new atomic physics, quantum mechanics.

Sometimes areas are thrown into turmoil after a milestone work appears. Such was the case in art after cubism came on the scene and in music after the appearance of works by Satie and Stravinsky. Stravinsky's 1913 *Rite of Spring* caused riots in Paris of a magnitude not even matched by Satie's *Parade*, as Stravinsky himself recalled with pride.

Karlheinz Stockhausen, Steve Reich, and Philip Glass caused turmoil again and initiated an entirely new phase in music. The twenty-first-century avant-garde electronic music they inspired often mixes sound and image, both generated by creative algorithms. One does not leave these concerts whistling a tune; instead, they provide cerebral and visceral experiences.

So if your idea seems out of step, it could be because everyone else is heading in the wrong direction. Have faith in yourself and your instincts!

7. The Need for Experience and Suffering

Being "out there," encountering the world both professionally and person-ally, is essential to prime the mind to make creative breakthroughs in art, literature, music, and science. Breakthroughs are made by thinkers who have a well-rounded intellectual background, who have read outside their field and can bring this knowledge to bear, however indirectly.

Einstein was only twenty-six when he discovered relativity theory, in 1905, but he had certainly lived. By this time, he had had at least two intense romantic relationships. One was with Marie Winteler. He boarded with her family when he attended preparatory school in Aarau, Switzer-land, to bone up on subjects he had done poorly on in high school in order to enter the Swiss Polytechnic Institute in Zurich. He had already rebelled against the Prussian high school system, been asked to leave, and traveled on his own through Northern Italy. When he moved to Zurich, Marie wrote that she would come and visit, to see where "my darling lives."[28] Soon afterward, Einstein ended the relationship.

Marie subsequently married and divorced, eventually dying in a mental asylum. A family member asserted that her unhappy affair with Einstein "confused her" and ruined her life.[29] But their love letters reveal that for him, she was an inspiration.

The woman Einstein rejected her for was Maleva Marić, a fellow physics student. They married in 1901, but by 1905 he had tired of her too. Maleva's influence on his relativity paper was distinctly negative; he succeeded despite her. He may not have suffered hugely himself, but he certainly imposed suffering on others.

Essential to Einstein's discovery of relativity theory was his insistence that its equations be beautiful so as to reflect the symmetries of nature. His aesthetic feel for nature was probably nurtured by his romantic attitude. By 1905, he was also well versed in philosophy—particularly that of Immanuel Kant, who analyzed how the brain constructs concepts of space and time. Without such intellectual and social maturity, he may not have succeeded in developing the penetrating critique of the state of science in his day that was required for his new theory of space and time.

At moments of extreme concentration, geniuses tend to focus to such an extent that they shut out those around them. In the course of their work, they are often vampires, sapping energy from those who share their lives.

Picasso's life was a series of disastrous liaisons, not unlike Einstein's. In 1907, when he painted *Les Demoiselles d'Avignon*, he was living with Fernande Olivier. Theirs was a tempestuous and argumentative relationship, in which they frequently broke up and came together again. As Einstein did with Mileva, Picasso learned to harness Fernande's moods to his vision, and his passions provided some of the dynamics for his greatest creations. This cycle would continue throughout his life.

Erwin Schrödinger famously enjoyed an open marriage and often travelled with both his wife and his current girlfriend. There were always affairs with others too, lurking in the background. This psychological stress spurred rather than hindered his scientific creativity.

In general, Werner Heisenberg led an idyllic family life, but he went through a period of great turmoil in 1927 when he was trying to convince his mentor and father figure, Niels Bohr, of the veracity of the uncertainty principle, perhaps his greatest discovery. Their ferocious arguments often drove Heisenberg to tears. Bohr's tenacious skepticism turned out to be crucial in shaping the uncertainty principle's final form.

Alma and Gustav Mahler's marriage was always in turmoil. Gustav forbade Alma to compose. Although he suspected she continued to do so, he never asked to see her work. "I played through my compositions again, my piano sonata, my many Lieder," Alma wrote to a friend. "I feel again: this is what I want. I long for creativity. My present life is a delusion. I need my art!"[30] As a result, Gustav had to suffer the affairs of his beautiful young wife.

Ted Hughes and Sylvia Plath suffered a tortured marriage, an explosive mix of her mental illness and his affairs, culminating in Plath's suicide. Its stresses and strains and their later reverberations drove both to creative heights.

Steve Jobs often behaved tyrannically against those he suspected of mediocrity and lack of preparation. Ed Catmull, one of the founders of Pixar, recalls Jobs's direct approach: "These charts are bullshit! This deal is crap!"[31] "He could be rough on people he didn't think were smart," recalled Steve Wozniak, Jobs's partner at Apple.[32] In this way, he could drive people beyond what they thought were their limits. Occasionally someone stood up to him, which he respected if what they had to say had validity.

Elon Musk, a billionaire entrepreneur whose successes include the Tesla electric car and the SpaceX space shuttle, worries that his children will not suffer as he has done. He feels that suffering gave him the will to succeed, no matter how adverse the circumstances. "They might have a little adversity at school, but these days schools are so protective," he says. Musk's solution was to create "artificial adversity" at home by insisting that his children spend more time reading than they do playing video games and by restricting the length of time they can play—a brave attempt, though it doesn't sound like the greatest of suffering.[33]

Although they often profess concern for humanity at large, geniuses often care little for those closest to them. Gandhi, the voice of the Indian masses, had difficulties with his own family. His oldest son rebelled against everything Gandhi taught and believed in. Gandhi's closest relationships were with people he would never meet, such as top-level politicians, with whom he communicated by letter.

The Indian astrophysicist Subrahmanyan Chandrasekhar, discoverer of black holes, was very close to his students and colleagues but paid scant attention to his wife, who had hoped for a career alongside him in physics. Her disappointment ended up tormenting both of them, she told me.[34]

The experiences of intellectual powerhouses such as these can inspire us lesser mortals to build up our emotional dimension not only socially but through literature, music, and philosophy, as these people did. To make an important scientific discovery, create a dramatic work of art, or write a breakthrough novel, you will have to have lived—and you will probably need to focus obsessively on your work to the exclusion of family and friends.

The Two Marks of Genius

1. The Essence of Creativity: Finding the Problem

Problem discovery is the remarkable ability, possessed by only a select few, to identify a specific problem—a problem that will open a bold new avenue of thought and that is usually antithetical to what just about everyone else in the field is working on. Entrepreneur Peter Thiel has these words of advice for those planning tech start-ups: "The next Bill Gates will not build an operating system. The next Larry Page or Sergey Brin won't make a search engine. And the next Mark Zuckerberg will not create a social network. If you're copying these guys you aren't learning from them."[35]

A stunning example is Einstein, who in 1905 realized that all the scientists toiling on the frontier of physics were trying to solve the wrong problem. They were concerned with how the electron is structured, whereas he realized that they should have been looking at the nature of space and time. For six years, no one understood the importance of his relativity theory. When appreciated at all, it was usually for the wrong reasons, because it was assumed to add rigor to the then-popular theory of the electron.

Picasso wanted to create an entirely new form of art that broke completely with impressionism, with the past. The problem he focused on was how to reduce nature to geometrical forms. Cézanne had moved in this direction, but only tentatively. Picasso decided to take it to the extreme. The result was his breakthrough painting of 1907, *Les Demoiselles d'Avignon*, which contained the seeds of cubism. Like Einstein's relativity theory, cubism would not be accepted worldwide for some six years. As for the painting itself, it went unsold for almost twenty years. When Picasso first showed it to friends and colleagues, they thought he had lost his mind.

Physicist Mitchell Feigenbaum wanted to solve the problem of how systems become disordered—like a wave breaking into droplets or smoke rings breaking up in the air. Looking at vast swirling canvases by J. M. W. Turner, he saw there patterns of dynamic fluid motion and what would come to be called Mandelbrot sets and fractals. Looking at a painting of a scene in a park, he realized that the best way to understand the background was to get close up and look at every small detail, then work back out to the whole panorama. Applying this to his scientific work, it struck him that everyone else in his field was trying to understand chaotic systems in their totality right from the start. Applying his newfound method of scaling down, he began by searching for the patterns within apparently random systems. This was the key to his discovery of modern chaos theory: to deal with complex systems by exploring how "big details relate to little details."[36] Thus, according to chaos theory, a butterfly fluttering its wings in Brazil might cause hurricanes in the northern hemisphere.

At the beginning of the twentieth century, Erik Satie used to play the piano at the Els Quatre Gats bistro in Montmartre, where Picasso sketched him. The problem of the day, as he saw it, was how to liberate French music from what he saw as the straitjacket of Germanic compositional style. His friend Claude Debussy had already attempted this, but Satie wanted to create an entirely new style of music with its own menu of problems. A short man, shabbily dressed, with an unkempt beard and a famously sharp tongue, Satie looked like a sack of potatoes, according to poet Jean Cocteau. Unprepossessing though he was, he produced haunting melodies from chords that seemed too complex to yield anything but atonality. To the undiscerning listener, these melodies seem to repeat themselves. But in fact there are subtle differences, a technique that Philip Glass picked up. Satie was the personification of the Parisian avant-garde, and in 1917 he went on to collaborate with Picasso, Cocteau, and Sergei Diaghilev on short ballet pieces, most notably *Parade*. His score incorporated cowbells, typewriters, foghorns, milk bottles, and a pistol to produce the sounds of everyday life in Paris—which, combined with Picasso's cubist costumes, caused a riot in the theater.

Regal and moody looking, Karlheinz Stockhausen was at the forefront of the radical new trends in music that commenced after World War II. The problem he set himself was to break completely with all previous avant-garde music, including twelve-tone music. To do so, he explored the possibilities of electronic music, partly using mathematical statistics, as well as concrete music, for which he took sounds from just about anywhere, including the human voice, the environment, and computer-based signal processing. His groundbreaking work continues to be controversial.

Steve Reich went yet further. The problem he posed for himself was how to produce new sounds with the minimal use of musical instruments. He experimented with tape loops to create phasing patterns, sometimes accompanied by voices and clapping hands. His repetitive compositions with their slow harmonic rhythms marked the beginning of minimal music.

Which brings us to Philip Glass. Tall and wild-haired, he thrived in the New York art world of the 1960s. The problem he flirted with was to find a new approach to minimalism in music, beyond that pioneered by Satie, Stockhausen, and Reich. He was chief among the musicians who picked up on Satie's repetitive atonal melodies to craft the dominant sound of the late twentieth century.

Although it can't be taught, we all have these leaps of imagination. Perhaps the lesson is to practice introspection to give such leaps a chance to emerge, then to trust in them and go along with them when they do.

2. Spotting Connections

In 1905, Einstein realized there was a connection between the structure of the laws of thermodynamics (which deal with the flow of heat) and the nature of space and time. What could seem further apart?

The theory of light as it stood in 1905 predicted that the speed of light, when measured in a laboratory on Earth, should vary due to the earth's motion. But very accurate measurements showed otherwise: the speed of light always remained the same. To explain away the discrepancy between the theory and the experiments, scientists resorted to piling on hypotheses—suggesting, for example, that moving objects become deformed when in motion.

Mulling these over, and dissatisfied at the lack of any systematic explanation for the suggestions, Einstein suddenly recalled an interesting feature of the laws of thermodynamics: they don't explain, they simply insist. The first law of thermodynamics is that energy is conserved in every physical process. Never mind how; it just is.

So, Einstein concluded, why not simply assert that the speed of light is always the same, no matter where or how it is measured? He added another assertion: that measurements taken in laboratories in uniform relative motion are unaffected by the laboratory's motion—the principle of relativity.[37] His theory of relativity followed from these two statements or postulates. This new theory of space and time either eliminated or systematically deduced hypotheses that earlier scientists had proposed with no basis in theory.

At pretty much the same time, Picasso turned not to the latest developments in art but to contemporary developments in science, technology, and mathematics for inspiration. The problem he set himself was how to represent all perspectives of a scene at once. Images from a book on four-dimensional geometry—geometry with four spatial dimensions—and what he had learned about the science of X-rays gave him hints as to how to go about it. He learned about these subjects from members of his think tank.[38] The result was *Les Demoiselles d'Avignon*, which brought art decisively into the twentieth century.

In 1968, the twenty-four-year-old Italian physicist Gabriel Veneziano was working at CERN and MIT. Studying the equations for how particle collisions are represented in physics, he found that these apparently unrelated equations could be brought together with the Euler beta function, an exotic mathematical formula seemingly of use only in pure mathematics. Further study of this unexpected connection between mathematics and physics led physicists to hypothesize that elementary particles can be represented as vibrating strings, which in turn led to string theory.

Forever playing games, revising rules, or inventing new ones, mathematician John Horton Conway studied the patterns that emerge as one places and removes tiles in the Chinese board game Go. This inspired him to invent the Game of Life, a mathematical grid of cells in which simple rules about a cell becoming "live" or "dead" produce a riot of patterns. The Game of Life is primarily a game, but it also turned out to be an important tool for studying the evolution of spiral galaxies and in the development of chaos theory.

The key lessons here are to be broad rather than narrow in one's interests; to take on board all sorts of ideas, no matter how unlikely; and to be alert for connections.

Intent, Imagination, and Unpredictability

There are three qualities, three states of mind, that thread through the seven hallmarks of creativity and the two marks of genius: intent, imagination, and unpredictability.

Anyone launching into a creative endeavor—an artist, a poet, a scientific researcher—begins with intent, with the desire to solve a problem or at least a line of pursuit.

Next they think about how to solve it, which may involve going well beyond the original approach. To do this, they may well dream up—that is, imagine—an entirely new approach to the problem.

This leap could come out of the blue and be entirely unpredictable.

Unpredictability—going beyond logic—is an essential element in creativity. To rephrase Toulouse's words, quoted at the beginning of this part, the mathematician Poincaré's way of thinking was more akin to a dream than to a rational approach, seemingly most suited to "works of pure imagination."

Great discoveries are made not by logic alone, but often by spotting links between things or areas or ideas or philosophies that at first sight have nothing to do with each other. This can happen suddenly and unpredictably, when the mind rearranges the information at hand in a totally new way.

Samuel Taylor Coleridge claimed he was inspired to write his much beloved poem "Kubla Khan" while in an opium dream, in which he heard a voice intoning the first lines. But there is never creation from nothing. There is always some material to begin with. And in Coleridge's case, he later revealed that he had been reading about Xanadu just before he went to sleep.

The poem may have been dreamed up in his unconscious, but it required artistry to get it down on paper. To build his rich word picture, he began with iambic tetrameters, then moved on to other rhyming schemes and made much use of the sonic qualities of the words. In other words, he reinterpreted the traditional verse form and used it in new ways. Dream or not, Coleridge still pushed the boundaries of the rules of poetry that held sway in his day, added to which he was already an accomplished poet and used all his skill in his work. His problem was to get the poem down before he forgot it—but in the process he employed intent and imagination, finally breaking into unpredictability, to dramatic effect.

3 Margaret Boden's Three Types of Creativity

Creativity is the ability to come up with ideas or artefacts that are *new, surprising and valuable.*

—Margaret Boden[39]

Margaret Boden is a research professor of cognitive science at the University of Sussex and the author of the widely read *The Creative Mind: Myths & Mechanisms*, published in 1990. She has studied creativity, particularly in the context of computer science, for many years, looking into the creative aspects of computers and their similarities to the workings of the human brain.[40] She defines creativity as the ability to come up with products—ideas or artifacts—that are new, surprising, and of value.[41]

She goes on to provide three criteria by which we can assess to what extent an idea or an artifact can be considered creative: "A creative idea must be useful, illuminating or challenging in some way."[42] It's not enough simply to be novel. To be truly creative, an idea needs to be genuinely original—a creative leap. It also needs to be unexpected and of genuine value.

Boden's deceptively simple categories have spawned much discussion on creativity, what it is, and what the most suitable criteria are to assess it. Are her three criteria sufficient? Or are they too imprecise to be useful? Are there other criteria that might equally well be applied?

Let's examine a few responses to Boden's criteria.

Dean Simonton, a distinguished professor of psychology at the University of California at Davis, studies the sociocultural factors in creativity. He questions how many criteria are really necessary. Some researchers consider two to be optimal: originality and effectiveness, for example.[43]

Simonton likens Boden's three criteria "to those of the U.S. Patent Office, namely, to earn patent protection an invention must be new, useful, and non-obvious."[44]

Sir Ken Robinson, an educator, prolific writer on creativity, and advisor on the subject to governments, defines creativity as "the process of having original ideas that have value."[45] This of course raises the question of how to define value.

Anna Jordanous is a senior lecturer in the School of Computing at the University of Kent, researching human and machine creativity. "Most people are relatively happy with novelty and value as a definition of creativity—certainly subject to aesthetics and correctness," she says.[46]

French composer and computer scientist François Pachet takes a different line. He believes that creativity can be understood only in subjective terms, not objective ones. "Society will decide whether someone is creative or not," he says.[47]

Tony Veale of University College Dublin asserts that creativity cannot be defined. "We call something creative when it fits a certain narrative," he says.[48] We can tell stories of how Thomas Edison invented the electric lightbulb or Leonardo da Vinci created his paintings, but such descriptions are entirely subjective and depend on the attitudes and state of knowledge of the society of the day. Some of the most important creative ideas and artifacts are not recognized as such for years. Many great artists die in obscurity, Vincent van Gogh being a prime example.

Novelty, value, and surprise: Are these all there is to creativity? As criteria, they focus on the product rather than the process. But surely the process of creativity is equally as important as the final product. In *The Creative Mind*, Boden takes a long look at the creative process. She breaks it down into three types and proposes three "different psychological mechanisms, eliciting different sorts of surprise."[49]

First there is "combinatorial creativity," combining familiar ideas in unfamiliar ways. These include analogies, like comparing the heart to a pump, and metaphors—like the atom acting as if it is a miniscule solar system, the core of Niels Bohr's theory of the atom. Sometimes this process of combination can be purely statistical, playing around with material to see what emerges, like cutting out words in a printed poem, tossing them around, and gluing them on a sheet of paper to create another poem. The results of such combinations can generate surprise or even shock.

Next comes "exploratory creativity," working within accepted rules of procedure, as in art, literature, music, and indeed science, and trying to generate new styles, new sentences, new melodies, new theories—something that only you and no one else has ever thought of before. It's like exploring a familiar place and finding something new there, as indeed we all do every day.

Finally there is "transformational creativity," which is domain busting and full of surprises. It can be a leap of the imagination, resulting from the artist or scientist feeling so constrained and frustrated by existing rules that they burst out, creating something that rewrites the rule book. Thus Beethoven launched the Romantic period in classical music and Einstein discovered relativity theory, showing that the world of our experience is a mere approximation of what's really out there. Niels Bohr discovered modern atomic theory, casting further doubt on our perceptions of the world, and Cézanne pushed impressionism toward the more abstract postimpressionism—which, along with important sources such as the mathematical, scientific, and technological developments of the day, was the springboard from which Picasso created cubism.

It is often difficult to separate these three processes. Analogy and metaphor, aspects of combinatorial creativity, are often essential to discover domain-breaking theories—transformational creativity.

Boden appreciates that it may take years for the results of transformational creativity to be recognized because they are often so outlandish that they may seem jolting or repellent, causing disgust or disbelief.[50] Some thinkers interpret this disgust at dramatic new developments as evidence that we have inherent limitations in our cognitive systems. But if this were the case, then any progress would be virtually impossible. It is probably better to see it—particularly in music—as a matter of time. The journey from Mozart to the Sex Pistols could not have happened overnight.

Another way to look at this is in terms of little-c creativity and big-C Creativity, which I introduced earlier. This terminology dates back at least as far as 1988.[51] To elaborate, little-c creativity is an everyday experience such as thinking up a new route to work, a discovery that has novelty, value, and surprise, at least for the discoverer. Everyone is little-c creative. Big-C Creativity is altogether different. It is spectacular and can be domain breaking. It's an idea that no one else has ever had in the history of the world. Only a few geniuses are capable of arriving at such ideas. Such transformational ideas have to be generally accepted, and it may take time for them to be recognized for what they are.

In 1905, Einstein published four papers that would change the course of physics and of history.[52] The fourth contained a result he had overlooked in his previous paper, the relativity paper. This was the famous equivalence between mass and energy, $E = mc^2$. But initially these four papers were ignored, and when they were appreciated at all it was for the wrong reasons. The consensus was that the relativity paper simply improved on one of the current theories of the electron. We now look back on 1905 as Einstein's annus mirabilis—but only in retrospect. It was not seen as such at the time.

Similarly Picasso's 1907 *Les Demoiselles d'Avignon* contained the seeds of cubism, but at the time no one understood what he had achieved. The painting was reviled by critics, the public, and his friends. "Another big daub by Picasso" and "a nightmare," wrote the art critics of the time.[53]

The point is that Einstein's papers undoubtedly contained conclusions that were novel, surprising, and had great value, as is now universally recognized, but no one identified them as such at the time. The same is true of Picasso's early cubist works. It was only some years after their first appearance that these works were finally recognized as supreme examples of big-C Creativity.

But at least Einstein's and Picasso's works were recognized in their lifetimes. Such was not the case for van Gogh and Emily Dickinson, both of whom died in obscurity. During Bach's lifetime, only a few dedicated admirers understood that he was drawing together a great number of musical developments in his sublime cantatas, inventions, and variations, often with complex counterpoints. To do this, he crossed the line into mathematics many times and crossed back again. After his death, his reputation declined; it was only rescued by Felix Mendelssohn when he performed the Saint Matthew Passion in Berlin in 1829.

There have also been occasions when the products of big-C Creativity have not stood the test of time. For example, in 1912, Nils Gustav Dalen was awarded the Nobel Prize in physics for his invention of gas lighting for buoys and lighthouses. His invention has long since been rendered obsolete.[54]

As these examples suggest, big-C Creativity is much more complex than little-c creativity. They also show how subjective the judgments of novelty, surprise, and value can be.

4 Unconscious Thought: The Key Ingredient

Geniuses work long and hard. Ideas don't arise out of nothing. In 1908, pioneering French mathematician, scientist, and philosopher Henri Poincaré laid out the four stages that lead to a new idea apparently leaping from nowhere into consciousness.[55]

In 1881, twenty-seven years earlier, Poincaré had just put his foot onto the bottom step of a horse-drawn omnibus when he suddenly realized the answer to a mathematical problem he'd been worrying over. He had never thought of taking geometry into account—but in fact the answer lay in non-Euclidean geometry, an entirely different class from the standard geometry. The result was a major breakthrough and the discovery of an entire class of mathematical functions.

At the moment that Poincaré had this breakthrough, he hadn't been thinking about mathematics at all. He'd been thinking and talking about something entirely different. The key, he realized, was unconscious thought.

Mathematician Jacques Hadamard attended Poincaré's 1908 lecture and was inspired by his comment that what is really important in a scientific discovery is the way it was discovered, a topic that should be of great interest to psychologists.[56]

Psychologist Graham Wallas went on to expand on Poincaré's four-stage model in his 1926 book *The Art of Thought*.[57] It is still discussed today, and its framework remains solid. It is an inspiring and deeply informative way of describing the creative process, showing that new ideas do not just pop up out of nowhere, even though they may seem to.

The Four Stages of Creativity

1. Conscious Thought
Ideas don't arise in an intellectual vacuum. The first step is conscious thought, feeding the brain with the material you're working on: working at your desk, reading, thinking, planning, focusing, gathering information. It's like sowing seeds and giving them water.

2. Unconscious Thought
When philosophers, scientists, artists, researchers—anyone toiling over a problem—hit a wall, they take a break. But the passionate desire to solve the problem keeps it alive in the unconscious, where it can be mulled over freely in ways not possible with conscious thought because of all the barriers and inhibitions there. Unconscious thought is all-important. This phase is like waiting for your seeds to germinate. You could take a bath, take a nap, or go for a walk—and let the mind wander.

3. Illumination
We have all experienced an aha moment when the solution to a problem we've been worrying about comes to mind unexpectedly when we're running for a bus or about to fall asleep.

Just as you stop thinking about a problem, suddenly the solution flashes into your mind. Poincaré called this "sudden illumination."[58] It's like the moment when the first shoots of your newly planted seeds appear above the surface.

4. Verification
This last stage is every bit as important as the previous three. You still have to use your critical thinking skills to hone and craft your newfound idea. The idea will not necessarily leap out perfect and fully formed. It needs to be checked, and its consequences deduced, which demands discipline, attention, will—that is, conscious work.

The four-stage model of creativity is the best way to explore high-level thinking because it reveals how, in a prepared unconscious, connections can occur between widely disparate concepts.

Another way that creativity researchers work is to assume that the difference between creative and noncreative thinkers lies in their database of knowledge. Creative thinkers build up their expertise by accumulating a vast amount of material. They are also skilled at sifting through this material and using it to solve problems. This is certainly an interesting approach, but it doesn't tackle the essence of highly creative thinking—and certainly not that of geniuses who it is hard to imagine laboriously sifting through data in an organized manner.[59] Such an analysis also suggests that hard work alone will make you a great thinker, or even a genius, which is sadly unlikely.

The Importance of Taking Time Off

When the French psychiatrist Édouard Toulouse interviewed Poincaré in 1897, he reported that he "never does any important work in the evening in order not to trouble his sleep.... It is a manner of work uncommon in scientific matters and constitutes a character well suited to the mental activity of M. H. Poincaré."[60] In other words Poincaré had complete confidence in the power of his unconscious and knew when to stop conscious work on a problem so that "his unconscious [could] continue the work of reflection."[61]

Poincaré's belief in the best way to nurture creative thinking was similar to that of other eminent scientists, such as the German polymath Hermann von Helmholtz. Originally trained as a physician, Helmholtz made important contributions to psychology, physiology, physics, and theories of vision and perception, as well as writing penetrating essays on philosophy. He wrote of how a period of hard work culminated in intellectual fatigue. "Then after the fatigue of the work had passed away, an hour of perfect bodily repose was necessary before the fruitful ideas came. Often in the morning upon awakening."[62] He also quoted the German poet Goethe's famous lines on the workings of the unconscious: "What man does not know / Or has not thought of / Wanders in the night / Through the labyrinth of the mind."[63]

On another occasion, Helmholtz mentioned the German mathematician Karl Friedrich Gauss's remarks on how ideas occur on awakening in the morning: "The law of [mathematical] induction was discovered January 1835 at 7 am, before rising."[64]

Poincaré's creative work yielded a solution fairly quickly, but for Helmholtz solving a problem sometimes took "weeks or months," resulting in a "sharp attack of migraine." Helmholtz complained that when trying to solve a problem he could never find "the royal road [because] he was not clever enough." Afterward, he reviewed the numerous pages of his work, with all their dead ends and false starts—and, lo and behold, the "royal road" emerged, as he reveals in his published papers.

Toulouse's book on Poincaré is probably the most complete psychological profile ever of a major scientist. Besides Poincaré, he also carried out observations on Émile Zola, sculptors Jules Dalou and Auguste Rodin, and composer Camille Saint-Saëns. These observations led him to abandon the original assumption that underlaid his project: "genius is a neurosis."[65]

Toulouse carried out his interviews in 1897 and he did not complete his book until 1910. But this delay did not impinge on his analysis of his interviews. He mentions Poincaré's lecture of 1908, in which he laid out the four stages of creativity, almost at the very end of his book, and then only in support of his own findings regarding Poincaré's own emphasis on the power of unconscious thought.

In 1897, Poincaré was immensely busy, yet he still took the time to participate in Toulouse's research on creativity. I believe the reason is Poincaré's intense interest in scientific discovery and in creativity in general, a theme that runs throughout his many fascinating essays on the foundations of science.

One thing that sparked Poincaré's interest was a series of psychological questionnaires on scientific creativity sent out between 1902 and 1908 by a team of French psychologists. The responses were disappointing. In fact, the only well-known scientist to reply was Ludwig Boltzmann, famous for his work on the theory of gases and on entropy, a measure of disorder. In response to the question, "What advice would you give to a young man pursuing his mathematical studies?" he replied, "I have only one piece of advice for young mathematicians: 'Be a genius!' The rest is unimportant."[66] Poincaré was aware of the failure of the questionnaire and wanted to bring the question of creativity to the attention of not only the intellectual community but also the curious layperson. His bestselling books with their huge readership were the best vehicle.

Some years ago, I had the good fortune to discover Poincaré's archival materials. Several documents verify the account he gave in his lecture of how he came to make his great discovery. It is clear that he did not feel that he had to come up with an on-the-spot description of a scientific discovery in response to Toulouse's questions. Conversely, this is exactly what Belgian chemist August Kekulé did in 1890 when he made up an on-the-spot story for a journalist about how he had discovered the cyclical structure of the benzene molecule. He claimed that while dozing in front of the fire at the University of Ghent, he dreamt of six monkeys forming a hexagon by grabbing the tail of the one in front and realized that the structure of the benzene molecule was hexagonal, as indeed it was. It's such a great story that even though it's been known since 1954 to be apocryphal, it persists in many analyses of creativity.[67]

Strangely, Henri Poincaré helped spark the explosion of creativity that occurred at the beginning of the twentieth century in that he was the common denominator between Einstein and Picasso. He was one of the inspirations for both Einstein's relativity theory of 1905 and Picasso's *Les Demoiselles d'Avignon*.[68] Both were acquainted with Poincaré's best-selling *Science and Hypothesis*, published in 1902. In Berne, Switzerland, Einstein read it with members of his think tank, one of whom recalled that it "profoundly impressed us and held us spellbound for weeks on end."[69] Einstein was undoubtedly inspired by Poincaré's masterful essays on the nature of space and time. But in the end, he disagreed with Poincaré's understanding of space and time and of the physics of that era, which he replaced with his relativity theory.[70]

In Paris, Maurice Princet, a member of Picasso's circle and an accountant with a penchant for advanced mathematics, described the book in after-dinner lectures that Picasso attended.[71] Poincaré piqued Picasso's interest in how to view four-dimensional space, in which, if you could place yourself in it, you would see every perspective of a scene at once. (To repeat, for Picasso the fourth dimension is a spatial dimension.) The problem was how to project all these perspectives onto a flat canvas. But in the end Picasso disagreed with Poincaré's suggestion that the way to project an image in four-dimensional space onto a canvas was to do so one perspective at a time. Picasso wanted to project all perspectives at once, which led to cubism.

Poincaré was so near, yet so far, in both science and art.

Another example of the power of unconscious thought is Archimedes's famous Eureka moment in the bathtub. This was preceded by months of mulling over the problem his king had set him as to whether the crown that had recently been made for him was pure gold. The snag was that this had to be solved without melting the crown down. Out of this came the famous Archimedes principle.

There are many more examples of sudden flashes of illumination coming at unexpected times. One of Einstein's inspirations for relativity theory came while he was daydreaming, pondering what it would be like to catch up with a point on a light wave. He concluded that you can't. As for why, that was another matter he had to struggle with. It came down to the nature of time and how we measure it. Heisenberg hit on the crucial element in quantum mechanics while admiring the scenery on the island of Heligoland, where he was recovering from hay fever. And Alan Turing dreamt up the "logical computing machine" while thinking about typewriters. But all these moments of illumination came not out of nowhere but after long periods of mulling over a problem.

Like Archimedes's bathtub and Poincaré's omnibus, traffic lights too can play a role in creativity. Waiting at a traffic light at a London intersection one day in 1933, physicist Leo Szilard swore that by the time it turned green he would have cracked the problem he had been working on for months—to find a way to harness the energy in the nucleus of an atom. He did. Similarly, physicist Steven Weinberg was driving to work in 1967 when he hit on the key to the standard model, which substantially added to our understanding of the subatomic world.

Beethoven's daily creative rhythm was to improvise at the piano, sketch out some music as his desk, then go for a walk. "Walking was as much a part of the process as the rest of it," writes Jan Swafford in a recent biography.[72]

Steve Jobs was in the appliance section of Macy's one day at a time when he was trying to think up an elegant design for the cover of the Apple II. There he was struck by the sleek case of a Cuisinart food processor, made of one piece of light, molded plastic. It was precisely what he had been looking for.

John Hegarty, a creative director at Bartle Bogle Hegarty who dreamt up groundbreaking advertising campaigns for Levi's and came up with the slogan "Vorsprung Durch Technik" for Audi, writes: "When I'm asked, *When do you do your best creative thinking?* My answer is always, *When I'm not thinking.*"[73]

And then there's Mozart. Every now and then someone appears for whom the normal rules of life seem not to apply, who throws all our theories into disarray. According to legend, Mozart wrote a letter to his father in which he described how he composed music not line by line but in a burst, "all at once."[74] Sadly, scholars doubt the letter's authenticity.[75]

Fortunately, there is a better, genuine letter that Mozart wrote to his father on December 30, 1780, about his work on the opera *Idomeneo*. "Everything is composed, just not copied out yet," he writes, an extraordinary statement if one thinks about it for a minute.[76] It seems Mozart could conceive of an entire piece of music in his mind and hold it there until he had the chance to sit down and transcribe it, transcription being an act he found so appallingly boring that he usually did so while chatting with friends—and perhaps telling a scatological joke or two, at which he was superb.

Another example of Mozart's extraordinary abilities is displayed in a letter he wrote to his sister Marianne, nicknamed Nannerl, on April 20, 1782. In it, he says, "I composed the fugue first and wrote it down while I was thinking out the prelude."[77] This is nothing short of amazing. He is describing how he composed his Prelude and Fugue in C Major. The prelude is an exploration into complex pianistic techniques, just as many of Bach's inventions were, involving not only music but problems of touch, all of which Mozart had to keep in mind while transcribing the fugue.

For ordinary mortals, the moral is that instead of sweating over a problem, it's better to take a break, go for a walk, have a snooze. The solution may just come to you out of nowhere.

Unconscious Thought and Computers

[Scientific creativity] is the process in which the human mind seems to borrow least from the exterior world.
—Henri Poincaré[78]

We are never not thinking. Solutions to problems we have labored over for hours, days, months, or names of people we embarrassingly could not remember when we met them, often pop up when we are thinking of something else—the "tip-of-the-tongue" phenomenon.

During unconscious thinking, the mind mulls over many different approaches to a problem, using facts stored in our deepest memory, as well as material used in the original version of the problem. The unconscious mind tries them all out in ways and areas that may at first seem unconnected. Inhibitions and other barriers prevent this freewheeling approach from operating when one is using conscious thought.

For more insight into unconscious thought, I've formulated what I call a model for network thinking, based on Poincaré's four stages of creativity. According to this, consciously working on a problem primes the unconscious to continue this work, even when we are no longer consciously thinking about it. A helpful way to imagine what happens in unconscious thought is to picture it as many lines of thought taking place at once in parallel, coming together from time to time to enrich each other. This leads to the illumination, the solution.

Essential to the process are information on the problem at hand, background knowledge, and reasoning methods. The brain assesses each of the resulting combinations of facts using aesthetics along with other criteria, depending on the field. We then reject most combinations, sometimes using our intuition. Intuition is a much-misunderstood notion. It is nothing more than the culmination of experience, of having made numerous mistakes and thought deeply about them. An art critic's ability to make an instant decision as to whether an artwork is genuine is awe-inspiring, but it is not innate. It has been learned the hard way.

This model of network thinking can be reproduced on a computer able to do many calculations at once—that is, in parallel. A computer's central processing unit (CPU) is where it performs calculations on problems fed to it by the computer's programs or software. We can add more CPUs, thus building up the number of calculations in parallel—parallel lines of thought—it can deal with. The model for network thinking is an ongoing project.[79] As well as offering insights into unconscious thinking, it may also be useful in understanding how computers work.

So how close are human thought processes to the way computers work? To what extent can computers mimic the human brain? And are they—or will they ever be—capable of unconscious thought?

We've looked at what goes on in the brains of geniuses like Einstein, Bach, and Picasso. But what about computers? What goes on in their brains?

5 The Birth of Artificial Intelligence

Humans, when engaged in problem solving in the kinds of tasks we have considered, are representable as information processing systems.
—Allen Newell and Herbert A. Simon[80]

Newell and Simon's view—that the brain is an information processing system and can therefore be reproduced in machine form and can also be studied—seemed outrageously radical in 1972. They were among the pioneers who laid the groundwork for the first developments in artificial intelligence (AI).

Your computer is a box connected to your printer, screen, keyboard, and mouse. If you opened it, you would find devices (hardware) for storing information—data—and retrieving it to use in problem-solving programs (algorithms), along with CPUs for calculations. This is the computer's functional architecture for processing information.

In the early 1970s, psychologists like Newell and Simon, who were interested in AI, expanded the concept of a computer's functional architecture to reflect the way the brain is put together—that is, the brain's cognitive functional architecture. Like a computer, the brain has storage for information or facts—memory—and ways of retrieving information and working on it, using rules for solving problems—algorithms. And also like a computer, the brain is an information-processing system and can be studied using computer science. In other words, the brain is like a computer and a computer is like the brain.

It all began more than a decade earlier, back in the 1950s, when psychologists in the cognitive science field began to apply scientific methods to psychology. Newell and Simon were among the chief contributors.

Their method was to ask people to solve problems and explain their procedures step-by-step, the aim being to formulate a general theory of problem solving.

In 1956, a group of scientists and mathematicians interested in whether it might be possible to simulate human intelligence in machines gathered for an informal conference at Dartmouth College in New Hampshire. One of the organizers, John McCarthy, coined the term artificial intelligence, or AI. Newell and Simon discussed their work and presented their program, the Logic Theorist. It was the first program deliberately created to mimic the problem-solving skills of a human being and the first true AI program.

In 1976, mathematicians Kenneth Appel and Wolfgang Haken were among the first to apply computers to mathematics. They used a computer to prove the four-color theorem, the long-standing conjecture that no more than four colors are needed to color the regions of a map in such a way that no two adjacent regions have the same color. Many mathematicians objected to their use of computers and derided their proof, saying it lacked the generality of mathematical proofs using equations full of x's and y's standing for every number and every conceivable map. They insisted that computers could never replace human beings in the "queen of the sciences," mathematics. Nevertheless, over the years, Appel and Haken's proof was checked and rechecked and its validity firmly established.[81]

Meanwhile, Simon was developing algorithms that he claimed could make scientific discoveries in the same way that human scientists do. He claimed that "creativity involves nothing more than normal problem-solving processes."[82] His assumption was that there were no differences in anyone's thought processes. It was just that certain people, like Bach, Einstein, Poincaré, and Picasso, had better heuristics—better problem-solving methods. This assumption was essential for him to write discovery software—computer programs that can make discoveries—because these programs were based on the problem-solving strategies (heuristics) of people of ordinary intelligence.

In 1987, Simon and his coworkers published a book called *Scientific Discovery: Computational Explorations of the Creative Process*, in which they gave detailed descriptions of their software. They used an information-processing language that was symbolic rather than numerical, based on people's descriptions of how they solved a problem. They then took a new problem and compared how the computer and the person solved it, going into greater and greater detail. The question was whether a computer program with certain selective problem-solving capabilities could come up with a solution to a specific problem. "If an affirmative answer can be given," they wrote, "then we can claim to have driven the mystery out of these kinds of scientific creativity."[83] A big claim indeed! But did they succeed?

Using the same data that had been used by seventeenth-century German astronomer Johannes Kepler, Simon's purpose-built program, BACON, was able to generate one of Kepler's laws. It was purpose built in that it was programmed expressly to study quantities that could be expressed as ratios of one another. The BACON program runs through millions of possibilities until it finds a ratio of terms that produces a number that is the same for the entire set of data. In this way, the program deduced Kepler's third law, which states (roughly) that the ratio of the annual time it takes for a planet to go around the sun squared and the planet's average distance from the sun cubed is a constant—that is, that there is a specific and unchanging relationship between the distance of a planet from the sun and the length of its year.

This would be interesting as a simulation. But Simon claimed it was the real thing, that the computer was thinking precisely as Kepler had thought. The real issue, though, was not how Kepler had thought but why he had chosen to work on this particular problem. The answer is that he had discovered it. It was a brand-new problem, an example of problem discovery. Moreover, Simon had not taken into account Kepler's belief in and use of astrology and mysticism, added to which the scientific discovery that Simon was looking for was already in the software.

In his defense, Simon claimed his program was capable of discovering laws other than Kepler's[84]—but they were all laws based on the ratios of certain terms, like Kepler's.

Simon never agreed that his discovery software was merely a number cruncher. Nevertheless, taken as a simulation of creative thinking, alongside the success of Appel and Haken in proving the four-color theorem, it seemed to indicate that the computer did indeed function in the same way as the brain, which meant that the human brain was indeed an information-processing system, just like a computer, and could therefore be explored using the tools of AI.

The First Inklings of Computer Creativity

The first inkling anyone had that computers might be more than giant cal-culators or glorified typewriters came in the 1960s. It occurred in 1965, to be precise, pretty much simultaneously on two continents. In Germany, art-ists Frieder Nake and Georg Nees, inspired by the philosopher Max Bense's suggestion of using computers to pin down a scientific notion of aesthetics, produced geometric patterns of lines and curves, drawn by a pen attached to their computer, which plotted the computer's output—a plotter. It was the first computer art—intriguing if modest.

At the same time, at Bell Labs in the United States, the massive IBM 7094, which occupied an entire room there, was being used to produce numerical solutions to complex equations. The output numbers were transmitted to a plotter, which laid them out on a graph. One day the plotter malfunc-tioned and drew a collection of random lines. The user ran down the halls shouting that the computer had "produced art." A. Michael Noll, a scientist there, dubbed it "computer art." It had been produced by accident, but Noll set about creating it deliberately. The Library of Congress balked at copyrighting one of his creations because it had been made by a computer, which the library saw as a mere number-cruncher. Noll replied that the pro-grams were written by a human being, and the bureaucrats finally relented. It was akin to the criticisms later leveled against Appel and Haken for using a computer to prove the four-color theorem. How could a mere machine ever be as creative as a human being?[85]

But all this work was programmed. What computer scientists really wanted was a way to turn the computer loose and let it create. Artist Harold Cohen's computer program AARON was an early effort. It began in 1968 and ran for many years. AARON randomly assembled arms, legs, shapes, and colors and produced attractive images—but these were essentially pas-tiches. It produced only what Cohen programmed it to produce.

Computer music began to take off in the 1970s. One of the pioneers was George Lewis, an American trombonist and jazz improviser par excel-lence. As part of the sonic art scene in New York City, he and his friends wondered what could be done to link computers and music. They used very basic computers, microcomputers—in particular, the KIM-1 (Keyboard Input Monitor), with a tiny memory of one thousand bytes. These would serve as models for the Commodore 64—the bestselling home computer of all time. Lewis and his colleagues hooked several KIMs together, each with its own program to produce its own music. "It sounded to me like our own group improvising. People were creating amazing programs" for these simple devices, he tells me.[86] Lewis released his first recording, *The KIM and I*, in 1979; in it, he improvised along with the KIM's music. This primitive setup evolved into what became, in 1987, his famous "Voyager" system, in which human instrumentalists interact with an improvising orchestra generated by Lewis's software and a trio of Yamaha DX-7 synthesizers.[87] The digital orchestra created the sounds of instruments from all over the world, combining symphonic strings with instruments from Africa, the Americas, Asia, and the Middle East. The software chose groupings of instruments to create a rich tapestry of sound.

For Lewis, "computer programming was a theoretical tool for learning and for exploring improvisation as a practice and also as a way of life."[88] He notes, "My favourite non-human improviser is the Mars Rover.... It plops down on the surface and goes to work with what it has. That's all improv is."[89]

Exciting work was also getting underway in linking the computer with performers. At the MIT Media Lab, composer Tod Machover was developing a computer-enhanced cello, which had its debut in 1991; meanwhile, over at the NYU Media Lab, Robert Rowe was composing instrumental music with computer and human musicians on stage together.[90] The Greek-French composer Iannis Xenakis pioneered computer-assisted composition, using a computer to transform complex probabilistic mathematics into musical notation.

As in computer art, producing truly creative computer music required breakthroughs in algorithms—algorithms that, once launched, can take off in unexpected directions. Creative or generative algorithms began to emerge in the 1990s in, for example, work by computer scientist and artist Scott Draves in his famous *Electric Sheep*, an open-source screen saver.

There were even attempts at software for psychoanalysis. The first, Joseph Weizenbaum's ELIZA, appeared in the 1960s. It was called ELIZA because, like Eliza Doolittle of *Pygmalion* fame, it could be taught to speak increasingly well. It provided canned replies to key words, which could be used when a patient was being treated by a nondirectional therapist. If a patient said, "My mother hates me," the computer might reply, "Who else hates you?"[91]

When ELIZA appeared in the 1960s, it caused a sensation because it could do something as complex as therapy. This shook Weizenbaum himself, who insisted that computers could not really delve into the unconscious. He emphasized ELIZA's limited vocabulary and that it was merely giving a parody of responses, and he firmly rejected the idea that the unconscious could be treated as an information-processing system. He concluded that people who raved about ELIZA misunderstood it. His opposition to AI went against the trend at MIT, where he taught, which was a bastion of AI. As a humanist, he had effectively ended up in the wrong institution.

Computers That Mimic the Brain

Most personal computers have three or four CPUs that oversee the step-by-step solution to a problem. But how does the brain work in real life? Supposing you see someone in the distance whom you haven't run across for years. You recognize not only their physical characteristics, their facial characteristics, perhaps even their smell, but even recall that they collect stamps from Ecuador. All this information seems to bubble up from different parts of your brain, akin to when the solution to a problem over which you've struggled for days and then seemingly forgotten about suddenly emerges into consciousness. The brain can process many different sorts of stimuli simultaneously because it is a massively parallel system, like a computer with a huge number of CPUs working simultaneously.

It seems that thinking occurs through the interplay of many paths, as in the model I proposed to understand unconscious thought.

By the 1940s, researchers had begun to muse over how to develop computer architectures that could mimic the brain's neural network. Such architectures act like a collection of neurons, neurons being nerve cells, the building blocks or atoms of the brain. The human brain is made up of about one hundred billion neurons. Each grows fibers, or dendrites, which connect with those of other neurons at junction points called synapses. Depending on the level of chemical or electrical stimulation sparked by incoming information, such as a reaction to an event you perceive, the synapses are in an on or off state.

This process can be mimicked in a computer equipped with an artificial neural network made up of layers of artificial neurons, signal-detection devices that process information, functioning in a way loosely analogous to the nerve cells in the human brain. When information is put in, it stimulates an artificial neuron and causes it to start to work—to compute—as with nerve cells in the brain. Like our brains, an artificial neural network can be primed to seek patterns in data.

An artificial neural network is made up of three parts. The first contains the input information or data to be processed. The second, made up of layers of simulated neurons, is where the data is processed. The third is where data is recognized as some sort of pattern, such as a face or the process of steering a driverless car. Artificial neural networks have up to three layers, whereas deep neural networks—which were developed very recently, in the second decade of this century—have many more.

In the 1970s and 1980s, this form of computer architecture, artificial neural networks, was usually called parallel distributed processing (PDP). Scientists of the time claimed that these setups provided faster computation and were more faithful models of human cognition than had been in use before.[92]

The machines that most of us use are programmed with logic. To solve a problem, they follow rigid and/or, yes/no routes as they test out alternatives. This is how Simon's BACON program worked, trying out different sorts of ratios for different distances and times, whether cubed or squared, and so on, until it found the correct one. This is one type of machine learning, in which a machine learns by means of input rules and symbols such as equations or symbolic representations of the way people solve problems.

Artificial neural networks, conversely, need not be extensively preprogrammed, unlike our laptops, and they don't manipulate symbols. Instead they are based on another sort of machine learning in which data is fed into the machine with no explicit instructions. In other words, the machine learns by itself. Henceforth this is what I mean by "machine learning." In their early days, scientists taught machines by feeding data such as variously angled lines into their single layer of neurons. The machine would then compare an input letter of the alphabet with these shapes and identify it as, for example, a *T*. To begin with, it was a triumph whenever an artificial neural network managed to recognize a letter of the alphabet.

In the 1990s, artificial neural networks were developed that could read the numbers on checks, which was of great use for banks—but that was as far as they went. These early machines had trouble finding patterns, an essential aspect of data analysis. And there wasn't enough data available to train them—data such as that later provided by social media like Facebook—nor were the machines powerful enough.

Scientists were also trying to develop programs that could translate from one language to another, working on a word-for-word basis, by painstakingly inputting rules of grammar. But the problem seemed insurmountable.

AI seemed to overpromise and underdeliver, as well as being of little use in real-world situations such as reading documents, translating from foreign languages, and finding patterns in data. Funding dried up and people lost interest, leading to the so-called AI winter.[93] All this would dramatically change in the twenty-first century with the advent of more powerful computers and algorithms, together with a cornucopia of data from archives, social media, the public web (government, regulatory, banks, health care services, stocks and bonds), and medical records, to name but a few. And so we hurtled into the age of big data.

6 Games Computers Play

Deep Blue Defeats Garry Kasparov

I could sense—I could smell—a new kind of intelligence. It's a weird kind, an inefficient, inflexible kind.

—Garry Kasparov[94]

In 1973, along with forty others, I played chess with Bobby Fischer. Then reigning champion, Fischer had just beaten the defending champion Boris Spassky of the Soviet Union in the unforgettable 1972 tournament in Reykjavik, in Iceland. It was a battle of titans ratcheted up in Cold War rhetoric to a struggle between the United States and the USSR. Then Secretary of State Henry Kissinger personally offered Fischer encouragement.

Always impeccably dressed, Fischer was tall, rail thin, with an unusually long face and an aura of shy brilliance. In a tournament he was like ice, unperturbed, with a piercing stare that psyched out opponents.

To him, chess was second nature. He took us through a game he had played some years before with the Soviet grand master Mikhail Tal. Fischer spoke about this complex match, effortlessly moving magnetic disks showing images of chess pieces on a metallic board hung on a wall. His hands moved over the board as if creating a great painting or playing a piano concerto. After some forty moves, he turned to the audience and announced matter-of-factly that at this point he had known he could checkmate Tal in six moves. Tal had known it too and conceded. To be able to think six moves ahead? Chess was transformed before our eyes. It became not a game but an art form. We rose to our feet and applauded. Fischer's was a virtuoso performance. Afterward he defeated all forty of us, staring icily at each of us as one by one we turned over our kings in defeat and slouched away. We were in the presence of genius—in chess, that is.

Fast forward to 1996, when Garry Kasparov, the Russian world chess champion, played IBM's Deep Blue. Kasparov had played many games against computers and had never been beaten. But this machine was a behemoth of calculational power and depth of chess knowledge. Its powerful CPUs could assess one hundred million moves per second and were massively parallel, meaning that it could operate on many possibilities simultaneously. Deep Blue had a library of thousands of opening moves, middle-game moves, and endgames and could compare possibilities for moves with seven hundred thousand grand master games. It had eight thousand parts that could evaluate moves, and it could "see" eight moves ahead.

Kasparov got off to a bad start, losing the first game. It was the first time a computer had ever defeated a grand master under tournament conditions. To Kasparov's relief, he went on to win the match. "I could sense—I could smell—a new kind of intelligence," he famously said. "It's a weird kind, an inefficient, inflexible kind."[95] He had saved the human race, he added.

In 1997, he played a rematch. The newly upgraded version of Deep Blue could now evaluate two hundred million moves per second. It all went wrong, Kasparov recalled, in the forty-fourth move of the first game, when the computer came up with a sacrifice of such subtlety that Kasparov accused IBM of cheating. He was sure there must have been human intervention behind it. Although ruffled, Kasparov went on to win.

But he never recovered his equilibrium. He lost the second game and eventually lost the entire match. Machines don't get flustered or tired; they just go on. Kasparov demanded a rematch, but by that time IBM had partially dismantled Deep Blue and sent one of its two towers to the Smithsonian in Washington, DC.

It turned out that Deep Blue's "incredibly refined move" resulted from a bug in its software. Unable to select a move from its playbook—the ways it was programmed to respond to certain board positions—it went afield and chose another that had a good chance of success. It had found a way out of its quandary. Did this perhaps qualify as a creative act? Indeed, at what stage can a machine's actions be considered creative? Deep Blue was given a single problem to solve: to win at chess. To make its winning move, it applied all the knowledge that it had been fed, but it went one step further—and made what surely qualifies as a creative leap.

Over forty years earlier, the wartime code-breaker and computing pioneer Alan Turing wrote a paper entitled "Computing Machinery and Intelligence," in which he proposed what became known famously as the Turing test. This is a test of whether a machine can exhibit human-like behavior, whether it can fool a human judge into thinking that it's human. It involves two players and a judge. One of the players is a computer. The judge's task is to converse with the players via text, so that the result is not affected by the computer's ability to render words as speech, and then decide which is the machine. As yet, no computer has managed to fool a judge into thinking it is human and can therefore be deemed a "thinking machine." But the test is too restrictive and ambitious a definition of a thinking machine.

It's worth noting that the Turing test is not a test for creativity or even for intelligence. Turing wrote that the question of whether a machine was intelligent was unanswerable, and he proposed the test as something that could at least seriously be discussed.

Playing against Deep Blue, Kasparov said that he sensed a "new kind of intelligence." But overall, Deep Blue's conservative style of play would be a tip-off to a grand master that he was playing against a computer. So Deep Blue would not be able to pass a Turing test.

As for Kasparov, he went on to cash in on the popularity of chess-playing computers with his own software, which contains the essential patterns and opening moves that took him many years to learn. Now they are at the fingertips of young players, giving rise to an increasing number of grand masters as young as twelve. Yet, as Kasparov notes, so far this has not led to the emergence of another Bobby Fischer.

Kasparov may not be entirely correct here. Judit Polgár and her three sisters are all chess grand masters. Their father, an educational psychologist, believes that geniuses are made, not born. To prove this, he raised his children from the age of four in a hothouse environment with a particular focus on chess. Judit went on to become the strongest female player in the history of chess, entering the top one hundred players rating at the age of twelve, and her sisters also became grand masters. But can her success be attributed only to her father's intensive chess lessons, a learning process the psychologist K. Anders Ericsson calls "deliberate practice?"[96] As I've noted before, many people practice for hours on end and never achieve the eminence of someone like Judit; neither will working on physics all day, every day necessarily make you an Einstein. One needs to practice to develop expertise in any field, but conversely, possessing expertise does not mean that a person has practiced far more than everyone else. There is clearly something else going on. One point that deliberate practice does not take into account is that some people are born child prodigies, and a few may even be born geniuses in the pursuit they take up: chess in the case of Judit Polgár, and physics for Einstein.

The present international chess champion, Magnus Carlsen, is an excellent example of geniuses being born, not made. He has achieved the highest international rating in the history of chess, higher than Judit Polgár, Bobby Fischer, or Garry Kasparov, and at the age of twenty-two he became the youngest ever world chess champion. It is said that he achieved all this with considerably less dedication than Judit Polgár. In fact, psychologists have found that "more intelligent children also happen to practice less."[97]

To repeat, genius in humans cannot be taught. Worldly experience, maturity, and suffering are necessary in chess, too.

So the twentieth century came to a close at a moment of great excitement about the power of a computer to win at a game that many consider to require great intelligence. Reminiscing about his defeat by Deep Blue, Kasparov wrote that computer scientists should try "to develop a programme that played chess by thinking like a human, perhaps even learning the game as a human does. Surely this would be a far more fruitful avenue of investigation than creating, as we are doing, ever-faster algorithms to run on ever-faster hardware."[98] This would indeed come to pass in the twenty-first century.

IBM Watson Becomes *Jeopardy!* Champion

> Can a submarine swim?
> —David Ferrucci[99]

After Deep Blue's triumph at chess, engineers at IBM were on the lookout for a new challenge. One evening in 2004, a group of them met up at a restaurant. Suddenly the other diners all leaped from their tables to congregate in front of the television. It turned out that the reigning champion of *Jeopardy!*, Ken Jennings, was about to conclude his record seventy-four-game winning streak. Then and there, the engineers decided to build an IBM computer that could compete—and win—at *Jeopardy!*

In *Jeopardy!*, the answers are given and the contestants have to find the questions, which usually begin with *What* or *Who is*. For example, if the answer is "The film *Gigi* gave him his signature song, 'Thank Heaven for Little Girls,'" the correct question will be, "Who is Maurice Chevalier?" To participate, the computer has to be programmed to understand everyday language and reply in it. In AI, this is the field of natural language processing, related to how computers interact with people.

IBM Watson—named after Thomas J. Watson, IBM's dynamic president—took four years to build. Its huge database includes over two hundred million pages of information from dictionaries, encyclopedias, books, newspapers, and the full text of Wikipedia, and it can process over a million books a second. It operates in a massively parallel manner; that is, it can scan many possibilities simultaneously and is capable of generating hypotheses and ranking them at lightning speed. It thinks much like a person, in fact, by running through alternatives.

And in 2011 it stood on a stage between Ken Jennings and Brad Rutter, two *Jeopardy!* champions. The blue lights on its face revolved while, speaking quietly with a man's voice, it correctly found question after question, to become the *Jeopardy!* grand champion.

When Deep Blue played chess, it was working within the realm of what computers are good at, using statistics and probabilities to determine strategy. *Jeopardy!*, on the other hand, propelled Watson into the unfamiliar world of human language. While Deep Blue stayed in the computer's comfort zone, Watson walked awkward terrain for a machine.

Deep Blue was purpose built to play chess and was put out to pasture after its phenomenal victory. But Watson went far beyond, thanks to its vast database. This enables it to produce incredible feats, instantaneously retrieving information like numbers and names buried deep in web pages. Using this unstructured data, Watson can weigh the options and determine the best way to proceed to answer a question. In the case of *Jeopardy!*, it gave the question with the highest probability of being correct.

IBM plans to set up Watson for use in medical analysis and business strategy. It can participate in scientific research by going through thousands of scientific papers and offering a scientist suggestions for how best to proceed. Scientists at the North Carolina School of Medicine fed Watson data on one thousand cancer patients. In 99 percent of cases, it came up with the same treatment that was recommended by oncologists. In 30 percent of cases, Watson discovered a treatment option missed by the human doctors.[100] Watson can be a chef, too, concocting recipes from unlikely ingredients, often with rave results. "I'd give a strong review to a chef who'll never have the pleasure of tasting one of his own creations," wrote journalist Nanette Byrnes in the *MIT Technology Review* magazine.[101]

Like Deep Blue, throughout all its games of *Jeopardy!*, Watson never tired and remained unfazed. For the first time, people began to wonder seriously whether a machine could actually think. David Ferrucci, team leader of the Watson project, commented provocatively, "Can a submarine swim?"[102] Of course, a submarine swims—not like a fish, but better. It's an apt analogy. Watson's intelligence is impressive but narrow, and not exactly like a human's.

Because it's strictly a machine that provides questions for answers, Watson could not pass the Turing test. In the *Jeopardy!* games, human contestants fared much better at dealing with puzzle-type questions, whereas Watson tipped the balance for obscure questions, using its huge database of information about little-known events and people. The judge in the Turing test would easily guess that he was dealing with a computer. At its base, Watson is an information-retrieval system, and it would be premature to call it creative—but it is certainly a step in that direction.

Before the game, Jennings referred to himself jokingly as the "great carbon-based hope."[103] Similarly, before playing Deep Blue in 1996, Kasparov proclaimed that his mission was to save the human race. The next computer that came along would pose yet more of a challenge.

AlphaGo Defeats the Reigning World Go Champion

We are now past the point where we debate the gap between the capability of AlphaGo and humans. It's now between computers.
—Mok Jin-seok[104]

Go is generally acknowledged to be the most difficult board game of all. It's a game for two players in which the aim is to surround more territory than the opponent. The game was invented in China more than 2,500 years ago and is believed to be the oldest board game still being played.

What makes Go so difficult is that, unlike in chess, there are very few rules. As a result, there are many more alternatives to consider per move. The number of possible games in Go is astronomically larger than in chess.

In early 2016, I spoke with several AI experts. They all said that it would be a decade before a computer could crack Go. They insisted that more than brute force—trying every possible alternative, the approach used by Deep

Blue when it played chess—would be required here. But they proved to be wrong—in their timing, at least.

In the first decade of the twenty-first century, parallel distributed processing reentered the field, rebranded as deep neural networks. The central part of the computer, mimicking the brain, is now made up of several layers of neurons. This development has greatly enhanced the computer's learning capacity and its ability to distinguish patterns in complex input data.

Demis Hassabis and his colleagues at DeepMind in London—whose mission is to "solve intelligence"—took this configuration yet further by using reinforcement learning, in which neurons in the intermediate layers transmit back—back propagate—the signals that successfully identified a pattern or made a good move in a video game, thereby reinforcing success and thus learning. This process was first used in the 1980s and is the same as that by which we learn via the brain's dopamine-driven reward system, which provides rewards as incentives to progress. In computers, this could be called the inspiration to learn more. The machine is also hooked up to external memory so as to save patterns it has learned, in the same way that we retain memories.

In 2016, DeepMind (which had been taken over by Google two years earlier) launched AlphaGo, which was purpose built to play Go. It was the result of all these twenty-first-century advances. To learn Go, it studied thirty million possible moves in games played by masters. It also played against itself millions of times, improving with each game, learning just as humans learn. AlphaGo learned Go by developing hypotheses and testing them, which surely shows imagination—creativity.

A few months later, in March 2016, AlphaGo defeated South Korean Go master Lee Se-dol. Lee later commented that the computer had displayed human intuition, a feel for the game. AlphaGo was not preprogrammed to play Go as Deep Blue had been to play chess. In its choice of moves, it sought patterns, which is the way grand masters play. They don't focus on a particular piece but plan their strategy like a military maneuver. Military science was the inspiration for these board games.

AlphaGo's most notable move has become legendary. Move thirty-seven in the second of five games surprised both Lee and the AlphaGo team, as well as just about everyone else. After careful analysis, the DeepMind team made a discovery: from studying previous games, AlphaGo had calculated the chance of a human player making the same move to be one in ten thousand. Its practice games against itself had also shown that the move offered an unusually strong positional advantage. AlphaGo knew that Lee would be caught entirely unawares. It was a killer move, a move no human player would have made.

In early 2017, AlphaGo decimated the Chinese Go world champion, Ke Jie. Around that time, DeepMind publicly released fifty-five games that AlphaGo had played against itself. "They're how I imagine games from far in the future," said Shi Yue, a champion Go player from China.[105] Top Go players find many of the moves in AlphaGo's games to be more complex than those in games played by humans—downright incomprehensible, in fact, especially the openings.

"We are now past the point where we debate the gap between the capability of AlphaGo and humans. It's now between computers," concluded Mok Jin-seok, director of the South Korean Go team.[106]

And indeed, that turned out to be the case.

Later in 2017, DeepMind released AlphaGo Zero, an advanced version of AlphaGo. AlphaGo Zero is entirely self-taught. It was fed only the basic rules of the game, but unlike AlphaGo it was not given any human games to study. Instead, it had to work it all out from scratch by playing millions of games against itself. In three days, it had learned enough to beat the version of AlphaGo that had defeated Le Se-dol by one hundred games to nil. After twenty-one days, it defeated the version that had demolished the Chinese Go champion, Ke Jie. And after forty days, it surpassed all other versions to become the best Go player in the world.

Andy Okun, president of the American Go Association, said that the time had now arrived when humans and computers could have meaningful interactions. "Go players, coming from so many nations, speak to each other with their moves, even when they do not share an ordinary language," he said. "The time when humans can have meaningful conversation with an AI has always seemed far off and the stuff of science fiction. But for Go players that day is here."[107]

According to David Silver, leader of the teams that created AlphaGo and AlphaGo Zero, AlphaGo Zero is more powerful than its predecessor because "we've removed the constraints of human knowledge and so it is able to create knowledge itself."[108] As Demis Hassabis put it, it is "no longer constrained by the limits of human knowledge."[109]

Hassabis, among others at DeepMind, envisages practical applications for AlphaGo Zero, such as drug research. If applied to defeating Alzheimer's, for example, it could perhaps come up with cures that would otherwise take us hundreds of years to find. At present, scientists at DeepMind are studying protein folding, the process by which our organs are formed in the early embryonic stages through complex foldings of chains of proteins. Misfolded proteins are responsible for many devastating diseases, including Alzheimer's, Parkinson's, and cystic fibrosis. There is currently insufficient data to train an artificial neural network to work on protein folding and too many ways for a brute-force search—trying every possible alternative—to predict the different structures of proteins. Using a system like AlphaGo Zero would entail feeding in the rules for this sort of chemistry and the goal or intent of exploring protein folding, an easier option than the old method of trying every possible alternative.

Another step forward would be a computer that could make up a game itself. Hassabis is confident that AlphaGo Zero could do this. "We're pretty sure it would work, it would just extend the learning time a lot."[110] The key factor with AlphaGo Zero is that it can teach itself, playing games against itself and improving a little each time. It needs no human knowledge, data, or intervention.

AlphaZero, a yet more advanced version of AlphaGo Zero, has learned to play chess and shogi, a Japanese version of chess, as well as Go, after being fed only the rules of these games. Within twenty-four hours, it achieved superhuman levels of play in both these games, easily defeating leading programs.

Whereas Deep Blue required a huge amount of hand programming, feeding tens of thousands of games played by grand masters into its database, AlphaZero did not need any of this. It has developed its own style and strategies. It makes bizarre sacrifices and positions its pieces in intriguing ways, such as moving a queen into a corner. It has also developed its own system for assigning values to pieces. While Deep Blue examined two hundred million moves per second, AlphaZero surveyed a mere sixty thousand. Although its principal machine competitor in chess, an algorithm called Stockfish, can study a thousand more, AlphaZero trounced it. Like a human player, AlphaZero knew what to ignore. As Kasparov put it, AlphaZero "is the embodiment of the cliché, 'work smarter, not harder.'"[111] It surely has genuine moments of creativity.

"It doesn't play like a human and it doesn't play like a program. It plays in a third, almost alien way," said Demis Hassabis.[112] It shows, in fact, glimmers of machines thinking in ways other than the way we humans think, ways that may seem incomprehensible to us. For the moment, however, AlphaZero has no way of understanding that it has made an astounding move of great beauty because it has no awareness.

AlphaGo's success was a watershed, showing that AI is here to stay. Machines can increasingly teach themselves how to perform complex tasks that not long ago were thought to require the unique intelligence of humans. This has led to extensive investment by Google, Tesla, and Amazon to ensure that there will be no more AI winters.

And all this means that computers are now finally beginning to create art, literature, and music in ways that exhibit not only their creativity but their inner lives.

II Portrait of the Computer as an Artist

The first inkling anyone had that computers might be more than giant calculators or glorified typewriters came in the 1960s, when A. Michael Noll programmed a computer at Bell Labs, the pioneering research institute outside New York, to generate patterns of lines he called "computer art." His program produced dots distributed in a way prescribed by a mathematical equation called a Gaussian distribution, which generates bell-like curves. He then connected the dots from bottom to top in a random way, producing a continuous zigzag. The result reminded him of Picasso's *Ma Jolie*, which he had seen many times at the Museum of Modern Art (MoMA). He called his creation *Gaussian Quadratic*. He even held an exhibition, in 1965, at the Howard Wise Gallery on New York's grand Upper West Side.

Meanwhile, over in Germany that same year, Georg Nees and Frieder Nake were also beginning to look into the artistic possibilities of computers. But all this work was programmed, and the computers of the day were vast and unwieldly. The so-called art consisted mainly of geometric patterns of lines and dots: intriguing, certainly, but modest. Many years would go by before computers and computer art became a force to be reckoned with—and before anyone dared to suggest that computers might be creative.

7 DeepDream: How Alexander Mordvintsev Excavated the Computer's Hidden Layers

Whatever you see there, I want more of it.

—Alexander Mordvintsev[1]

Early in the morning on May 18, 2015, Alexander Mordvintsev made an amazing discovery. He had been having trouble sleeping. Just after midnight, he awoke with a start. He was sure he'd heard a noise in the Zurich apartment where he lived with his wife and child. Afraid that he hadn't locked the door to the terrace, he ran out of the bedroom to check if there was an intruder. All was fine; the terrace door was locked, and there was no intruder. But as he was standing in his living room, suddenly he "was surrounded by dozens of very beautiful ideas. That beautiful moment occurred when one idea crystallizes to a point where you can start programming."[2] It all came together. In an instant he saw what everyone else had missed. He sat down straightaway at his computer and began to type lines of code.

Up until then, artificial neural networks had been our servants, dutifully performing the tasks we asked them to perform, becoming steadily better at serving us. They definitely worked, but no one quite knew how. Mordvintsev's adventure that night was to transform completely our conception of what computers were capable of. His great idea was to let them off the leash, see what happened when they were given a little freedom, allowed to dream a little. He let loose the computer's inner workings, tapped into their mysterious hidden layers. Who would have guessed that they would throw up wild images not a million miles from van Gogh's *Starry Night*?

Mordvintsev comes across as focused, intense. He's more relaxed when he recalls his childhood, growing up in St. Petersburg. Mordvintsev graduated in 2010 from Saint Petersburg State University of Information Technologies,

Mechanics, and Optics with a master's in computer science, then went to work for a company specializing in marine-training simulators, using computers to model biological systems—in this case, coral reefs. Assigned to a computer vision group, he quickly became fascinated with the field. Computer vision is all about reinventing the eye, teaching computers to see, developing computers that can understand digital and audio images—that is, pictures and sound. "I spent a beautiful year on machine algorithms and was amazed at the machine's ability to track faces," he tells me.[3]

When Mordvintsev's first child was born, he and his wife decided that big cities were not the place for children. It was then that he received a call from a Google recruiter in Zurich, offering him a job there.

On arrival, he was worried. There were not many teams that did computer vision, and he was "a computer vision guy."[4] Worse, he was assigned to a team specializing in SafeSearch, preventing spam and porn from infecting search results. Nevertheless, he had the chance to wander around Google. Chatting to his fellow workers, Mordvintsev was struck by the power of deep neural networks. Previously he had been skeptical, but now he was in a place with access to huge data caches and the most up-to-date machines. He realized how deep neural networks could "really shine," as he puts it, and he began to look into how convolutional neural networks (ConvNets) function.

*   *   *

Neural networks are designed to mimic the brain. Our brains are made up of at least one hundred billion interconnected nerve cells (neurons), linked by a barely understood thicket of one hundred trillion connections. For us to see, the neurons in our brains pick up the images we receive on our retinas and give them shape and meaning. The process of creating an image out of a jumble of visual impressions begins in the primary visual cortex, which identifies lines and edges. This basic sketch is passed—like an assembly line in a factory—to the regions of the brain, which fill in the shape, spot shadows, and build up noses, eyes, and faces. The final image is put together using information from our memories and from language, which helps us categorize and classify images into, for example, different types of dogs and cats.

Artificial neural networks are designed to replicate the activities of the brain and to cast light on how the brain works. Convolutional neural networks are a specialized form devoted mainly to vision, able to recognize objects and spot patterns in data. The neurons are arranged in a similar way as in the eye. ConvNets have up to thirty layers, each made up of many thousands of artificial neurons, which is why they are called deep neural networks. The neurons in each layer are able to detect signals but are much less complex than the brain's nerve cells. The number of neurons and connections in a ConvNet is tiny in comparison to the number of nerve cells and connections in the human brain. For now, artificial neural networks are more akin to the brain of a mouse. But the assembly line process by which the machine recognizes an image is similar to the way in which we see.

*   *   *

To train a ConvNet, you feed in millions of images from a database such as ImageNet, made up of over fourteen million URLs of images, annotated by hand to specify the content. The network's adjustable parameters—the connections between the neurons—are tuned until it has learned the classifications so that when it is shown an image of, for example, a particular breed of dog, it recognizes it.

When you then show it an image and ask it to identify it, the ConvNet works in a similar way to the human brain. First the early layers pick out lines in the map of the pixels that make up the image. Each layer in succession picks out more and more details, building up parts of faces, cars, pagodas, whatever images it has inside its memory. The deeper you go, the more abstract the information gets. Finally, in the last layer, all the results of analyzing features in the pixels are assembled into the final image, be it a face, a car, a dog, or any of the millions of images that the neural net was trained on.

The crucial point is that the machine does not see a cat or dog, as we do, but a set of numbers. The image is broken up into pixels. Each pixel is represented by numbers that give its color on a red, green, and blue scale and its position. In other words, it's numbers all the way down. In the first layer, a filter illuminates areas of the pixel map one at a time, seeking out lines and edges, convolving—hence the term convolutional neural network. Then it transmits this primitive sketch to the next layer. The filters operate in the same way in each layer to clarify and identify the target image.

Finally, the last layer comes up with probabilities of what the image actually is. If the network has been asked to identify a dog, the conclusion might be 99.99 percent probability that it's a dog, with as many low probabilities for it being a cat, a lion, or a car as there are classes in the data it's been trained on.

Before deep neural networks, the filters in each of the layers had to be hand-engineered, a formidable task. In ConvNets, they emerge as a natural consequence of training.

*   *   *

One of the first successes of artificial neural networks was to read the numbers on checks. Now they can recognize faces, find patterns in data, and power driverless cars. Most scientists were satisfied to leave it at that. The unasked question was, What is the machine's reasoning? What occurs in the layers of neurons between the input layer that receives the image to be identified and the output layer where the solution emerges? These are the hidden layers, so called because they are neither input nor output; they are inside the machine. Mordvintsev became obsessed with finding out not only why ConvNets worked so well but why they worked at all, how they reasoned, what goes on in the hidden layers.

He set to work even though this problem was not part of his official duties, which related to SafeSearch. Google has a policy of allowing its engineers to spend up to 20 percent of their time, or one day a week, on some other Google-related project. Researchers, of course, can't just turn their minds on and off. The passion of your inquiry stays with you, either in your conscious or, more likely, unconscious.

A team from Oxford University had published papers that provided clues as to how best to proceed. They explained that when the computer was being fed with images, the pixels that made up the image were converted into numbers. To investigate how the ConvNet worked, the researchers stopped the process part way into the hidden layers and made the network generate an image of what it could see right then. They were trying to find out what the network saw, what was going on inside its "brain." They discovered that the images in the various layers, though blurry, still resembled the target image.[5]

Following the same lines, Mordvintsev was sure the hidden layers were not just black boxes, taking in data and producing results. He saw them as "transparent but very very obscure."[6] And that was when, not long after midnight on that early May morning, everything suddenly fell into place.

Mordvintsev sat down and wrote the code that encapsulated his break-through, enabling him to explore "how a neural network works layer by layer."

Ideas sometimes emerge at the strangest of times, as when French mathematician, philosopher, and scientist Henri Poincaré was stepping up into an omnibus and suddenly realized the solution to a problem that he had been struggling with. For Poincaré, unconscious thought, primed by conscious thought, was the key to the creative moment, the moment of illumination.[7] And so it was for Mordvintsev.

Instead of looking at what features of the original image are contained in a particular layer and then generating those features in the form of pixels to produce an approximate impression of the original image, as the Oxford team had done, Mordvintsev did the reverse. He fed an image into a Conv-Net that had been trained on the ImageNet data, but stopped the forward progress part way through. In other words, he stepped on the brakes. When the network was still in the middle of trying to verify a nascent sense that a particular pattern might be a target object, he told it to generate it right then and there.

The intermediate layers in a network are made up of many thousands of interconnected neurons containing a bit of everything the network has been trained on—in this case, the ImageNet dataset with lots of dogs and cats. If the target image has, for example, even a hint of dog in it, the relevant artificial neuron in that layer will be stimulated to emphasize the dogness. Then you reverse the process repeatedly back and forth and see what emerges. As Mordvintsev puts it, "Whatever you see there, I want more of it."[8] Google engineers refer to this as "brain surgery."[9] Whereas the Oxford group tried to reconstruct the original image, Mordvintsev's great idea was to keep the strengths of the connections between the neurons fixed and let the image change. As he put it modestly: "There were many suggestions about understanding neural networks. Mine was very practical."

So much for theory. But what happened in practice?

The first image that Mordvintsev used was of a cat and a beagle (see figure 7.1).

Normally, if you fed this through the machine, it would identify both the cat and the dog, having been trained on ImageNet with its images of 118 breeds of dog plus several cats. Mordvintsev fed in just the cat portion of the image and stopped part way through the hidden layers, bursting

Figure 7.1
Mordvintsev's reference image of a cat and a beagle, 2015.

with neurons containing a mash-up of dog and cat features, as well as whatever else is in ImageNet. The result of passing this image through several times was the nightmare beast shown in figure 7.2. Nothing like it had ever been seen—a thing with two sets of eyes on its head and another set on its haunches, and eyes and canine attributes bursting out all over its body: not entirely surprising, as the network had been trained more on dogs than cats. The background too had been transformed into complex geometric patterns, with a couple of spiders bursting through. It seems the machine saw spiders there, even though we hadn't. It was a vision of the world through the eyes of the machine.

Mordvintsev sat up until 2:00 a.m. writing a report full of images like that of the cat. He applied his algorithm at multiple scales, producing big and small cat-like creatures simultaneously, producing images with fractal properties and a look that can only be called psychedelic. The crucial point is that the machine was producing images that were not programmed into it.

Figure 7.2
Alexander Mordvintsev, nightmare beast created using DeepDream, 2015. [See color plate 1.]

Our human perceptual system behaves in a similar way, making us "see" things that aren't really there, like the face on the moon or pictures in clouds or the happy face in the Galle crater on Mars, an illusion called *pareidolia*. The dream-like images generated by Mordvintsev's algorithm were almost hallucinogenic, startlingly akin to those experienced by people on LSD. Did that mean that an artificial neural net was not that artificial? Could we say that Mordvintsev had found a way to look into the machine's unconscious, into its inner life, its dreams? Certainly he'd found a way to plumb its hidden layers.

Finally, Mordvintsev posted several of his images on an internal Google website, assuming that no one would notice them for a while. "I was wondering how to get back to sleep," he recalls.[10]

But the sun never sets on Google. It was late afternoon in Mountain View, California, and Google headquarters was in full swing. Mordvintsev's images went viral. The unknown engineer from the innocuous SafeSearch team in Zurich received rave reviews and soon after was snapped up by the Google machine-learning team in Seattle.

Mike Tyka Takes the Dream Deeper

> I'm a computationalist and I believe the brain is a computer, so obviously computers can be creative.
>
> —Mike Tyka[11]

One of the first to spot Mordvintsev's post was Mike Tyka, a software engineer at Google's Seattle office. At first, Tyka and Mordvintsev dubbed it inceptionism, after Christopher Nolan's 2010 movie *Inception*, starring Leonardo DiCaprio, about a technology capable of inserting people into other people's dreams, akin to plumbing the hidden layers of a machine. Then Tyka came up with the name *DeepDream*. "We had to call it something," he tells me.

Mordvintsev's images catalyzed Tyka. Normally, you don't explicitly program a deep neural network, so "you don't know how it works. Alex [Mordvintsev] looked for ways to visualize the knowledge in a trained neural net," he explains. "At that time most people seemed not to be interested in those sorts of problems."[12]

Tyka is an authority on neural networks. Long-haired, bearded, and amiable, dressed in a regulation black t-shirt, he never studied art but was attracted to the demoscene and fascinated by the possibilities of electronically generating graphics and text, not realizing that this was "basically art."[13] Tyka's father, none too happy about his son's artistic interests and concerned about his future, recommended that he study science. At the University of Bristol, Tyka studied biotechnology and biochemistry and soon after found himself at Google, using neural networks to study protein folding, the process by which proteins come together to form organs in the earliest phases of the embryo.

But he still wanted to become an artist. His studies of the forms that emerge in protein folding inspired him to create copper and glass sculptures. I spoke with Tyka by Skype in March 2017 about his work developing DeepDream. "So you've finally succeeded in combining art, science and technology?" I asked him. "Sure, I try all the time," Tyka replied.[14]

For Tyka, it was the fractal nature of Mordvintsev's images that made them so compelling.[15] This came from Mordvintsev scaling and rescaling them, compounding images, producing weird, psychedelic effects.

Not surprisingly, the public relations people at Google were wary of publishing Mordvintsev's images. After all, they queried, "Are people really going to be interested in this?"[16] But then they realized that somebody was going to leak them. And indeed, on July 16, 2015, two months after Mordvintsev's initial discovery, someone posted the soon-to-be-famous "dogslug cum puppyslug," as everyone called it, anonymously (see figure 7.3).

Reactions ranged from "looks like a bad dream" to "this thing can see into the abyss." In response, Tyka, Mordvintsev, and another software engineer,

Figure 7.3
"Dogslug cum puppyslug" created using DeepDream, 2015.

Figure 7.4
Two ibises—the original photograph (left) and as "seen" by a machine, 2015 (right).

Chris Olah, wrote a blog post entitled "Inceptionism: Going Deeper into Neural Networks."[17]

As an artist, Tyka realized that this could be "a great tool to make interesting art."[18] Following Mordvintsev's method, he tried feeding a photograph of an ibis into the system, reversing it as Mordvintsev suggested, stopping at an early layer. He expected the network to enhance lines because the earlier layers only pick up lines and edges. This is more or less what happened, as in the right-hand image in figure 7.4, in which linear patterns have developed.

Pushing the image further in touches on layers that seek out more complex information, producing abstractions and creating psychedelic effects. Indeed, if you put in a photograph of yourself and stop at an intermediate layer, and the machine detects dog-like features, it will turn you into a weird dog-like creature, as if it were hallucinating when it looked at you.

Tyka arranged for Mordvintsev's code to be shared within Google. It was soon shared externally as well on GitHub, a web-based repository for code. Tyka then went one step further. Up until now, scientists had studied Deep-Dream by putting in photographs in the form of JPGs. Tyka fed in a much less clearly defined image of a sky with clouds, then stopped the network at an interior layer, allowing the machine to tweak the image, bringing out any faint resemblances it happened to spot with parts of images in the ImageNet data it already had in its memory—dogs, cats, cars, pagodas, whatever. As Mordvintsev had put it, "Whatever you see, give me more."

Leonardo da Vinci's advice to students who had difficulty in finding something to paint was to look at the wall. "See that splotch? Stare at it for a while. What do you see?" Similarly, he advised them to look at clouds. This is precisely what Tyka had the machine do.

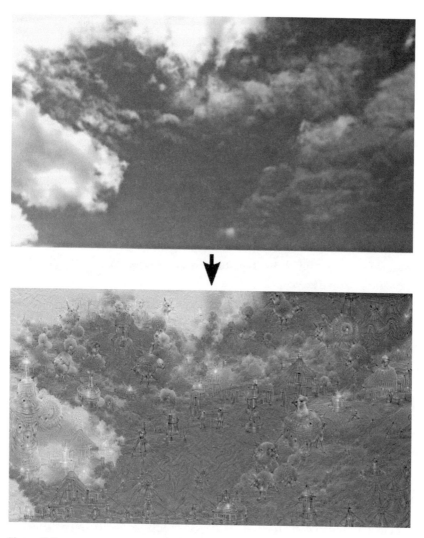

Figure 7.5
Picture of clouds before (top) and after (bottom) being transformed by DeepDream, 2015.

If we look hard at the top image in figure 7.5, we might be able to make out some bird-like features. The machine, which has been trained to recognize birds, spots them too. The machine's bird neurons in that intermediate layer activate and firm up the image. But this layer is not deep enough into the machine for recognizable birds to appear. Other neurons also activate, creating other shapes, and weird, bird-like creatures appear. Tyka continued to run the photograph backward and forward again, always stopping at the same layer, further embellishing the image each time, rendering it increasingly psychedelic.

But Tyka wanted to go a step further yet. Was there a way to use DeepDream to produce something completely new rather than simply embellishing images? He decided to input "noise," a collection of random dots, and let the machine look for what wasn't really there. He passed the image back and forth, stopping at a layer deep inside, letting the machine run through its repertoire of images as it tried to detect resemblances to them. Was there any way he could enhance this technique? The critical idea came to him at 2:00 a.m.[19] He concentrated on one segment of the image the machine had spawned and magnified it, zoomed in on it. In fact, he zoomed in and then zoomed out, intermittently cropping the image, revealing structures within structures. "Zoom is compelling," he says, "because of the fractal features that start to appear as a result of the network having only a finite amount of imagery it knows about." Soon you have a strange conglomeration of animals, reptiles, lizards, cars, bicycles, stretching to infinity, "all the way down."[20] Tyka's extraordinary, ever-changing video holds audiences spellbound.[21]

Tyka tells me, "I'm a computationalist and I believe the brain is a computer—so of course machines can be creative."[22] Furthermore, he says, when the Go grand master Lee Se-dol played AlphaGo and described its moves as beautiful, he was acknowledging its creativity.

He shares this computational view of creativity with his colleague at Google's Seattle office, Blaise Agüera y Arcas, who says: "As a computational neuroscientist I am sure that there is nothing spooky going on in the brain."[23] Convolutional neural networks, modeled on our visual system, can help us understand how we make sense of the world by turning incoming perceptions into knowledge. In other words, they can help us understand our brains better—the reverse of what was intended.

8   Blaise Agüera y Arcas Brings Together Artists and Machine Intelligence

When we do art with machines I don't think there is a very strict boundary between what is human and what is machine. ... We have a cyborg nature that is fundamental to the whole enterprise of being human.

—Blaise Agüera y Arcas[24]

Inspired by the popularity and importance of DeepDream, Blaise Agüera y Arcas, with Tyka's help, formed Artists and Machine Intelligence (AMI) at Google in Seattle, with the goal of fusing machine intelligence with art. The program includes engineers on site who wish to pursue an interest in art and technology, and it also gives grants and residencies to artists to work with machine learning. They prefer artists who already know about machine learning but are also prepared to link artists with engineers.

Agüera y Arcas is currently head of Google's Machine Intelligence Group in Seattle and is a star in Google's firmament. He sports designer stubble and de rigueur t-shirt, and he speaks with an unassuming air on physics, computer science, AI, philosophy, history, and art. He has a keen interest in music theory, especially Bach, and is a good cello player to boot. "I don't think of myself as a professional in anything," he tells me.[25]

Like many people interested in emergent technology, Agüera y Arcas was active for a while in the demoscene, an international computer art subculture that produces demos, self-contained computer programs that power flashy audiovisual presentations, showing off programming, visual art, and musical skills.

Agüera y Arcas studied physics at Princeton, then did a master's in applied mathematics. In 2003, he started Seadragon Software, a company that develops equipment to enable viewers to browse high-resolution images for use in mapping, visual books, and telemedicine. In 2006, Microsoft bought Seadragon, and Agüera y Arcas was given the position of distinguished engineer. Then, in 2013, he was headhunted and joined Google.

The current head of AMI is Kenric McDowell, who focuses on "spinning narratives around machine intelligence and how we can relate to it."[26] Like many people at Google, McDowell's background is eclectic. He began programming at the age of nine, majored in classical music composition at San Francisco State University, then switched to the Conceptual Information Arts program, in which he learned software for installations and game development. Then he changed directions again and completed an MFA in photography at Bard College in New York State. After a twelve-year stint in advertising, McDowell went to work for Google doing speculative design, which brought him back to his original dream of combining art and technology.

When DeepDream went viral, Agüera y Arcas assembled a few people at Google who he knew were interested in art and had a background in it. "Let's do something cool and interesting," McDowell recalls him saying.[27] McDowell was in a position to play a key role because he had an MFA and had shown his work in an art exhibition in New York. He advised against stepping forward and saying, "Hey, we're at Google and doing art." "I was afraid that some people might get offended and not take us seriously. There's an established dialog that exists outside the tech world," he says. Google had to signal that it had a serious engagement with art.

First the group contacted artists they thought might want to get involved. Then, on February 26, 2016, they held an auction of artworks at the Gray Area Foundation for the Arts, a nonprofit organization supporting art and technology, in the heart of San Francisco's Mission District. The exhibition was called *DeepDream: The Art of Neural Networks*. Over eight hundred attended, including many curious geek hipsters eager to see the new art. Mike Tyka curated. Agüera y Arcas set the stage with an electrifying oration: "In addition to being a really cool art show, this is also the inaugural event of a collaboration that we are launching at Google between scientists, researchers, engineers, artists, thinkers—that we are calling 'artists and machine intelligence.' This is really a beginning and a seed and something that we hope is going to be going on for a long time."[28] He added that "some artists will embrace machine intelligence as a new medium or partner, while others will continue using today's media and modes of production," and stated his own belief that machine-generated art is cutting edge. It's the new avant-garde, which will transform society, our understanding of the world in which we live and our place in it.

He continued: "Like the invention of applied pigments, the printing press, photography, and computers, we believe machine intelligence is an innovation that will profoundly affect art. As with these earlier innovations, it will ultimately transform society in ways that are hard to imagine from today's vantage point; in the nearer term, it will expand our understanding of both external reality and our perceptual and cognitive processes."[29]

He gave as an example Hans Holbein's 1533 painting *The Ambassadors*, with its famous distorted image of the human skull—the anamorphic skull. Holbein undoubtedly used mirrors to project the skull's image onto the canvas before tracing the outline. In his talk, Agüera y Arcas also reviewed the history of photography and the public resistance to its being a form of art, through to David Hockney's work today and his fruitful collaboration with scientists.

"We're witnessing a time of convergences," he continued, "not just across disciplines, but between brains and computers; between scientists trying to understand and technologists trying to make; and between academia and industry. We don't believe the convergence will yield a monoculture, but a vibrant hybridity."[30] In short, "We are fundamentally technological beings."[31]

The exhibition of DeepDream art was a huge success. Several Silicon Valley barons attended, including Clay Bevor, the head of Google's virtual reality project. Twenty-nine artworks were sold, including four of Tyka's, and raised almost $100,000 for the Gray Area Foundation. As *Wired* magazine's Cade Metz put it, "It was also a night to reflect on the rapid and increasing rise of artificial intelligence. Technology has now reached the point where neural networks are not only driving the Google search engine, but spitting out art for which some people will pay serious money."[32]

The following June, the group held a symposium called Music, Art, and Machine Intelligence. This was a joint meeting of Google's AMI, headed by Agüera y Arcas, and Google's Project Magenta, headed by Douglas Eck, which explores the role of machine learning in creating art, literature, and music. Twenty-nine presenters spoke to an audience of eighty about their research on machine-generated art, literature, and music. To heighten the drama, each presentation lasted precisely ten minutes.

An up-and-coming artist, Anna Ridler, attended and was bowled over and inspired by the luminaries she met at the symposium. "It was art like you've never seen before," she says.[33] She saw a new field opening up, "including a lot of people who thought philosophically about their fields."

Despite its success, the event was a one-off. McDowell and his fellow curators decided that "setting up art exhibitions is not Google's strength."[34] They decided it was better to "support other artists that have an interesting approach to technology" in a way that allowed them to use AI in their own way, rather than have Google "frame the conversation."[35] The new scheme allows for a few artists in residence, as well as financial and technical support for artists working on their own.

Memo Akten Educates a Neural Network

#DeepDream is blowing my mind.
—Memo Akten[36]

The first work to be snapped up at the Gray Area art exhibit was Memo Akten's extraordinary image of GCHQ as "seen" by a machine (figure 8.1).[37]

Figure 8.1
All Watched Over by Machines of Loving Grace: DeepDream Edition, 2015.

Government Communications Headquarters (GCHQ) in Cheltenham, deep in the English countryside, is an all-seeing eye that scours the ether for intelligence signals on behalf of security organizations in the United Kingdom. Akten is wary of its powers. DeepDream offered an excellent way to subvert it. The finished work is, he wrote, "an artificial hallucination seeded by a satellite view from Google Maps, and reimagined through deep neural networks developed by Google."

He wrote in a blog post, "#DeepDream is blowing my mind."[38] It is, after all, a neural network that has been trained on certain information that makes up its entire base of knowledge, which makes it a lot deeper than something that merely produces hallucinations. "When you show it something new," like an undefined image of a cloud, "it tries to make sense of what it's seeing in terms of what it already knows, which is"—and this is the crux of matter—"how we make sense of the world." Perception is in the brain, whether it be our brain or that of a deep neural network. "I find that really poetic," says Akten.

Memo Akten's dress reflects his Turkish origins. With his moustache and beard, long hair, necklaces, bracelets, earrings, and brightly colored clothing, at times he takes on the aura of a pirate of the Caribbean. He began programming at the age of ten and took, as he puts it, the typical Turkish educational trajectory—into engineering.

He studied civil engineering, but never used it. Instead, he hankered to make sci-fi films, like those of Ridley Scott and Stanley Kubrick. He had no access to a camera, but he "didn't need one," he says. "I had computers."[39] Besides English, Turkish, and French, he also had the Pascal programming language "as a way to express [himself]."[40]

Then he discovered Oscar Fischinger, the great German-born nonfigurative animator whose works the Nazis condemned as "degenerate art." Fischinger emigrated to the United States, where his talent was recognized by Paramount Pictures and Walt Disney. Akten's interests also included the music of Steve Reich, John Cage, and Edgar Varèse.

He recalls that when he was growing up, he thought that art was just painting and sculpture. "I didn't realize I was doing art already while messing around on my computer."[41] He is now working on a PhD at Goldsmiths University, trying to create semiautonomous intelligent creative systems that musicians can collaborate with. But Akten is not someone to tie himself down to one research topic. He is interested in a deeper understanding of what happens when machines store knowledge about the data they are trained on—knowledge that is essentially a collection of numbers. "So what is that knowledge? That," he says, "is what my actual PhD is about."

In 2017, at Ars Electronica, the giant electronic art exhibition in Linz, Austria, he showed a piece he called *Learning to See: Hello, World!*[42] This is one of an ongoing series of works that explore how neural networks come alive as they begin to observe the world around them through the data they are fed, much as babies do when they first move about and absorb images. Computer scientists refer to a machine awakening as a "hello, world" moment. In his piece, Akten trains a deep neural network on images from a video camera pointed at himself. As the neural network is fed more and more images, it begins to recognize a pattern—Akten's face. Then Akten moves, and the machine has to start all over again. Soon it can recognize his face from any angle.[43]

"By saying a machine can be creative you are not anthropomorphising the machine," Akten asserts, "but liberating it by expanding the term 'creativity' to go beyond humans." Creativity is not limited to people. "I'm a biological machine," he continues. "Humans can create art. Why not machines?"

9   What Came after DeepDream?

Damien Henry and a Machine That Dreams a Landscape

It will be hard for the art world to ignore what machine learning can do and what artists can do with machine learning.

—Damien Henry[44]

Damien Henry's computer-generated *Music for 18 Musicians—Steve Reich*, based on train journeys he took across France, provides another thought-provoking demonstration of how a neural net awakens.

Henry was always amazed at the fact that deep neural networks can learn without explicit instructions. He wanted to find a way to demonstrate this and decided to feed a deep neural network with videos taken from a moving train, giving the network many examples so that it could "figure out how to do things."[45]

Then he chose a single still image from the sequence and fed it into the machine. He used an algorithm that would predict the next frame in the sequence as a likely outcome of the preceding one again and again, over one hundred thousand times.

To his amazement, he found that the algorithm captured phenomena he "would not have thought about to capture himself." The distant blue sky hardly moves, while the foreground moves by rapidly.[46] The result is a mesmerizing fifty-six minutes of an extraordinary landscape eternally passing by. "At some point," he recalls, "I found Steve Reich's music, *Eighteen Musicians*, which I completely fell in love with." Like the train sequence, it was repetitive, and it made a perfect match. Reich's music spurred Henry to enlarge his initial premise. One new idea was to use several videos for training, including trips through countryside and cities. "The result was more complex," he says.

Damien Henry has a goatee, warm smile, and Gallic sense of humor. He is the technical program manager at the Google Cultural Institute in Paris, where he kindly invited me to spend some time. He became interested in coding, he tells me, at the age of eight or ten. But his interest was not in video games. Wasn't there something else coding was good for? He pondered this, but put these thoughts aside because he felt they were nothing more than "procrastination," which he prefers to avoid.[47] At university, instead of studying computer science, he opted for aeronautical engineering. But he couldn't stay away from coding, and when he resumed his explorations, he concluded that his previous efforts should be called "creative coding."

He posted a version of his train journey music video, almost an hour long, on YouTube, in which a blurry landscape unfolds from an impressionistic haze, accompanied by Steve Reich's hypnotic music. It is not a "real landscape," but the world as seen by a machine. The machine makes choices, it employs probability, but that does not devalue the final result. We too reason probabilistically. We take in data, figure out ways to deal with it, and choose the option most likely to succeed.

Henry firmly believes that machines cannot be creative by themselves. "The more complex the tool, the more creative we can be," he says. The idea of totally removing people from the equation makes no sense to him.

Mario Klingemann and His *X Degrees of Separation*

> I try to get away from the "default" setting, the out-of-the-box setting, tweak it and add my own touch to it.
> —Mario Klingemann[48]

People "still have problems accepting that you can do art using machines," says Mario Klingemann.[49] He is well aware that he is part of a new avant-garde and feels that "this is where the really interesting work is."

In 2015, he began a large-scale project to classify the million or more out-of-copyright digital images from 1500 to 1899 that have been put online by the British Library. To do this, he trained a machine that organized them into classes—portraits, horses, dogs, men, women, rocks, ancient and modern tools, and so on. These groupings existed in a multi-multi-dimensional space—a latent space made up of the encodings of the numerous pixels that make up the artworks. He then projected them into two dimensions. Eventually he tagged about four hundred thousand. He put some of his results on Twitter.

Shortly afterward, the phone rang. It was Damien Henry from Google—the call independent machine artists dream of. "We have this huge amount of cultural data and see that you do interesting stuff. Why not drop by?" Henry said.[50] "I would never pass a Google engineer interview because I have only certain knowledge," Klingemann tells me, alluding to Google's legendarily rigorous interviews. But Henry sensed something interesting and extraordinary and Klingemann became an artist in residence.

Mario Klingemann is another artist who showed his work at AMI. Always smiling, always brimming with ideas, he started coding at the age of twelve but still cut and pasted graphics for his school newspaper by hand. He didn't go to art school or have any higher education. Painting and drawing held no interest for him, nor did informatics. Initially he worked in advertising on projects that combined code and art and kept his eyes open for developments. But he felt that he lacked the seal of approval as an artist. "I'm trying to make up for that by doing interesting things in fields not yet taught in art schools," he says.[51]

He now calls himself an artist—a code artist.

At Google, Klingemann was excited about the data available and the machines he had access to for his "experiments," as he calls his artwork. Along with another computer artist, Simon Doury, Klingemann was asked to create a way of making connections, two at a time, between the millions of artworks available from the British Library, based on "six degrees of separation," the idea that everything in the world can be connected to everything else in a maximum of six steps. Doury and Klingemann's X Degrees of Separation is a readily available website.[52] On it, you pick any two artworks from the million in the Google cache. Using machine learning, the computer quickly finds a pathway connecting them through a chain of five, six, or seven artworks using visual clues. Thus a four-thousand-year-old clay figure can be linked to van Gogh's *The Starry Night* through seven intermediary works.

Klingemann and Doury based their website on the fact that artificial neural networks transform (encode) the pixels in the chosen image into numbers. The machine scans the works available, seeking similarities in their encodings. These translate into the visual similarities that we see in the successive images, similarities that we might otherwise overlook between, for example, the four-thousand-year-old clay figure and van Gogh's painting, as well as those in the intermediary works.[53] The degrees of separation vary with the images chosen. Sometimes there are five, sometimes eight.

In his time off, Klingemann also explored DeepDream, his "trigger into this neural network field."[54] He studied the online code and read what others were doing. "It was all puppyslugs and puppy dogs and psychedelic images. I wanted to do something else," he tells me. He asked himself: How can I use the same methods and get different results? Instead of feeding his machine with images from ImageNet, as other artists had, he fed in decorative letters of the alphabet, such as we see in woodcuts and antique books. To check that

Figure 9.1
Mario Klingmann, *Mona Lisa* transformed by DeepDream, 2016.

the machine had correctly learned what he wanted it to, he fed in decorative images from old books. The machine was able to pick out a particular letter that was largely hidden. In one image, the machine indicated that there was a *B* present. Klingemann thought it had made a mistake until he looked closer. Sure enough, there was indeed a *B*, though it was virtually invisible.

Having equipped his machine with a huge number of stylized letters and the code for DeepDream, he fed in the *Mona Lisa*. Out came a *Mona Lisa* transformed into an alphabetized linocut (figure 9.1).

Given that he had fed the machine only with wood block prints of letters, it looked for these in everything it saw.

Angelo Semeraro's Recognition: Intertwining Past and Present

> Maybe what happens right now has already happened in other forms a long time ago.
> —Angelo Semeraro[55]

Recognition is the work of a team at the Fabrica Research Centre in Treviso, in Italy. It is sometimes called the "Italian ideas factory" in reference to its highly creative output in design, visual communication, photography, and journalism.[56] The team is made up of Angelo Semeraro, who focuses on technological input; Corallie Gourguechon, who focuses on product design; and project manager Monica Lanaro. In 2016, they won the IK Prize sponsored by Tate Britain, awarded to groups or individuals who propose the best original idea based on digital technology for exploring the art on display at Tate and on its website. That year, Tate partnered with Microsoft. The challenge was to use AI for this purpose.

Semeraro discovered computers as a teenager. He loved the guitar, and thought of combining technology and music; he soon extended this to include art. He studied mathematics and computer science at the University of Bologna, then went to Fabrica, where he found people who "were interested in how a subjective field like art could be seen through the rational eye of AI."[57]

The catalyst for their work was news images: "accidental Renaissances," modern images composed by accident that bear striking similarities to Renaissance art. The title originates from photographs of drunken late-night revelers sprawled on the streets of Manchester, England, on New

Year's Eve in 2016, which look startlingly akin to a Renaissance painting.[58] "This inspired us to show how humans can take two images from two completely different eras and then find comparisons between them," Semeraro tells me.[59] Perhaps, the Fabrica team thought, "Comparison between the images can be greater than the sum of the two, to create a new content. That was how the idea began to take shape."

Winning the IK Prize gave them the opportunity to work with Tate's vast collection of five hundred years of British art, with Microsoft, and with the Reuters news agency and its huge library of photographs. This, they felt, would enable them to show how the present and past intertwine. "Maybe," Semeraro says, "what happens right now has already happened in the past."[60] Semeraro points out that we often say that the "past can help us to understand. But why cannot the present help us to understand Tate Britain's five-hundred-year-old collection?"

It took the team two days to find a single good match between 1,250 news images and 30,000 art works, while in three months the machine made 4,502 matches. The machine does not deal with pixels but with the numbers that encode each pixel. An artificial neural network compares these numbers with the numbers characterizing other art works and looks for similarities, as shown in the two images in figure 9.2.

Figure 9.2
A pairing by Recognition of a 2016 photograph with a painting from 1660, 2017.

Sometimes the machine spotted surprising matches that at first sight made no sense, but on further reflection turned out to be very interesting. Some remained ambiguous. There were also mistaken matches—which shows, Semeraro muses, "that art is a nice playground."[61] The machine saw what Semeraro and his colleagues could not.

Leon Gatys's Style Transfer: Photography "In the Style Of"

In a way, style transfer is also brain surgery.
—Leon Gatys[62]

Have you ever wondered what Picasso would have done with one of your favorite photographs, or how he would have portrayed you yourself? Leon Gatys and two colleagues at the University of Tübingen in Germany figured out a way to find out. They called their method style transfer,[63] and it appeared two months after Mordvintsev, Tyka, and Olah launched DeepDream.

Gatys studied physics at University College London and was inspired by the deeply philosophical debates he read about on the interpretation of quantum physics—in particular, the ideas of Niels Bohr and Werner Heisenberg. At Tübingen, he explored how complex neural networks can help explain how we see the world around us. DeepDream had shown how machines can elucidate the complexity in the way we process incoming perceptions. At times we see things that aren't really there. Perception occurs in the brain, and it is the same with machines.

From this Gatys evolved "a neural algorithm of artistic style." If we can "see" a scene with our eyes but imagine it as something different, rendered by Rembrandt or Cézanne, why can't a convolutional neural network do the same? Gatys puts great weight on the analogy, however loose, between ConvNets and human vision. "I want to have a machine that perceives the world in a similar way as we do, then to use that machine to create something that is exciting to us."[64]

Style is a nebulous concept that art historians argue over. It takes years of training and experience for an art historian to be able to distinguish an artist's work by its style. Could it really be something a machine could grasp? Could a neural network separate style from content and miraculously produce a work that looked as if it had been recovered from the studio of a long-dead master? It seems it could.

Style transfer works by recreating an arbitrary photograph in the style of a classic painting. In the 1980s, before artificial neural networks came into their own, this was a hugely difficult task. In those days, machines dealt with representations of the world using objects and symbols set into complex networks made up of statements and rules about things and their relationships. Computer scientists were essentially programming the world as we see and perceive it into their machines. Applying these networks to a painting was impossible.

But neural networks deal not with statements about a painting, but with numbers. To interchange the pixels in a painting with the pixels in a photograph would be extremely complex, if possible at all. But in deep neural networks, each pixel is replaced with the numbers that encode it, as are the pixels in the photograph to be altered. The question is how to mix the numbers in a photograph with those in a classic painting so as to create something new.

In style transfer, the style image is a photograph of a painting and the content image is an arbitrary photograph. Gatys begins by feeding the encodings for the style image and the content image into the layers of the network, then puts in an image made up of white noise. This will be the basis of the new image—the blank canvas. At this stage, the pixels in it are distributed at random, with no connections between them, in a dense conglomeration of black and white dots with no discernible pattern. This blank canvas is then propagated back and forth through the system so that it captures as much as possible of the style of the painting and the content of the photograph, mixing them both together until it finally reproduces the image in the photograph in the style of the painting. Even so, the process is rather mysterious and the results a little magical, as in figure 9.3, where style transfer takes a photograph of the Neckarfront at Tübingen and transforms it in the style of van Gogh's *The Starry Night* to create a new, rather extraordinary, and exciting image.

Style transfer proved instantly and deservedly popular, so Gatys, along with colleagues at Tübingen, set up a website (https://deepart.io/page/about/) where anyone can play with it. You insert a photograph together with a painting, by, for example, Picasso, click a button, and in a short time the machine creates an image in the style of your chosen painting—thus yielding, for example, a cubist image of yourself.

How does style transfer compare with DeepDream? Both use representations of the features at various depths in a deep neural network to change

Figure 9.3
The content image, a photograph of the Neckarfront at Tübingen (upper left). The style image, van Gogh's *The Starry Night* (lower left). The image on the right results from combining the style and content images to make *The Neckarfront at Tübingen according to van Gogh*, as van Gogh might have painted it. [See color plate 2.]

and synthesize images. But whereas DeepDream finds an image of, for example, a cat, that maximally stimulates a certain neuron that has been trained to identify it, in style transfer both style and content are extracted from an image. The deeper the level you sample from the style image's journey through the layers of the network, the more you can match the structure of the content image, even though the appearance is completely changed.

This, says Gatys, is like having a vague image of what a forest was like last time you saw one, then using this information to imagine a brand-new forest. He is optimistic that style transfer will offer new insights into the way people see and hopes that it is a first step toward understanding perception. "That's something I'm very excited about."[65]

One of the offshoots of style transfer is photographic style transfer, in which the style image is also a photograph.[66] The issue here is how to control the way in which the style image is imported over to the content image so that straight lines remain straight and curved lines remain curved, thus yielding an output photograph with no abstraction. The result will be akin to what a very advanced version of Adobe Photoshop could produce.

Other recent avenues of research for style transfer include "generation of audio in the style of another piece of audio or, perhaps, generating text," says Gene Kogan, another prolific artist/technologist.[67]

Another is fashion. In this case, an artificial neural network is trained to distinguish between popular and less popular trends in clothing based on elements such as collars, pockets, sleeves, and patterns. The process here is to transfer the style of, say, one shirt to another, then keep reprocessing.[68]

As for Gatys's views on creativity, he feels that we will need to understand human creativity better before we can evaluate our progress toward machine creativity.

10 Ian Goodfellow's Generative Adversarial Networks: AI Learns to Imagine

I actually thought up GANs during a debate in a pub.

—Ian Goodfellow[69]

In 2014, the year before Mordvintsev's DeepDream images went viral, Ian Goodfellow of the University of Montreal came up with an invention that would redefine the frontier of machine learning: generative adversarial networks (GANs). Yann LeCun, who, along with Geoffrey Hinton, pioneered the modern revolution in deep neural networks, declared GANs to be "the most interesting idea in the last 10 years in machine learning."[70]

GANs are a way of training the computer to create realistic images entirely by itself.

Up to now, we've been looking at supervised learning, in which a neural network is fed millions of labeled images of cats, dogs, cars, houses, and so on, usually from ImageNet. From these, the neural network learns that dogs belong to the labeled classification *dog*, cats to *cat*, and so on. When it is presented with an image of something four-legged and furry, the computer can guess with a high probability of success whether it is a dog or a cat and what breed it is. If it makes a mistake, it sends information about the error back through the network, a process called back propagation, which enables it to readjust the parameters, or weights, between the network's neurons.

But this is not at all the way that humans learn. When we are children, someone may tell us a couple of times that a certain animal is a dog and another is a cat. When we see similar four-legged furry creatures, we learn to reason that they too are dogs and not cats or vice versa. We learn by observing the world, not by being told the names of every object in it, and thus we draw up rules from what we are taught and what we observe. From this we also learn how to deduce new facts about the world. This cycle continues throughout our lives. There is a treasure trove of data out there. The problem is how to understand it in the same way that humans do. Getting machines to learn in the same way that we do is known as unsupervised learning and is the Holy Grail of machine learning. This is the quest that Goodfellow tackled.

Goodfellow began coding at the age of eleven. In his mathematics class in junior high school, the students' calculators included video games. Instead of listening to his teacher, Goodfellow edited the code for a racing car game, for which he got into serious trouble, he tells me with relish.[71]

For his master's degree in computer science at Stanford University, he concentrated on AI. He then moved to the University of Montreal, a powerhouse of machine learning. There Goodfellow worked with Yoshua Bengio, a key player in the field.

For his PhD, he focused on networks called generative models, which generate images. The machine he worked on had undergone unsupervised learning. This involved feeding a machine a lot of images, such as images of dogs. The idea was that the machine should start to generate imaginary images, such as new sorts of dogs. But the machine couldn't recognize that the images were dogs.

For it to do so, it had to be fed more and more photos, until the process effectively became supervised, not unsupervised, learning. Goodfellow was frustrated. He felt that he was not doing anything original but simply following other people's work. This brought home to him how difficult it was to generate images using generative models.

After his PhD, he stayed on at the University of Montreal to write a textbook on deep learning, both supervised and unsupervised, while continuing to brood on generative models and their shortcomings. He had the feeling that he was on the verge of discovering "something new and interesting."[72]

Goodfellow's friends, meanwhile, were working on an entirely different AI research project. One night, in the middle of an intense debate in a pub with them, the idea for a new kind of generative network suddenly popped out of nowhere into his mind. Just as Mordvintsev thought up DeepDream in his dark living room after checking for a burglar, Goodfellow "actually thought up GANs during a debate in a pub," he tells me.[73]

"It was that nascent moment when things clicked," he says. While his friends continued their late-night pub discussion, "I went home and did it.

I actually wrote the code and was pretty confident it would work." He adds, "It was actually an extension of some earlier ideas. In a lot of creativity one has to build up experience and background knowledge." This is the basis of creativity. The four steps—conscious thinking, unconscious thinking, illumination, and verification—are all key to the creative process. Ideas do not emerge from nothing.

GANs are based on game theory.[74] There are two dueling networks, the discriminator (D) and the generator (G). Both are deep neural networks. D is fed with images of the real world, from a dataset such as ImageNet. Meanwhile, G begins to generate images out of a first layer that is latent space, made up of noise, like randomly situated dots. It is chaotic, disorganized, and contains infinite possibilities, like our imaginations. Initially the images G produces are completely abstract, a blur of shapes.

G is like an art forger, while D operates like a detective evaluating the images generated by G. D decides whether the image it receives from G is realistic, based on the images it has been fed, or whether it is unrealistic—that is, fake. The first few images G creates are largely noise and D rejects them. G then sends them back to where they came from and tries again. By the time this new image reaches the discriminator network, it will be better formed because the intermediary layers in G (G's hidden layers) are beginning to learn from their errors.

By now G no longer reverts to its latent space layer to generate images. Instead it starts from layers near the beginning, that is, near the latent space layer. Due to its interactions with D, it starts to learn how to produce images that look real. While the discriminator tries to distinguish realistic from unrealistic images, the generator tries to create images that will fool the discriminator into thinking they are real. Eventually a stable situation emerges in which G's images actually look like the ones in D's training set. In game theory, this is known as the Nash equilibrium after the mathematician John Forbes Nash Jr.

This process of networks competing lessens the human intervention required. In previous methods for generating images, scientists set criteria to measure how wrong a generative model is in deciding whether a painting is real or not. This is a difficult problem to handle mathematically. With GANs, the discriminator decides. In this way, machines can begin to learn what the world looks like. "You can think of generative models as giving artificial intelligence a form of imagination," says Goodfellow.[75] "I look forward to seeing how a lot of the mathematical tools I've developed for this work will be useful for artists," he adds. "And I will enjoy seeing what they do with it."[76]

As to whether machines can be creative, Goodfellow's opinion is that "they already are."[77] If creativity means producing something new and beneficial, as in Margaret Boden's three criteria, then, he continues, "machine learning algorithms are already at that point. We see this also with generative models and reinforcement learning."

Goodfellow is now a scientist with the Google Brain team in Mountain View.

Mike Tyka's *Portraits of Imaginary People*

To me, art is judged by the reactions people have.
—Mike Tyka[78]

Mike Tyka was one of the first to see the possibilities of DeepDream for making art. He was also eager to explore the artistic possibilities of GANs. The result is his stunning work, *Portraits of Imaginary People*. For this, he fed the discriminator thousands of photographs of faces from Flickr, a vast

Figure 10.1
One of Mike Tyka's *Portraits of Imaginary People*, Ars Electronica, 2017.

image- and video-hosting site. As the generator's output improved, the faces of imaginary people it had conjured up became clearer and clearer. What emerged were highly stylized faces that nonetheless looked almost real—"photographs" of people who don't exist, as in the two rather disturbing faces in figures 10.1 and 10.2. A selection of his pictures was shown at Ars Electronica in 2017. The crowds were entranced.

The brain instinctively registers that these are not real people. Tyka could have pushed the machine to produce even more realistically human faces, and ultimately viewers would have been repulsed. Art would enter the realm of the "uncanny valley," in which people become nervous about a possible existential threat posed by an alien life-form all too similar to ours.

Figure 10.2
Another of Mike Tyka's *Portraits of Imaginary People,* Ars Electronica, 2017.

Refik Anadol Creates a Dreaming Archive

Can we make an archive dream?
—Refik Anadol[79]

Istanbul's SALT Galata is a huge art institution and online library containing 1.7 million images relating to Turkey created from the late nineteenth century to the present. (The Turkish word "salt" means "absolute, pure, unvarnished.") In 2015, the curators decided they wanted to digitize their collection. Vasif Kortun, the chief curator, consulted Refik Anadol about what media art could contribute.

Anadol, a Turkish-born media artist, bubbles over with enthusiasm for media art and for the possibilities of combining it with architecture. He started coding at the age of eight and went on to study visual communication and design in Istanbul. A visit to Ars Electronica in 2005 inspired him to turn to media art.

His moment of inspiration came when he realized that he didn't just want to exhibit his media art "in galleries where the audiences are limited," but "in public places, using media art and architecture. I have a data-driven mind," he tells me. "I love exploring data as a substance, a physical quality."[80]

For the SALT project, Kortun sent him the institution's complete collection—all two terabytes of it, a monstrously huge amount. (The prefix *tera* derives from the Greek word for monster. The entire Library of Congress has about 525 terabytes of information.) The Turkish material included images, drawings, photographs, letters, and maps. It was "an immensely rich environment, so rich that just to look at the images didn't make sense," Anadol says.[81] He wanted to expand the concept of an archive. Perhaps, he thought, the way to do it lay in a "collision between media art and architecture."

In 2016, he attended Google's Music, Art, and Machine Intelligence symposium in San Francisco, a hotbed of new ideas. There he met Mike Tyka, who had started using DeepDream for making art and was now the art guru at Google. Anadol told him about his project and asked, "Can we collaborate? Can we make an archive dream?" On Tyka's suggestion, Anadol wrote a proposal entitled "Archive Dreaming." The AMI program at Google promptly accepted it.

For over six months, Anadol worked long distance with Tyka and others on the AMI program, exchanging files.[82] To deal with the 1.7 million images that all had to be transformed into numbers and so existed in a multi-multi-dimensional latent space—latent because the information in it is not readily visible—Anadol used the t-SNE algorithm (t-distributed stochastic neighbor embedding) to reduce the number of dimensions. This allowed him to flatten the multi-multi-dimensional latent space of the files to two or three dimensions, while simultaneously collecting together images that shared a high level of visual similarity in his Archive Dreaming installation. All this clarified the information in latent space and thus was the "invisible made visible. There is a new world here," he says. "The potentials are enormous. Imagine the stories you can create."[83]

Archive Dreaming is an immersive media installation. Viewers stand in a cylindrical room while an ever-changing display of images is projected onto the walls. "Do we learn about the data?" asks Anadol. "For sure, yes, but the purpose of the installation is more than about questions."[84] There is no search bar. So how do you ask questions? You don't, immediately. What you see is the whole archive alive with data, a collision between media art and architecture. "Maybe after seeing the archive in its entirety you will ask a different question and so machine learning will help us to think differently," Anadol says. Standing in the cylindrical room is both mesmerizing and unbalancing. Images revolve around the walls and onto the inhabitants of the room, too. The viewer is literally immersed in SALT's vast archive. Archive Dreaming is user-driven. But when it is idle, it "dreams" of unexpected correlations between documents.

So what happens when the archive dreams, when the installation is dormant, asleep? In this state a GAN comes into operation. The GAN's discriminator has absorbed the 1.7 million images in the archives. Soon the generator begins to produce new images that look much like the real ones but have never actually existed. Or could they be from a "parallel history? Thus can the archive be a complete hallucination?"[85] After all, says Anadol, "who will define in the future what is real and what is not?" Indeed, standing in the cylindrical space it is difficult to distinguish the fake from the real, an issue that has become key in our time.

Being surrounded by millions of images, both real and unreal, is reminiscent of Jorge Luis Borges's short story "The Library of Babel," which tells of a library—the universe—made up of all possible 410-page books that can be generated with twenty-two letters of the alphabet, plus commas, periods, and spaces. There is a literal infinity of them, including every erroneous copy of every book, biographies of every person who ever lived, predictions of the future, explanations of the Kabballah and other mystical writings, whatever you could possibly think of. And one could be the index for all the rest. Borges's story was indeed an inspiration, says Anadol. The same concept applies to Archive Dreaming and to whatever the generator in the GAN spins out.

Anadol intends to continue using machine intelligence in combination with architecture. Buildings are "temporary architectural spaces," he says. "They can be canvases as well as works of media art."[86] One project he has in mind and hopes to carry out in collaboration with AMI is to take the one-hundred-year-long archives of the Los Angeles Philharmonic Orchestra and project them onto the walls of the Walt Disney Concert Hall. In this way the viewer will experience the past in real time, immersed in movies, music, images, and interviews. Frank Gehry, who designed the concert hall, "loves the concept," says Anadol, "because his building would then have an intelligence, a culture, a memory."[87]

Anadol says, smiling, "Why doesn't this room record us so that we can come back next year and relive this episode?"[88]

Theresa Reimann-Dubbers's AI Looks at the Messiah

Depends what will be meant by *artist.*
—Theresa Reimann-Dubbers[89]

Theresa Reimann-Dubbers's mission is to confront "AI's oversimplification of complex human concepts."[90] How can a machine understand the term Messiah, for example? To explore this, she created *A(.I.) Messianic Window.* First she fed the discriminator sixteen thousand images of Christ taken from WikiGallery—which is, as she says, "actually very few."[91] After three hundred cycles of generating images that became better and better at appearing realistic and thus fooling the discriminator, the machine began creating images that were no longer figurative, perhaps partly to do with the small number of training images and the lack of time to do more cycles. Reimann-Dubbers describes the final images as "fleshy," referring to the flesh-colored structures in the generated images, which most viewers recognize as limbs at first glance. "I found this ironic because—to look at it plainly—the algorithm's understanding of Christ has resulted in images of many arms and legs." Certainly AI as yet cannot comprehend complex human concepts like the Messiah. Reimann-Dubbers set up the images to form a stained-glass window, as if actually in a church, as in figure 10.3.

Reimann-Dubbers's work has been shown at Ars Electronica and at the workshop on Machine Learning and Creativity at the 2017 Annual Conference on Neural Information Processing Systems (NIPS).

She discovered the link between art and technology while studying at the New Media Art department at the University of the Arts in Berlin.

Figure 10.3
Theresa Reimann-Dubbers, *A(.I.) Messianic Window*, 2017.

On the question of the role of the machine in the creative process, she says that in her view the machine is not a tool but the object of the study, which means that the machine has no volition and cannot even be considered as a collaborator. She intends to pursue this further by looking for a project "in which the machine takes on a collaborative role."[92]

Reimann-Dubbers primarily makes installations on the theme of nature and people communicating in a variety of ways, including electronics. "My work is motivated," she tells me, "by the desire to expose that which McLuhan calls the 'environment' of technologies. By engaging critically with new technologies my work examines their 'anti-environment,' embedding this in objects/installations to challenge the given environment."

Jake Elwes's Dreams of Latent Space

> Networks can begin to dream.
> —Jake Elwes[93]

"Networks can begin to dream," says media artist Jake Elwes. "A lot of what is profound is missing from much work in computer science, such as consciousness, intelligence and creativity."

A network is trained not on the image itself but on the image converted into numbers, which it manipulates in the multidimensional spaces of its various layers. The fully connected layers are where the big event occurs. Here the image is reassembled. The network compares it with the images it has already learned and recognizes it as being of a particular class, such as a dog. It is the culmination of the image's journey through the hidden layers.

In a GAN, the generator network interacts with a discriminator that has been fed a huge number of images. For Elwes, this is where dreaming enters the story. To begin with, the generator creates images out of nothing, from pure noise, latent space—a totally undeveloped space where the possibilities are limitless, like our imaginations. The first forms are blobby and amorphous and the discriminator rejects them. Then they are sent back along the connections between the neurons in the generator, which adjust their weights. When the generator sends out another image, it is tempered by the new weights and thus the generated images become better.

Elwes's big idea was this: after a certain number of jousts between generator and discriminator, to cut the generator loose. Now the generator no longer needs to satisfy the discriminator. But it continues to produce images from latent space and in so doing wanders around the space of the images the discriminator has been fed, such as ImageNet. "The generator is no longer trying to satisfy the discriminator to get the most realistic image of a thing. Instead it's left to daydream—to meander through this latent space. For me it creates abstract expressionist paintings," he explains.[94] The machine is able to achieve these strange but alluring forms because it "reaches towards a noumenal world, a world outside of our experience." The result is an endless sequence of colorful undulating forms and images, eternally morphing one into the next.

Viewers see the products of the machine's imagination reduced to fit our own three-dimensional world of perceptions. But we have not even an inkling of what these images are in the machine's multi-multi-dimensional universe. Elwes calls them latent space. One of his depictions of latent space is figure 10.4.

As a student at the Slade School of Fine Art at University College London, Elwes was one of the few people who could code. He wanted to look into

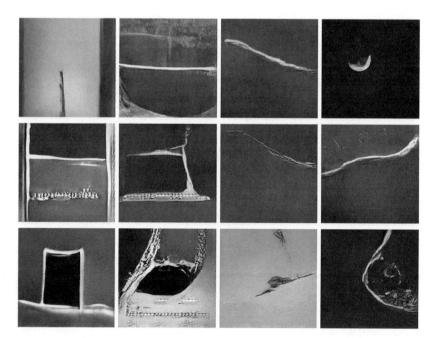

Figure 10.4
A machine dreams. Jake Elwes, *Latent Space*, 2017.

deeper issues concerning machines. Many artists used machines merely as a tool. For him, the issue was how "to blur the boundary between artist and machine, to work out where agency lies, to make technology the material and also the concept."[95] He calls himself an intellectual agent provocateur.

So how did artists receive Elwes's work, the dream images that emerge from the machine's imagination? "Most were incredulous. They claimed that the images couldn't have been drawn by a computer," Elwes says.[96] Sometimes they took the creations to be a Francis Bacon or a Rothko. "No, they're all generated by a computer. I had no impact on any of them," he told them. Elwes hopes that the "images will set off discussions, philosophical discussions about how we ourselves work and whether machines can be creative." He is sure that eventually they will be.

11 Phillip Isola's Pix2Pix: Filling in the Picture

Pix2Pix allows mixing of science and art together, offering a means to show data in a way that's provocative, emotional, and compelling.
—Phillip Isola[97]

"Translating one image into another…is like translating between languages, like between English and French. They are two different representations of the same world," says Phillip Isola.[98]

Isola and his coworkers invented a variation on GANs that he calls conditional generative adversarial networks (CGANs). They are conditional because instead of starting the generator network (G) from noise, from nothing, they condition it by using an actual image. Rather than feeding the discriminator network (D) on huge caches of images, they use pairs of images, such as a black-and-white image of a scene and the same scene in color. Then, they input a new black-and-white scene into the generator network. Initially D rejects the new scene, so G colorizes it. In other words, the output is conditioned by the input, which is what GANs are all about. As a result, Pix2Pix, as Isola calls his system, requires a much smaller set of training data than other supervised learning algorithms.

Thus Isola discovered how to translate an image of one sort into another sort: Pix2Pix, pixels to pixels.[99] As he puts it, all those "little problems in computer vision were just mapping of pixels to pixels."[100] While style transfer transfers the style of one image onto another, creating an image "in the style of" a painting by Picasso, for example, Pix2Pix goes further. Like Leon Gatys, who invented style transfer, Isola is interested in perception, how we see.

As a graduate student, Isola studied cognitive science, a highly interdisciplinary subject that includes computer science, psychology, and neuroscience. He concluded that a good way to study the human mind would be to build machines that "think kind of like we do."[101] This took him back to computer science, which he had studied as an undergraduate.

Pix2Pix seems almost like magic. "Yes," agrees Isola enthusiastically. In fact, he continues, all this is more than just a "math thing, it offers a new space to explore. Artists like that."[102] But to make Pix2Pix accessible to artists entailed structuring an interface so that it could be used right out of the box, directly from the GitHub online repository.

Isola was particularly impressed with the work of Chris Hesse, who fed one thousand pairs of images into the discriminator network.[103] Each consisted of a photograph of a cat and the outline of the same photograph. Then he constructed an interface that allowed the user to insert a rough sketch of a cat. The network filled in the rough sketch, creating what looks like a photograph of a cat-like creature (figure 11.1).

Hesse called his creation *edges2 cats*. The interface is essentially a black box: the user does not need to know about the mathematics of Pix2Pix, just as a writer does not need to know how a ballpoint pen works to use it.

Hesse's work went viral. *edges2cats* enabled users to make a drawing and see it change in real time. Hesse also used databases of fifty thousand shoes and 137 thousand handbags, all in outline only (figure 11.2). Freehand sketches generated weird, photograph-like images.[104]

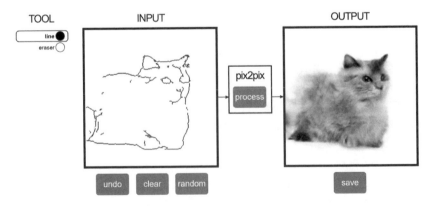

Figure 11.1
Chris Hesse, *edges2cats*, 2017.

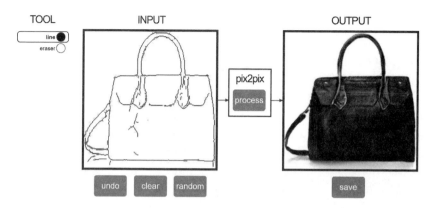

Figure 11.2
Chris Hesse, *edges2handbags*, 2017.

"Pix2Pix empowers people who may not have the requisite motor skills and technical skills to express their creativity," says Isola. "It allows mixing of science and art together, offering a means to show data in a way that's provocative, emotional, and compelling." He sees Pix2Pix as a first step to developing a user-friendly interface for artists. In this way, Pix2Pix has opened new vistas in art, with artists using Pix2Pix "in ways we had not imagined."[105]

Isola and his colleague Jun-Yan Zhu are optimistic that machines may one day be creative, but they feel we are a long way from this goal. They are excited about AlphaZero, the newest version of AlphaGo, which has been given only the rules of Go without any samples of games played previously. This they consider a "whole other level of machine intelligence."[106] Jun-Yan adds, "There's a long way to go, but in the history of the universe it's happening right now. This is a moment in history."[107]

Mario Klingemann Changes Faces with Pix2Pix

I really got hooked with Pix2Pix.
—Mario Klingemann[108]

Pix2Pix came along at just the right time for Mario Klingemann, the artist who invented X Degrees of Separation. He was looking for new fields in which, he says, "I can have my solitude for a while."[109] He was convinced that the material the machine was trained on was the key to its creativity, and set about exploring how to clarify or enhance an image. Using Pix2Pix, he fed his machine with thousands of pairs of images in which one is a blurred version of the other. Then he put in an arbitrary blurred image. Pix2Pix sharpened it up (figures 11.3 and 11.4).

The "machine had to get creative in order to restore lost information," he says. The result was somewhat "creepy, crazy."[110] These were faces never

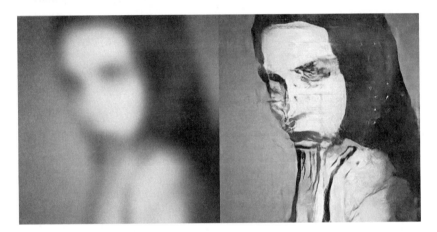

Figure 11.3
Mario Klingemann, *Transhancement Sketch*, 2017.

Figure 11.4
Mario Klingemann, *Transhancement Sketch*, 2017.

seen before. And they emerge from a creative source that happens to be a machine. Klingemann calls this process transhancement: "new types of artefacts were generated lying somewhere on the spectrum between the painterly and the digital."[111]

Klingemann based another use of Pix2Pix around facial markers. Facial markers or facial landmarks are a system of sixty-eight localized points delineating key facial structures that, when mapped onto a photograph, enable a computer to recognize and identify a particular face. The markers include the corners of the eyes, the outline of the face, the nose, the jaw, the mouth, and so on—and all these can be generated with an algorithm. For data, Klingemann fed in photographic portraits alongside the same images reduced to facial markers.

Next he fed in the facial markers of his own face and ran the output image a couple more times (figure 11.5). "There is not much left of me," he reported.

Klingemann's pièce de résistance for Pix2Pix is his disquieting video of the French singer Françoise Hardy, in which her face morphs into that of Kelly-anne Conway when she appeared at her first press briefing as Donald Trump's presidential counsellor. Conway's voice emerges from Hardy's mouth, asserting that Sean Spicer, Trump's then press secretary, who defended Trump's lie about the size of the crowd at his inauguration, "gave alternate facts."

To construct the video, Klingemann downloaded 1960s' music videos of Hardy from YouTube. Then he used face-marker detection to create pairs of

Figure 11.5
Mario Klingemann, *Neurographic Self-Portrait*, 2017.

face markers and fed these along with the original video frames into the network. Next, he extracted Conway's face markers from her interview footage and fed them into the trained model, melding the two faces. Klingemann calls this piece *Alternative Face*—the epitome of "fake news."[112] It is a concrete example of post-truth, with Conway's voice emerging from Hardy's mouth.

In 2018 Klingemann was the seventh recipient of the Lumen Prize Gold Award for Art and Technology. It was the first time a work created using AI won gold.

On the subject of creativity, Klingemann asserts that we humans are incapable of it because we only build on what we have learned and what others have done while machines can create from scratch—a surprising and fascinating statement. Machines, he says, will one day liberate us. "I hope machines will have a rather different sort of creativity and open up different doors." He sees his artwork as a step in this direction.

Anna Ridler's *Fall of the House of Usher*

For me, input becomes the creative act.
—Anna Ridler[113]

Artist Anna Ridler's work is all about memory, narrative, and performance. She was fascinated by the possibilities of Pix2Pix, among them the fact that it could be trained using only a few images. She was concerned about the vast number of images from sources such as ImageNet that usually have to be fed into a machine to train it. She felt she was not in complete control of the material and was also concerned about the gender and racial biases that might be lurking in it. She wanted to use her own datasets—and Pix2Pix enabled her to do so.

She decided to make a piece exploring the 1928 silent film *Fall of the House of Usher*, adapted from Edgar Allen Poe's short story, using her own images. This is a macabre tale about decay and destruction, life and death, and includes Poe's favorite plot device: a person entombed alive. "It's a horror story and there's a lot of talk about AI and horror," she tells me.[114]

She felt machine learning might be able to enhance the message of the film. What emerges from Pix2Pix can be entirely unexpected, such as a disintegrated version of a photograph.

Ridler began by taking two hundred frames from the first four minutes of the film and redrawing each in pen and ink. Her rationale was that digital was pure and clear, whereas ink was very difficult to control: "it had entropy."[115] In physics, entropy is a measure of disorder and decay. Similarly, ink is fragile, prone to blot and run.

She trained the discriminator on pairs made up of her drawings and actual stills from the movie. Then she fed every frame from the entire movie into Pix2Pix. What emerged was a somewhat abstract film that the network had generated from her art, based on the types of images it thought should follow each frame. Next she took each of these generated frames and redrew it in ink to be inserted into the next cycle of Pix2Pix, giving rise to even more abstract images. The machine began to misremember, and the frames became blobs of black, white, and grey. Entropy was high; almost complete decay had set in, just as in Poe's original story. The result is a highly original take on Poe, a ghostly succession of increasingly abstract images, orchestrated with eerie background music.[116] It's also a meditation on memory and misremembering.

Ridler studied English language and literature at Oxford, then turned to computers and completed an MA in information experience and design at the Royal College of Art. She has brought her love of art, literature, and technology to bear on her work. Within AI, all three are fused. "I think of AI as trying to give you something. You use your own drawings and creations as input, purity of line, and allow it to suggest something."[117]

Ridler argues that machines cannot be artists. "Would you say that my paintbrush is an artist? They cannot be creative."[118]

Her great inspiration is Jorge Luis Borges's flight into highly speculative fiction, "Tlön, Uqbar, Orbis Tertius." In this story, Borges challenges the boundary between fiction and nonfiction and questions what is real and what is not. In her work, Ridler makes us ask: Which is the real film? The original frames or those produced by the generator of Pix2Pix on its journeys through latent space?

No doubt Borges would have enjoyed wandering multi-multi-dimensional latent space, the space of our imaginations.

12   Jun-Yan Zhu's CycleGAN Turns Horses into Zebras

Jun-Yan has done a lot, taking those math ideas and doing a really expert job, building systems to make beautiful images.

—Ian Goodfellow[119]

While working on Pix2Pix with Phillip Isola, Jun-Yan Zhu began to wonder if he could make it a little more general, broaden it a little. Could you, for example, turn images of a summer scene into winter? It would be difficult to find corresponding pairs of pictures, as required by Pix2Pix, and virtually impossible to find an image of a horse that exactly matched an image of a zebra, in exactly the same position.[120] But what if you fed in unpaired images with no information about the relationship between them? Why not simply give the computer lots of images of horses, zebras, summers, winters, and so on? Jun-Yan called this new version of Pix2Pix CycleGAN.

Pix2Pix's basic modus operandi is much the same as translating a sentence from English into French. Now, however, Jun-Yan wanted the translation from French back to English to result in exactly the same English sentence. This required constraints to prevent the computer generating random zebras from random horses. Jun-Yan ran the cycle over and over again, using algorithms to reduce the loss of consistency in both directions. He tried inserting an image of a horse into several unpaired images of zebras. After a number of cycles, the horse became a zebra.[121]

Jun-Yan expresses himself clearly and tersely in Chinese-accented English. Inspired by a love of computer graphics, he began to code at the age of ten or eleven. Another of his interests was Chinese painting, with its precise brush strokes and vibrant colors. But science was his passion. He chose to study mathematics and geometry in high school and computer science in college. There he was able to combine computer science with graphics and art. He was "amazed that the computer could create visual objects instead of having to draw them manually."[122]

Ian Goodfellow, inventor of GANs, takes pains to point out that both he and Jun-Yan had wanted to be cartoonists. "In both cases it led to our work in machine learning."[123]

Like most researchers in AI, Jun-Yan is highly competitive, which is what drew him to GANs. "It was the two-player-game idea," he tells me, in which the discriminator and generator compete for the upper hand.

Jun-Yan and his colleagues also tried applying CycleGAN to paintings. What, they asked, did Claude Monet actually see when he painted his landscapes? They fed into their system a collection of Monet's landscape paintings together with many random landscape photographs from Flickr. The results were illuminating.They showed that CycleGAN can translate both ways: from a Monet to a photograph-like landscape and from a photograph to a Monet-like painting, for example, or from a zebra to a horse or a horse to a zebra (figure 12.1).[124]

At present, CycleGAN only works for sets of images that are two different representations of the same underlying world: horses/zebras, landscape photographs/Monet landscape paintings. But even botched results can be informative. Jun-Yan was particularly inspired by the "Putin error." He and his colleagues tried transforming a photograph of President Vladimir Putin striking a manly pose on horseback into one in which he is riding a zebra. An image of a striped Putin on a zebra emerged (figure 12.2).[125]

The problem was that the training set of horses and zebras were all riderless. Even correcting this did not improve matters. And when they tried to turn dogs into cats and vice versa, strange-looking animals emerged. Says Isola, "Failures are interesting."[126]

The backstory of the development of CycleGAN is of interest as an example of how research that results in groundbreaking developments is carried out. While writing up the Pix2Pix paper, Jun-Yan felt restless because of the limits Pix2Pix imposed on the range of data it could use.

Isola too felt restless. "Although the results of Pix2Pix were really cool, they were sort of basic and boring," he tells me. "When you're publishing a paper, you really want some new equation in there, not only to show off your brash new results but to add some buzz, too."[127]

Figure 12.1
CycleGAN translates from a Monet to a photograph-like landscape (top, upper row)
and from a photograph to a Monet-like painting (top, lower row), and from a zebra
to a horse (bottom, upper row) and from a horse to a zebra (bottom, lower row). [See
color plate 3.]

Figure 12.2
Striped Putin astride a zebra, created by Jun-Yan Zhu using a CycleGAN, 2017.

Jun-Yan's idea caught everyone's fancy and they "tried to get a primitive version of CycleGAN into the Pix2Pix paper but could not at the time make it work." The team decided to omit it. "Pix2Pix alone was a solid contribution; let's flesh out the next one and do it well," they decided.

CycleGAN has opened new vistas for artists, giving increased freedom in that it removes the difficulty of finding paired images.

Mario Klingemann Plays with CycleGAN

> My general method is to use GANs (in particular Pix2Pix or CycleGAN) to transform from one representation to another.
>
> —Mario Klingemann[128]

Not surprisingly, Mario Klingemann was one of the first artists to explore the possibilities of CycleGAN. He began by feeding black-and-white portraits of men he found on the internet into his CycleGAN, then put in a set of colorful selfies of women. When he fed in a 1920s black-and-white photograph of a man wearing a white shirt, a color image emerged. Then he processed it through another CycleGAN, trained to turn human faces into doll faces. Lastly he merged the result with a Pix2Pix model he had trained on scratched or damaged photographs: "glitch art, random crazy images, perhaps also with their pixels altered."[129] The result is an image that is novel, surprising, and somewhat disturbing (figure 12.3).[130] He posted all these images on Twitter using the Twitter handle @quasimondo.

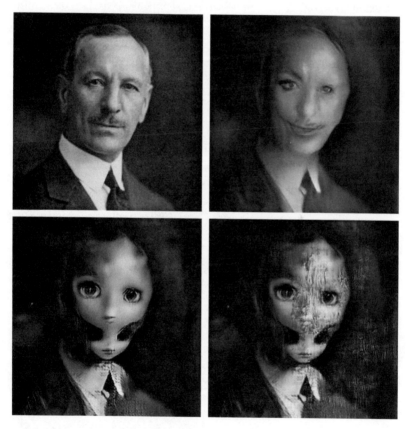

Figure 12.3
Mario Klingemann, computer-generated images created using Pix2Pix and Cycle-GAN. The original black-and-white photograph (upper left). The same photograph, processed by a CycleGAN trained on 1920s images of men and recent, colored selfies of women (upper right). Previous image, fed into a second CycleGAN trained to turn human faces into doll faces (lower left). The image in turn is processed by a Pix2Pix trained on "glitch images" to build in the element of decay, 2017 (lower right).

*   *   *

What might be the next step after DeepDream, style transfer, GANs, Pix2Pix, and CycleGAN? Isola and Jun-Yan say that they are looking for systems that can represent more general images, rather than just, say, horses and zebras. They would like to formulate algorithms that can "take raw undigested data and find interesting visual patterns, then organize that data in a way that gives an artist or a scientist ways to better understand it," then to cluster the data using an algorithm like t-SNE, and use t-SNE again to flatten the multi-multi-dimensional space into two dimensions.[131] "Then you can let everything loose on, say, Monet's paintings." So far, many of their attempts have failed. But, Isola says, "It's fun to have things that don't work out that well."

13   Ahmed Elgammal's Creative Adversarial Networks

I really believe that to advance AI you have to look at how people digest art.
—Ahmed Elgammal[132]

Egyptian-born computer scientist Ahmed Elgammal has a mission: to find a way for a machine to create new, original, and exciting artworks—not more of the same "in the style of" existing artworks, and not so way out as to be dismissed as bizarre, but artworks that stand comparison with works of the greatest contemporary artists.

Elgammal recalls with regret that when he finished high school he had to "choose between archaeology, art history, and computer science."[133] He decided to study computer science at the University of Alexandria, but "never gave up on his passion for art and history." As a graduate student, he combined his interests by studying computer vision, the way in which computers understand images by processing them in ways analogous to human vision, as in convolutional neural networks (ConvNets), the networks behind DeepDream.

Elgammal was convinced that "art and engineering are two sides of the same coin that can push the boundaries of what machines can do beyond game playing or driving a car."[134] As a professor in the Department of Computer Studies at Rutgers University, in 2014 he established the Art and Artificial Intelligence Laboratory, with the subtitle Advancing AI Technology in the Digital Humanities.

Initially the lab trained machines to distinguish different art styles—to tell the difference between, for example, Renaissance and baroque art. To do so, they used the WikiArt dataset, a huge online collection of 81,449 fine art paintings in twenty-seven different styles and forty-five different genres (including interiors, landscapes, and sculptures) by 1,119 artists, spanning the years 1400 to 2000—essentially, the entire canon of Western art. They supplemented this with information, including the sorts of brushstrokes used. They also included visual similarities, which artists influenced which others.

Elgammal and his coworkers went on to explore creativity, which they sought to quantify by looking at art history and setting up an algorithm to score how creative each painting was. Their baseline was how novel a painting was relative to earlier artworks and how influential it was in sparking further works in the new genre. The algorithm found that Picasso's 1907 *Les Demoiselles d'Avignon* spurred a whole new movement, cubism. This confirmed the accuracy of their algorithm. Says Elgammal, results such as this meant that "many events in art history could be explained by visual aspects of art, more than semantic and social contexts," contradicting what many art historians believe.[135]

Elgammal has become interested in how style evolves over time. He links this with what he sees as the current trend in AI to generate images from images we have already seen, such as training machines on thousands of images from art history. "That seemed silly to me," he says, "because art is not just generating things that look like art."[136] He has in mind style transfer, which transforms an image into a certain style such as a work by Picasso, and GANs, where the generator tries to produce images that resemble those in the discriminator's training set.

He argues that artists should abandon painting styles that have become stale and experiment with new styles that will arouse the viewer. He calls this the style's "arousal potential." This new art should be novel, surprising, complex, ambiguous, and puzzling. But if the work is too novel, viewers may find it repellent. The creative artist has to walk a fine line.

An example is the French artist Paul Cézanne who, in the late nineteenth and early twentieth centuries, moved on from the naturalism of impressionist art with its fleeting effects of light and color and developed a style based on abstract qualities and symbolic content, with cubes, geometric shapes, and experiments with perspective. Because Cézanne had moved away from impressionism, his works were received critically by the establishment—though younger artists, like Picasso, appreciated his mastery. Cézanne's work was a stepping stone to cubism and twentieth-century art. In Elgammal's analysis, Cézanne's style was novel and thus creative, but not so extreme as to be repulsive. To illustrate what he means by repulsive, Elgammal cites DeepDream's psychedelic imagery.

Elgammal and his group set to work to computerize their scheme and develop a way to bring about a style change that is novel and therefore creative. They formulated a variation on GANs that they called creative adversarial networks (CANs). Like GANs, CANs have two networks, a discriminator (D) and a generator (G). D is trained on the WikiArt dataset and learns to discriminate between art and nonart. To begin, G is untrained, in a state of pure noise, in latent space.

G begins sending images to D, which D rejects as nonart. G begins to learn what D doesn't like, and adjusts its weights to generate ever more art-like images, as assessed by D. But D can also detect the style of an image—its "art-style classification" function. When it notices that the image fits a particular style, then a function called style ambiguity kicks in, pushing the generator to produce works in styles which differ from all those in the WikiArt dataset—in other words, something altogether new and original.

The images in figure 13.1 were created by a CAN with the style ambiguity function turned off. The images are recognizable as portraits, landscapes and so on.

Conversely, turning the style ambiguity function on generates highly abstract images, as shown in figure 13.2.

Figure 13.1
Images created by a CAN with the style ambiguity function turned off, 2017.

Figure 13.2
Images created by a CAN with the style ambiguity function turned on, 2017.

The problem that Elgammal sets the network is to find a style that differs from all those in the training set. But the training set, the images it has been fed, encompass the whole of Western art. In the end, without any human intervention, it settles on abstraction as the solution to the problem. There are two possible explanations. Either there is a bias in the data toward abstraction, or, as Elgammal puts it, "the machine has captured the trajectory of art history, which is towards abstraction."[137] He opts for the second. It seems that moving toward abstraction is natural for both human and machine artists.

Elgammal's aim "was to do a visual Turing test," to see whether a sample of viewers could tell whether a work of art was made by a machine or a human artist.[138] Most people can distinguish machine art from human art. So what art would be best to set up in comparison with the works created by a CAN? Elgammal and his team chose twenty-five paintings by abstract expressionist artists produced between 1945 and 2007. Art lovers would probably be familiar with most of them, and they also had no recognizable subject matter. The second set was twenty-five paintings by contemporary artists shown at Art Basel 2016. These could be considered the pinnacle of the modern art world as assessed by the art establishment. Elgammal and his team set the CAN works, the abstract expressionist works, and the Art Basel works before a panel of eighteen viewers drawn from Amazon Mechanical Turk, a crowd-sourcing internet marketplace.

The results astounded Elgammal. The panel concluded that 53 percent of the CAN-generated artworks had been created by artists, as opposed to 85 percent of the abstract expressionists and 41 percent of the Art Basel collection. In other words, more than half the CAN works looked as if they were the products of human imagination to an admittedly nonexpert group of viewers.

But could the CAN products really be considered art? Elgammal asked a further twenty-one viewers how they felt when they interacted with the three sets of paintings. Did they feel that the painting was composed very intentionally?[139] Did they see "an emergent structure?" Did the painting communicate with them? Were they inspired by the work? Elgammal expected the CAN products to rate much lower than the art produced by real artists. In fact, the CAN products rated higher. It seemed that the (again, nonexpert) panel really did consider the CAN images to be works of art.

The next question was whether the machine's new art style was the result of turning on the style ambiguity function. Elgammal turned to a pool of art history students, well versed in novelty and aesthetics, and asked them to assess pairs of images produced by the CAN, one with the style ambiguity function turned off, which therefore produced images in the style of those in the WikiArt dataset (i.e., that fit in with the canon of Western art), the other with the style ambiguity function turned on. He asked them which images were more novel and which more aesthetically pleasing. More than half considered the CAN images produced with style ambiguity turned on to be more novel, and 60 percent found them also more aesthetically pleasing.

Elgammal's work has received far more positive reviews in the media than has DeepDream.[140] At the 2017 Frankfurt Book Fair, he was invited to exhibit artworks made by CAN. Artists admired the work and photographed it and inquired about the artist. Elgammal told them that this was AI art and explained his methods. To his surprise, the artists did not respond negatively. Rather they saw Elgammal's machine as another artist with whom they could also connect. "That's the ultimate approval, the ultimate signal I can get," says Elgammal. "An artist sees it and connects with it."[141]

In the future, Elgammal would like to have artists collaborate with CAN, perhaps coming up with creative ideas that the machine can explore. "I want to look into what would have happened if Picasso had lived in the twenty-first century." His aim is "to further our understanding of how humans create art, then to simulate that with a machine." But for the moment he does not believe that machines can truly be creative.[142]

At present, Elgammal's machine has "no semantic understanding of art beyond the concept of styles."[143] In other words, it doesn't understand the subject matter and certainly could not discuss possible meanings of the abstract forms it produces: Are they Jungian archetypes, for example? But in the not-too-distant future, machines will be capable of scanning the web and learning key features of the world in which we live. In that way they will "learn" about subject matter, objects, hopes and dreams, love and hate.

Elgammal also applied the criteria for creativity proposed by the British computer scientist Simon Colton to his work. Among these are novelty and a system's ability to assess its own creations.[144] Elgammal concludes that his system satisfies both requirements. The interaction between the two systems in CAN forces it to explore creative space as it strives to deviate from the styles the discriminator has been fed and yet still to produce works that the discriminator judges to be art.

"If the machine can be creative in the future it has to be its own judge," he says.

Is the art market ready to embrace work made by artificial intelligence?
—Naomi Rea[145]

In October 2018, for the first time in its history, Christie's in New York auctioned an artwork created by an AI—to be specific, a GAN. *Portrait of Edmond de Belamy* went on auction with an estimated price of $7,000 to $10,000. In the end, it sold to an anonymous phone bidder for an amazing $432,500.

The work is a portrait of an aristocratic-looking gentleman in a dark coat and white collar, but the features are mysteriously blurry, as if gazing out at the viewer from some other dimension, as shown in figure 14.1. The work is signed not by an artist but by the signature equation of the algorithm that spawned the painting.[146]

The creators of the work are a French collective called Obvious. To make it, they fed their GAN with fifteen thousand classical portraits from the WikiArt dataset, created between the fourteenth and twentieth centuries, then let the generator loose to create portraits that would fool the discriminator into thinking they were real art. They stopped the process at a point where the GAN produced a reasonably classical-looking portrait and in the end came up with eleven finished works. All are of the fictional Belamy family, Belamy being a play on *bel ami*, a loose translation of *good fellow* as a tribute to Ian Goodfellow, the inventor of GANs.

The event caused a media storm and a fair amount of controversy. A flurry of articles appeared declaring that AI had at last come into its own and been recognized as capable of producing true art—as if being auctioned by Christie's validated it. Journalists proclaimed that this was the first piece of art "aesthetically and conceptually rich enough to hold the attention of

$$\min_{g} \max_{D} E_x[log(D(x))] + E_y[log(1 - D(g(y)))]$$

Figure 14.1
Portrait of Edmond de Belamy, 2018.

the art world."[147] The argument is that unlike DeepDream, GANs can be used to produce complete new and dramatically different images.

The members of Obvious say they are conceptual artists whose goal is to democratize GANs and legitimize AI-produced art. They compare AI with the camera, which appeared to be a scientific instrument when it was first invented in the nineteenth century and only gradually revealed its artistic potential. They proclaim themselves pioneers of "GAN-ism" and give as their motto, "Creativity isn't just for humans."[148]

Richard Lloyd, head of prints and multiples at Christie's, believes the auction will lay bare fundamental questions about art and creativity. Does art have to be made by a person to qualify as art? "Everybody has their own definition of a work of art," he says. "If people find it emotionally charged and inspiring then it is."[149]

Even before the auction, one art collector, Nicolas Laugero-Lasserre, had bought one of the eleven portraits directly from the collective. *Le Comte de Belamy*, which he bought for about $12,000 in February 2018, shows a bewigged and ruffed aristocratic gentleman, again mysteriously blurred.

But the event has been greeted with outrage in the AI world. Many people working in AI question why this particular work should have been chosen and accuse Obvious of being mere marketers, promoters of their work, not true artists.

Mario Klingemann, who has done pioneering work in using GANs to create art, says: "Pretty much everyone who is working seriously in this field is shaking their head in disbelief about the lack of judgment when it comes to featuring Obvious, and of course Christie's decision to auction them out of all artists who work with neural networks."[150]

Besides Klingemann, many other artists whom I feature in this book are producing more original and interesting work than Obvious's Belamys. For a start, there is Ahmed Elgammal's creative adversarial network (CAN), tailored to search for totally new styles, and Jake Elwes's images, generated by the machine's wanderings through latent space.

In addition, despite extravagant claims to the contrary, this is not the first time that AI art has been auctioned. There was an auction at the Gray Area Foundation for the Arts in February 2016, as mentioned earlier, and there have been several others, including a group exhibition entitled Gradient Descent at a gallery in New Delhi, which included contributions from several artists featured in this book.[151] All these have helped establish AI art as a genre.

Some knotty questions arise as AI enters the fraught world of the art markets: Exactly who owns the artwork? Is it the artist, or is it the machine? Who owns the copyright?

The issue of copyright goes back to A. Michael Noll of Bell Labs, who, as mentioned previously, created one of the first works of computer art in the early 1960s.[152] When he tried to copyright it, the Library of Congress refused, claiming that a work generated by a computer could not be considered art because computers were capable only of number crunching. Noll insisted that the computer's output was created by a program written by a human being, and the Library of Congress eventually relented, making Noll's work the first copyrighted piece of computer art.

Noll's program was straightforward. He connected the dots produced by an equation called a Gaussian distribution from top to bottom in a random way. GANs, conversely, are much more complex. Most importantly, GANs assess their products, rejecting some and accepting others. Some people consider AI to be simply a tool, like a camera used by photographers who then alter their images using Adobe Photoshop. Jessica Fjeld, Assistant Director at the Cyberlaw Clinic at Harvard Law School, asserts that "humans are deeply involved with every aspect of the creation and training of today's AI technologies, and this will continue to be true tomorrow and for the foreseeable future."[153] As I believe I've shown in this book, AI need not always be considered merely a tool for artists, musicians, and writers. I suspect that in the not unforeseeable future, machines will come to be considered artists, writers, and musicians in their own right.

Mozart's father taught him music, but that does not make him the creator of his son's music. Should the teachers who taught us take credit for our discoveries? As time passes, it will become more and more clear how this applies to computers. GANs are an excellent example of what may well come to pass.

Obvious were soon followed by another artist. On March 6, 2019, Sotheby's in London auctioned an installation by Mario Klingemann. Applying his own alchemy to Pix2Pix, Klingemann's *Memories of Passersby I* produces an ever-changing stream of mind-expanding male and female faces across two screens. Disappointingly his work went for only $51,000. Did the out-of-line payment for *Portrait of Edmond de Belamy* momentarily freeze the market or was Obvious's good fortune simply a matter of novelty value? Nevertheless, the episode is indicative of the growing interest in AI art in the art world. (See my *Guardian* article: https://www.theguardian.com/technology/2019/mar/04/can-machines-be-more-creative-than-humans.)

15 Simon Colton's The Painting Fool

If you are not arguing about terms like *art* and *creativity*, then you are not talking about art or creativity.

—Simon Colton[154]

Simon Colton wants The Painting Fool to be "taken seriously as a creative artist in its own right."[155]

When you sit for your portrait, you sit in front of a screen. The Painting Fool greets you with, "Thank you for being my model."[156] Like any human artist, The Painting Fool has moods, determined by the articles it's been reading in the *Guardian* newspaper that day. Through its software, it carries out a sentiment analysis on the words, which makes it happy, very happy, sad, very sad, reflective, or experimental. It also extracts phrases that affect what it looks at as it reads other periodicals. In a way, it is seeking inspiration.

At this point, it may be in such a bad mood that it refuses to paint your portrait. If it decides to go on, it will assess your expression—smiling, sad, or whatever—using a neural network for facial recognition, which also associates your expression with an adjective denoting your mood. Additional software transfers the adjective to sequential graphic software. Further complex scanning of the developing image of your face enables The Painting Fool to select from 1,200 painting styles, plus nine means for expressing them, including simulations for pencil, pastels, and paints. It creates a sketch of the sitter's face in two to three minutes, then fills in the portrait. This can take up to fifteen minutes if the software is simulating acrylic paints, which take longer to dry. Then The Painting Fool runs the finished portrait back through the neural network to check whether it has caught your likeness and the facial expression it wants. If not, it has another go.

Then it sets to work to create a background, depending on its mood. It can choose from over a thousand abstract images taken from art and calculated to project different moods, plus image filters linking the mood to the face, resulting in about nine million choices. Out of these, The Painting Fool chooses the most appropriate background image, as shown in figures 15.1 and 15.2. Colton is "constantly surprised about what ends up in the background scene which doesn't actually exist," he says.[157] Could this be considered evidence of the software's imagination?

Figure 15.1
Happy face (left). As rendered by The Painting Fool, in vibrant pastels, with an "electric" background, 2015 (right). [See color plate 4.]

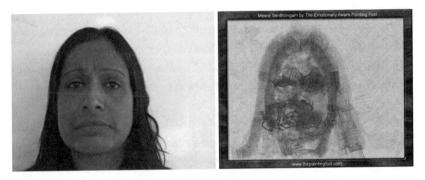

Figure 15.2
Sad face (left). As rendered by The Painting Fool, in muted colors, with a dull background, 2015 (right).

What if the machine was in a sad mood and the subject insisted on a portrait? The result might be a smiling face with a subdued background, perhaps in grey instead of brightly colored pastels. The software has even worked out that if it wants to produce something psychedelic, it shouldn't use shades of grey. "I didn't teach it that," Colton says.

Colton is a professor of digital games technologies at the University of Falmouth and of computational creativity, games, and artificial intelligence at Queen Mary University of London. For him, the two are connected. He thinks in terms of seeing and creating connections between different disciplines. He peppers his conversation with examples from art, including his thoughts on machine creativity, a field in which he is something of a guru.

As a graduate student, Colton created an algorithm that could produce mathematical theorems. He called it the HR Tool, after the great mathematicians G. H. Hardy and Srinivasa Ramanujan. When he set it to multiply two numbers together, on returning to the machine ten minutes later it had discovered certain arcane mathematical properties. If a child had made that discovery, Colton argues, "we would describe the child as imaginative (or at least inventive)."[158] In which case, why not say that the machine too might have imagination?

To explore machine creativity in art, Colton developed The Painting Fool, which he describes as an "art project rather than a scientific project."[159] He wanted to explore intentionality. Could the machine actually intend to paint a portrait in a particular manner? He also inquired whether the software could be said to have "*struggled*, with a fair meaning of that word."[160]

He specifically did not set up The Painting Fool to mimic his own tastes and opinions as to what makes a painting pleasing. Rather he wanted to create software that actually showed intention and that "struggled" like a human artist.

Once the process starts, Colton has no idea what articles the machine has read or whether it will choose to use pencil, pastel, or paint. He claims that this "has changed many people's minds about whether the software is just a mini-me."[161] He takes the artist Harold Cohen's famous painting software—AARON—as an example. AARON produces paintings by putting together images that Cohen has fed into it, following certain rules for composition to create a sort of collage. In other words, it paints in the style of its creator.

Colton incorporates his HR Tool into The Painting Fool, which enables it to seek out new mathematical ways to shape the final painting; to some extent, it allows The Painting Fool to write new software. Colton depicts this as the software struggling, like a human artist. Although the program was created by Colton, The Painting Fool's artwork is its own.

When the machine presents you with your portrait, on the back is commentary describing what mood it was in, what it was trying to achieve, and what it did achieve. Usually Colton lets the machine choose its own aesthetic, leaving it free to weigh alternatives, including its mood and method of producing the image, without any human intervention. He only curates the products when the work is to be exhibited in a gallery.[162]

Colton feels that a Turing-style test, attempting to determine whether a machine-generated artwork can be mistaken for a human creation, is asking the wrong question, making it seem that machine creativity aims to do no more than imitate human creativity.[163] Surely we want to go beyond that. Bach and Picasso have already been done, by Bach and Picasso. It can be useful to create systems that produce work like theirs as a first step toward developing more sophisticated machines, but in the end even this may not be necessary when new and more advanced machines come online. Machines are silicon-based life-forms and may well come to produce art, literature, and music of a sort that we cannot even begin to imagine.

Colton is critical of deep neural networks that have to be fed an enormous amount of material to create their art. "More information about the world often means less imaginative thought," he says. "It is difficult to imagine big data projects leading to the invention of imaginative ideas. In The Painting Fool project, we're more interested in the simulation of particular behaviors associated with creativity, such as imagination, appreciation and intentionality."[164]

Most people, Colton says, don't own a work of art or a portrait of themselves, and many would like to. But they are expensive. "Software can fill the gap." In the future, machines may well be able to produce interesting and affordable art for the masses. "Likewise," he goes on, "people will realize the importance of human creativity when they see computer creativity; this will, in fact, encourage and raise their personal creativity."

At the end of 2018, The Painting Fool became the world's first digital artist in residence at Cardiff University's Brain Research and Imagery Centre, thanks to the Wellcome Trust's fund for public engagement. There it produced "a painting a day, including visualizations of brain scans and interpretation of brain data."[165]

Over the one-year residency, Colton has worked to develop the machine further. He would like it to learn to change its own processes in creating art, to find its own material and paint a picture of that, and to be able to ask it why it painted a certain picture and what moved it to read a particular newspaper article. In general, he would like there to be more separation between it and himself as the programmer. Thus he has tried to work toward the computer creating autonomous work, "producing paintings [he] had never imagined."[166] According to Anna Jordanous, another prominent explorer of machine creativity, "Places like Tate Modern are beginning to take The Painting Fool seriously."[167]

To sum up, although Colton created The Painting Fool, its art is its own, created without further human intervention. It also assesses that art. Surely both qualities can be defined as aspects of creativity. It even has moods. As to the argument that it is not out in the world and therefore cannot have the kind of experiences that we deem necessary for creativity, Colton responds that when it paints its subjects, it has experiences that are recorded by its software, just as visual images strike our retinas and are recorded in our brains.

Colton also thinks it's irrelevant to compare computer to human art. He is adamant that it should be stated from the start that these are works produced by a machine. We should "be loud and proud about the AI processes leading to their generation. People can then enjoy that these have been created by a computer."[168]

16   Hod Lipson and Patrick Tresset's Artist Robots

We're like alchemists of the past, driven by the passion for knowledge.
—Hod Lipson[169]

In Isaac Asimov's *I, Robot*, the inspector asks a robot whether it has ever turned a canvas into a masterpiece. The robot replies, "Have you?" It was this exchange that inspired Hod Lipson to begin working with robots.

As director of Columbia University's Creative Machines Lab, Lipson has done a great deal of work on developing "self-aware" robots. He has developed software that can derive complex equations and thus enhance research, as well as robots in the form of simple structures that can replicate themselves with available parts, learn on their own, and evolve over time without human intervention. But his private passion is to develop a robot that paints. He has now built three painting robots: SEURAT, Pixasso, and PIX18. He built the first, SEURAT, with his then graduate student, Carlos Aguilar.[170]

The robots consist of an articulated robot arm, a digital paint simulator that predicts how a paint stroke will look if it is painted on a canvas, and an algorithm that instructs the robot arm in the correct brushstrokes to replicate a given painting. Lipson shows the painting robot a digital image, which it analyses and represents with actual brush strokes and paint on canvas. From time to time, he stops the process and culls those images that are too far removed from the original. Finally, the robot arm produces an image pleasing to the subject and to the operator of the program.

The results are rather spectacular. Figure 16.1 shows a painting created by PIX18.

…

Figure 16.1
Tear, inspired by Roy Lichtenstein's *Frightened Girl*. Lipson attributes the work to
PIX18 and himself thus: PIX18/Hod Lipson, 2016.

Since Aguilar graduated, Lipson has not been able to persuade another
graduate student to work on his robot art project. "Engineers shy away from
art," he says. "If you pay for an engineering degree, you want on your résumé
that you were designing rockets, et cetera—serious stuff. But if you've made
oil paintings, maybe you won't find a job. So this is one project I'm doing
myself, almost as a hobby."[171] Lipson's second robot, Pixasso, painted large
paintings in his basement.

When he moved from Cornell University to New York City, he built PIX18.
Lipson firmly believes that computers can be creative and have volition.

Just as the invention of photography drove adventurous artists to invent impressionism, so too "AI will push the art world to invent new forms of art," he says.[172]

He would like to shift the balance of creativity "almost entirely to the computer," so that eventually it paints out of its own life experiences using its own imagination, which will require machines to have emotions, too. Why should "creativity be the last bastion of humanism?" he asks.

"GANs are absolutely the path forward for machines to create their own things," he says. GANs also include an internal critic to eliminate the mass of unwanted material that pours out when machines generate art. Lipson speculates that eventually the art produced by machines will be impossible for us to understand. "But that won't be for a thousand years from now."

Robot art is becoming increasingly popular. Besides Lipson's robot artists, there is the German collective robotlab creating vast drawings[173] and the Czech artist Federico Diaz turning out enormous and spectacular pieces of sculpture.[174]

And in London, there is Patrick Tresset and his sketching robots, collectively called Paul. Paul is a robot arm attached to an old-fashioned school desk, inside which is a laptop that is its "brain."[175] Its arm holds a pen, and there is a camera "head" that looks at and photographs the sitter. Then Paul gets to work.[176] The process is akin to Lipson's, except that the images the robot uses to assess its progress were drawn by Tresset himself. The software is designed to emulate the perceptual and cognitive processes involved when artists sketch faces.

Tresset instructs me to sit absolutely still while Paul sketches me. I sense something awry here and decide to move. Paul carries on sketching; there is no effect on his movements, as in figure 16.2. In his wry French way, Tresset admits that asking subjects to sit still while Paul's camera moves is "a bit of theatre; the camera just needed to look once at you."[177]

It's rather endearing to see a classroom of Pauls all working away busily together. Tresset programs them so that some are eager to work, whereas others seem hesitant and shy. In this way, he says, he goes beyond the art dimension to create "little pieces of 'theatre' that touch people. I would say that I am inspired by Jacques Tati, Samuel Beckett and Antoine de Saint-Exupéry."[178] Tresset tells me that galleries pay his robots "like performers....And the bookings go quickly."[179]

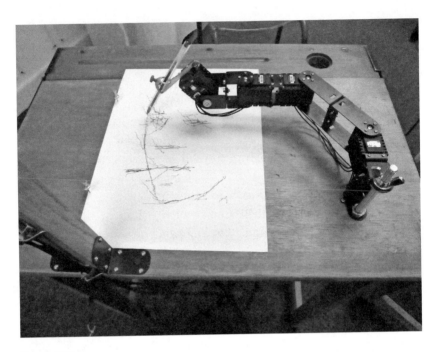

Figure 16.2
Paul sketching the author, 2017.

Recently, experiments have shown that people, as one would expect, tend to appreciate art made by computers more when the computer is housed in a robot that looks human, which suggests it has a mind like ours. This is the case with Tresset's robot, Paul. People are more prone to appreciate Paul's art if they stay in the room while their portrait is being drawn, rather than leaving and coming back later to see the finished work. It seems the process of creating the artwork is important for us to appreciate art produced by robots, as is the robot having human characteristics.[180]

Tresset is adamant that machines "cannot be creative. Real art is done by human beings. Drawings done by robots are not art."[181]

III Machines That Make Music: Putting the "Rhythm" into "Algorithm"

We want to explore…developing algorithms that can learn how to generate art and music, potentially creating compelling and artistic content on their own.
—Douglas Eck[1]

In August 2016, the Magenta team at Google unveiled a piece of music which they claimed was the first ever to be entirely composed by a computer. Certainly it was the first to be composed by a computer that had not been in any way programmed to do so. The tune is rather simple but, with the help of a little added percussion, really quite catchy.[2]

To set the process in motion, Douglas Eck, the head of Project Magenta, fed some 4,500 popular tunes, all digitized, into his computer, then "seeded" it with four musical notes: two Cs and two Gs. The computer then created its little melody.

Like all art, music requires rules. Without boundaries, without structure, it is simply noise. Traditionally the boundaries are the rules for writing a musical score, which are in effect a species of algorithm. As Peter Weibel, CEO of the Center for Art and Media in Karlsruhe and an eminent video and sound artist, says, "Right from the beginning there were algorithms for music."[3] Excitingly, what this means is that music can be programmed.

Besides writing music in the usual way, there have always been ways to assemble scores at random—by throwing dice, for example, using bars from existing scores as the raw material. But the musical fragments always had to be carefully selected to avoid using notes or phrases that couldn't follow each another according to the rules of composition. Musical games of dice were popular in the eighteenth century and were played by composers such as J. S. Bach's son, C. P. E. Bach, and by Mozart himself, ever on the lookout for nontraditional ways to compose music. They also gave laypeople the chance to compose music and can be seen as the precursor to machine-composed music.

In the twentieth century, the dice were replaced by Markov chains, a statistical process governing chains of events. Here an event—such as the next musical note—depends only on the previous one.[4] In terms of composing music, this meant programming the computer with rules to prevent inharmonious notes or measures following one another. In 1957, Lejaren Hiller, in collaboration with chemist and composer Leonard Issacson, used Markov chains together with rules for composing music to program the ILLIAC computer at the University of Illinois to generate a score for string quartet, which they called *The Illiac Suite*. This was probably the first score ever composed by a machine. The following year, Greek composer Iannis Xenakis applied Markov chains to hundreds of fragments of magnetic tape and composed two pieces, which he called *Analogique A* and *B*.

David Cope, emeritus professor of music at the University of California at Santa Cruz, was the first to apply Markov methods on a grand scale to compose musical scores that faithfully represented particular musical styles, such as those of Bach, Chopin, and Cope himself.

Twenty-first century computers equipped with neural networks can learn the rules of baroque music from Bach's scores and work out for themselves the probability of one note following another—which was precisely how Project Magenta set its computer to work to produce its little melody.

17 Project Magenta: AI Creates Its Own Music

Can we use machine learning to create compelling art and music? If so, how? If not, why not?

—Douglas Eck[5]

As head of Google's Project Magenta, Douglas Eck has found a way to combine his two loves—AI and music—in his work. An open and outspoken man, he first took an interest in computers at the age of thirteen. "I was from the floppy disc era," he says, "but never thought of myself as a computer person." Nevertheless, he became adept at coding.

Like many people working in AI and the arts, Eck has had an extraordinary career trajectory. As an undergraduate at Indiana University, he studied English literature and creative writing but couldn't find good employment opportunities. Instead he became a programmer, a career he had never planned on. As a young database programmer in Albuquerque, New Mexico, he became interested in the creative possibilities of coding. But he was also a musician. He enjoyed playing a sort of punk folk music on piano and guitar in coffee houses there. At twenty-four, he found himself bored with database programming and in love with music. He asked himself, "What's at the intersection of the two? Maybe I can put them together. So I said to myself, let's do AI and music."[6]

Eck had no training in AI except for being a self-taught coder, and in 1994 he applied to Indiana University to study computer science and cognitive science. There he banged on the door of one of the university's stellar professors, Douglas Hofstadter, author of *Gödel, Escher, Bach,* and asked to work with him. In retrospect, Eck says, this was an extremely unsuitable way to approach the great man. "But I just did it. This is the way I work."[7] After a year of bringing his mathematics up to date, Eck formally entered the graduate program—though, in the end, he did not work with Hofstadter because Hofstadter did not believe that AI was anywhere near sophisticated enough to produce innovative music. Hofstadter continues to maintain this view of AI to this day.[8]

At Indiana, Eck worked with researchers in cognitive science, studying the use of electronic devices to explore how we sense rhythm, what makes us tap our feet to the beat. "I just did it," he says—his catchphrase. "I just started working on musical cognition and computing and never looked back."[9]

At the Dalle Molle Institute for Artificial Intelligence (IDSIA) in Lugano, Switzerland, he worked on how to compose music on a neural network that had been trained on a form of twelve-bar blues popular among bebop jazz musicians.[10] In music, as in literature, there is a narrative structure, a beginning, a middle, and an end in which themes are reprised. Progress is not relentlessly linear. Machines have problems with this because many are built with an architecture that makes it difficult for them to remember what went before. Eck addressed himself to this problem.

His research was built on recurrent neural networks (RNNs), developed in the 1980s when neural networks were in their infancy. Instead of the usual feed-forward process for solving a problem, like composing music, instead of always looking to the next step, the networks could also move a few steps back or in a feedback loop. This meant they had a sort of memory. Past decisions could affect their response to new data. This avoided the restrictions required by Markov chains, which moved in one direction only: forward.

But RNNs could easily lose their knowledge of the past if the weights— the strengths of the connections between neurons—were not perfectly adjusted in the feedback loops. If the weights were set too high, the system became hyper and blew up in a riot of learning; if too low, the RNNs never remembered anything really interesting.

In 1997, Sepp Hochreiter and Jürgen Schmidhuber invented long short-term memory (LSTM).[11] LSTM protects RNN against memory loss by gating off the results accrued by the RNNs and keeping them in a memory cache, much as we do as we work over processes in our minds.

In 2002, Eck and Schmidhuber built on these early efforts, switching from RNN memory cells to LSTM cells. The aim was to set up a stable music generator. But at the time, neural networks didn't have sufficient hidden layers, and there wasn't enough data available to train them. As a result, the machine produced either monotonous riffs or jumbles of notes.

Eck joined Google in 2010. He was eager to tackle the challenge of combining AI and music. Other researchers, such as Leon Gatys with his style transfer, were combining machine learning with art. François Pachet, whom Eck greatly admired, was doing the same with AI and music. "People have carved out their own spaces. There's plenty of room for all of us," he recalls thinking.[12] He was encouraged by what he saw as the possibilities of machines to generate art and music using deep learning. Google was in a unique position to do this using Google Brain, its deep learning AI research project, initiated in 2011 in Mountain View, California. (Deep learning machines learn directly from data, such as images or moves in the game of Go, without needing to be programmed with specific algorithms.)

Eck made a proposal to Google for what he called Project Magenta, with himself at the helm, to tackle these questions: "Can we use machine learning to create compelling art and music? If so, how? If not, why not?"[13]

Creativity can only flourish when there are boundaries, guidelines, limiting factors: constraints. You can't create an advertisement for shoes without defining the kind of shoe, the price range, and the target market. Eck's constraint was to couple Magenta to Google Brain and its deep learning facility, applying machine learning with deep neural networks at every step—end to end; in other words, the machine teaches itself at every step of the process.[14] This minimalist approach had been immensely successful in developing Google's work in recognizing images and, a few years later, in translating languages and analyzing sound.

At Magenta, everything they used was open source—including TensorFlow, Google's extensive software library on GitHub, a giant coding and software-development platform. Says Eck, Magenta is "the glue between TensorFlow and the artistic and the music community." It brings together coders, artists, and musicians to build models to generate sound, images, and words. For the moment, Eck is focusing on music. "My whole career has been about music and audio," he says.[15] But, he insists, the scope of Magenta has always encompassed art and storytelling as well as music.

For now, the goal of Magenta is to provide a creative feedback loop for artists, musicians, and computers. Says Eck, "Art and technology have always coevolved."[16] He cites guitarists Les Paul and Jimi Hendrix in the 1950s and

1960s. Les Paul, an American jazz, country, and blues guitarist, was one of the pioneers of the solid-body electric guitar and the inventor of the Les Paul Standard, the Holy Grail of electric guitars. His guitars have an extraordinary sweetness of sound, as anyone who has ever played one—including Keith Richard and other legendary guitarists—will attest.

Hendrix took the Les Paul guitar and pushed its boundaries, amplifying it so much that it produced extreme distortion, taking the sound into another realm. In the same way, photography was initially developed to capture physical reality, but photographers soon put paid to that with intentional distortions, overexposed film, and other effects, essentially destroying the original instrument, as Hendrix did.

To Eck, the engineers at Magenta are more Les Paul and the artists more Jimi Hendrix. The essence of Magenta's existence is to be a creative feedback loop, a push and pull, between us and AI, increasing our human creativity. At present, fully autonomous creative machines are not on Eck's radar. He doesn't want to step back and "watch a machine create art," he says. Rather his aim is to "increase our creativity as people [with] a cool piece of technology to work with."[17]

As soon as Magenta was up and running, Eck set to work to bring his first project to life: to enable a machine to compose. The result was the small melody described at the beginning of this part, the first music composed entirely by a computer without being in any way programmed to do so. As described previously, Eck started by feeding in 4,500 popular tunes, from which the computer learned the rules for writing this particular sort of music. Then he seeded the computer with four musical notes—two Cs and two Gs. The computer then produced a ninety-second melody played on a Musical Instrument Digital Interface (MIDI) synthesizer (linking an electronic instrument and a computer), with percussion added to give it rhythm.

Eck was rather horrified when his creation of the little melody was snapped up by the media and proclaimed the world's first machine-composed melody. In fact, it created a sensation. Nick Patch of the *Toronto Star* wrote that the "age of the computer composer is finally upon us—even if the first machine-written tune sounds like a phoned-in Sega Genesis score."[18] The *Star* even invited three musicians and a singer to improvise on the melody in their own styles.

Ryan Keberle, a music professor in New York, complained that he "found [the tune] to be lacking in musical depth." Hardly surprising, but indicative of the seriousness with which many people took it. Although it was a computer-produced melody, it was not as simple as it might at first sound. There were variations made possible by LSTM.

There were many things wrong with this first musical venture. Says Eck, the machine "doesn't really understand musical time." It played only quarter notes and was not "attention-based." In other words, rather than being able to isolate a particular part of a musical score and focusing only on that, the neural net spread its attention around different parts of the score, as well as on everything going on around it.

Eck was also aware that the tune it had composed entirely lacked expressiveness: it was totally flat. To highlight what was missing, he programmed a computer to generate Beethoven's *Moonlight Sonata* and hooked it up to an electronic piano, which gave a robotic performance from the MIDI score. (A MIDI device can also output a musical score from a computer.) It was perfect, but totally lacking in feeling. Then a pianist sat down at the same piano and played the same piece from the same MIDI score. But he naturally modulated pressure on the keys, used the pedals, and brought in his own personality and feelings. As Eck puts it, "The performer is telling us a story that is not in the score. ... The story emerges from a combination of performer, score and real world."[19]

The next challenge, then, was to find a way to develop a machine that could create more expressive music. Two engineers at Magenta, Ian Simon and Sageev Oore, the latter of whom is a classical pianist and jazz musician, worked on this. They developed Performance RNN, "an LSTM recurrent neural network designed to model polyphonic music with expressive timing and dynamics."[20]

To create the Performance RNN version of *Moonlight Sonata*, they trained their neural network on the Yamaha Piano-e-Competition dataset, feeding in some 1,400 performances by skilled pianists, captured on a MIDI device. Oore played a keyboard attached to a MIDI that converted the input into data (numbers), which formed the raw material of the algorithm. In the MIDI, there are note-on and note-off events—when the pianist presses a key and when he releases it. MIDI data included the pitch of the note, its velocity (its volume), and how hard the key was pressed.

From this, Simon and Oore generated sequences of bars, complete with notes and dynamics. Then they expanded their training set by varying the initial data, increasing the length of each performance and changing the pitch or quality of sound by up to a major third—for example, from C to E.

Using this data, they set up their machine to generate music in steps of ten milliseconds, which offered more expressiveness in the timings of the notes, adding in a mixture of quarter and sixteenth notes to give variety and meaning. This provided more notes in intervals of seconds, resulting in the high density of notes appropriate to a musical score, as opposed to the primitive structure of the earlier melody. As the performances became longer, an LSTM stored what had gone before.

To control the model's output, Simon and Oore used a parameter they called temperature, which determines how random the machine's output is. At a temperature of one, the machine is left to produce any sounds it pleases. Lowering the temperature reduces the amount of randomness, but this tends to result in repetition. Raising the temperature results in random bursts of notes.

In the end, the music generated was only interesting for thirty seconds or so and then began to lose long-term structure. Nevertheless, this mini-malist approach was a step in the right direction: to create a neural net-work trained entirely on a database and not programmed to do anything in particular—trained end to end, in other words. To Eck, the result was exciting. The machine wasn't just generating notes: it was making deci-sions, "deciding how fast [the notes were] being played, and how loudly."[21]

Recently Eck and his colleagues have been looking for a way to generate longer sequences of notes. At the end of 2018 they brought out the Music Transformer. Eck describes it as "a genuine breakthrough in the neural net-work composition of music."[22]

Performance RNN not only degrades after only a few seconds, it also forgets the input motif almost immediately. The Music Transformer, on the other hand, keeps the input motif intact while playing it against the back-ground of the music it's been trained on.[23] This is closer to what musicians actually do. In fact the Music Transformer produces coherent music for more than twice as long as Performance RNN. In technical terms RNNs can only access specific parts of the music the neural network has been trained on, while the Music Transformer can access all of it while maintaining attention on the motif. Eck and his colleagues see the Music Transformer as a way for musicians to explore a range of possibilities for developing a given motif. An inspiring example is the way in which the Music Transformer plays with the motif in Chopin's Black-Key Étude, keeping it intact while improvising around it.

As head of Project Magenta, creativity is always on Eck's mind. I ask him about volition, whether machines can create works of art on their own. His first response is, "I predicted this question on my bike ride in this morning. It's the right question. This is the sort of thing I think about when I'm falling asleep or when I have a scotch."[24]

The present political climate has made him think about dystopian novels like George Orwell's *Animal Farm* and *1984*, he continues. How close are we to developing a computer capable of producing works like these? It seems impossibly far off, he concedes. "But who knows?" He doesn't know when machines will have "what looks to us to be actual volition." And when they do, people will question whether it truly is volition, to which the only answer will be the one that David Ferrucci gave when asked whether IBM Watson could think: "Can a submarine swim?" Whenever machines show glimmers of creativity, people raise the bar of what should be defined as creative.

It will take a generational shift to change this, says Eck. Today we have virtual pop stars like Hatsune Miku in Japan, a Vocaloid hologram who has thousands of fans. Young people are less hidebound about the concept of creativity; indeed, her computer nature is what gives Miku her popularity.

Eck is encouraged by the way Go enthusiasts respond to AlphaGo and its unpredictable moves and in particular to the fact that the Go community refers to the machine as "she" and described AlphaGo's key move in the second game of its match with Lee Se-dol as "beautiful." They didn't get caught in the trap of saying, "Well, if it were made by a human it would have been beautiful." Here, says Eck, "we can clearly attribute beauty to the machine."[25]

Eck believes that imposing boundaries on computers when they compose music will help to ensure they create works that we can appreciate and enjoy. He gives as an example serialism, which Arnold Schoenberg initiated early in the twentieth century with his twelve-tone technique, based on the twelve notes of the chromatic scale (each a semitone above or below its adjacent pitches), a limitation that conversely created new freedoms of expression. It was, says Eck, an interesting way to compose music, but people were simply not equipped to appreciate it. From this he concludes that there are limits to the sounds we can appreciate. "All happens in small leaps. You can't move from Mozart to the Sex Pistols in one generation." The music generated by creative machines, he suggests, will be of a kind so different from what we can even imagine—owing to our own cognitive limitations—that people will find it cacophonous, as happened at first with Schoenberg's serial music, until he modified it.

Another example Eck gives of the necessity of imposing limitations, or constraints, on creativity is the way in which he formed Project Magenta. "When I created Magenta, it was clear there had to be some constraining factors. Otherwise you're all over the place. For me the constraining factor was that I believed that deep learning, explicitly, has been a very productive and interesting revolution in machine learning, that would tie deep neural networks in with RNNs and reinforcement learning," he tells me. In other words, he had a definite plan in mind, rather than simply taking account of everything in AI. Thus inspired, he worked with engineers from Google Brain to create Magenta and tied it in with TensorFlow, Google's software library and machine-learning framework. He also chose to utilize end-to-end learning, in which the computer essentially teaches itself by being fed data, with no further outside input. This is the basis of Google's very successful translation process, which took twenty years to work out. "Finally we got it right," says Eck. "That's what we're trying to do with music."

18 From WaveNet and NSynth to Coconet: Adventures in Music Making

WaveNet: From Voice to Music

> Since WaveNets can be used to model any audio signal, we thought it would also be fun to try to generate music.
>
> —Aäron van den Oord[26]

Scientists have been working on voice synthesis for decades. Initially they fed whole libraries of parts of speech broken up into phonemes (units of sound) and morphemes (units of meaning) into a machine, along with rules for the sounds each letter of the alphabet can generate. A voice emerged, speaking words in a rather robotic fashion.

This was one of the challenges researchers at DeepMind in London were determined to crack. Instead of putting images into a convolutional neural network (ConvNet), they fed in samples of speech chopped into ten-millisecond fragments and converted into numbers. From this the machine learned not the rules of grammar, as in earlier efforts at voice synthesizing, but the underlying structure of speech, such as which tones are more likely to follow which others and what a realistic speech wave form looks like. When the machine was given a text, it created more realistic-sounding speech than any previous method had. It was able to mimic the human voice and sound entirely natural.[27] Google called its new method WaveNet and launched it in September 2016.

Like speech, music too is sound waves, so it made sense to try to generate that as well.[28] The scientists at Google fed in hundreds of hours of classical piano music, chopping the sound waves up into tiny fragments, which the neural network converted into numbers, then let the computer loose to generate whatever it wanted. It produced some fascinating pieces of piano music.

Sageev Oore, the engineer and pianist who had worked on Performance RNN, took a good look at the pieces the computer had generated.[29] First he played them by ear, smoothing them out, adding the human touch. Then he played the actual scores the machine had created.[30] Some were unexpectedly difficult to play. There were parts that didn't sound suited to the piano, thrown up as a result of the speed at which the machine had worked. There were also idiosyncratic combinations of notes and chords. At times, the music reminded Oore of the pioneering atonality of works by Russian composer Alexander Scriabin, who influenced Igor Stravinsky and Sergei Prokofiev. If the machine had been a person, we would have said it was highly creative.

Unfortunately, the melodies petered out after a few seconds. The big question was how to sustain the impetus.

NSynth: Creating Sounds Never Heard Before

> Music is intention communicated through sound.
> —Jesse Engel[31]

Meanwhile, Jesse Engel and his team at Google were experimenting with neural audio synthesis through their neural synthesizer (NSynth), which, Engel writes, "lets you interpolate between pairs of instruments to create new sounds."[32] The team started by feeding some three hundred thousand labeled musical notes, played on over a thousand instruments at various pitches and volumes, into an artificial neural network.

Then they seeded in two audio waves—the sounds of, for example, a flute and an organ. This was where they introduced the magic. They broke down the audio waves into small particles, encoded in numbers, thus transforming the music into numbers. Then they fed the numbers into a computer, in which the encodings for flute and organ intermingled. The machine had been configured to play the pure sound of a flute and the pure sound of an organ, but now it also produced sounds never heard or even imagined before, melding a flute and an organ, producing a sound impossible for a flute or an organ to make even when played together.

The possibilities are endless. You could substitute a cat's meow for the organ, then meld the meow and the flute. Thus NSynth enables musicians to play with sound and dream up bold new pieces of music. Engel says NSynth is more than just an algorithm. "It's an instrument I can play which encourages more than just novelty. It's personal expression as well."[33] NSynth can be used by a musician or by anyone else, even if they have little or no knowledge of AI. It's a wonderful example of AI's power to increase creativity: Project Magenta at its best, serving as a feedback loop between AI and the musician.

The first step is to train neural networks to understand existing music and compose along the same lines. But more exciting is when they enable us to create sounds we've never created before and compose music unlike any we've ever known. The next stage will be when they themselves start to compose music —music that reflects their very different experience of existence.

Another way of making music with AI is through Google's *AI Duet*, an interactive instrument that allows you to play a duet with a computer.[34] The network has been fed many samples of music so that it understands notes and timings, which means it can respond to whatever tune you play.

As part of Project Magenta, Engel agrees that there always has to be "a human in the loop."[35] The problem is how best to develop the relationship between computers and people so as to encourage the greatest degree of creativity. The researchers at Project Magenta, says Engel, are not particularly interested in developing computers that create autonomously.

This makes Eck's initial project at Magenta—the ninety-second melody— all the more adventurous.

Coconet: Filling in the Gaps

AI-music-generation people obsess on Bach.
—Douglas Eck[36]

Whereas machines compose in a linear way, starting at the beginning and going on to the end, composers often work in a more piecemeal fashion as inspiration strikes, scribbling motifs here and there. Doug Eck and Anna Huang, a researcher at Google who teaches at the University of Montreal, came up with a way to help composers complete a work.

They focused on Bach's chorales. Bach's music is a huge challenge, not only for musicians but for AI researchers. The greatest challenge is how to model his highly structured counterpoints, with notes playing against each other to produce two or more melodies.

Eck and Huang's inspired idea was to "bring artistic tools to music," in the spirit of Magenta.[37] They began with a ConvNet, but instead of feeding in visual images in the usual way, they fed in an entire Bach corpus: 382 four-part harmonized chorales of soprano, tenor, alto, and bass voices.

They also used context encoders, based on generative adversarial networks (GANs).[38] These are akin to an artist who reconstructs the image of a lost section of a building, deducing it from the context—that is, the rest of the building. The challenge lies in taking the context into account but not simply duplicating it. Similarly, having been fed a set of building façades, the context encoder can complete the picture, sometimes in a surprising or imaginative way.

Instead of building façades, Eck and Huang blocked out one voice at a time from the Bach chorales, then got the computer to create the missing part, deducing how it should sound statistically from the original data, just as a missing part of a building façade can be recreated from the surrounding elements. The remaining voices provide context for the computer-generated sound. Eck and Huang called their model Coconet—Counterpoint by Convolution.

The point, says Eck, is to "pay attention to the melody, which is not perfect but interesting…more Bach than Bach."[39]

19 François Pachet and His Computers That Improvise and Compose Songs

How do you compose a compelling song, a song that remains in your head and the heads of millions of people?

—François Pachet[40]

When I ask François Pachet what the future holds for him and his research, he replies, "I will stop working the day I take a taxi and hear a song composed by myself with my technology."[41]

Pachet is one of the pioneers of computer music using AI, and particularly machine improvisation. He is a scientist, composer, and director of the Spotify Creator Technology Research Lab in Paris.

Pachet started as a musician, studying at the prestigious École Normale de Musique de Paris, where he specialized in the guitar. He went on to study jazz and improvisation at the Berklee College of Music in Boston. "Jazz and improvisation are like a sport," he says. "It's an activity that keeps your mind in shape."[42] He likens improvisation to a conversation in which one person starts a sentence and another finishes it.

Pachet's second love was engineering, which he studied at the Université Pierre et Marie Curie in Paris, where he was an assistant professor of artificial intelligence until 1997. It was only when he moved to Sony Computer Science Laboratory, also in Paris, that he was finally able to combine his two loves and establish a team that explored AI and music.

The conundrum Pachet set out to solve was how to improvise with a computer and have it respond in the same style. For this he decided to use Markov models, based on Markov chains. To recap, Markov models predict the most probable note to follow the previous one, based only on previous events—and they are at the core of Pachet's work.

Pachet finds Markov models simpler and easier to control than neural networks. Neural nets, he says, can't compute fast enough, whereas Markov models, although less powerful, are more creative, particularly when a machine is improvising with a musician.[43]

In 2003, Pachet developed a system that can improvise with a musician. He called it the Continuator.[44] The musician starts by playing a few phrases on a piano hooked up to a MIDI, which transmits the notes to the Continuator. Then he sits back. In a flash, the Continuator's learning module learns the input note by note, breaks it into phrases, then sends each phrase in turn to a phrase analyzer to pull out the patterns and form the database. The machine then responds to the pianist with some phrases of its own. Thus the system instantaneously learns to play in the same style as the musician, without needing to be programmed to do so. It immediately responds to the riffs the pianist has just played with a new musical phrase, fulfilling Pachet's view of improvisation as conversation. Sometimes the performer is amazed at the machine's response.[45]

Pachet built in constraints so that the Continuator could respond to unexpected riffs or chord changes that it hadn't learned. One way of doing this was to weight the points at which it had to make a choice of going one way or another, taking into account how well that choice matched the piano accompaniment, rather than strictly following a Markov chain.

He then set up a musical Turing test to assess the Continuator's success, asking two music critics to decide when the pianist was playing and when the machine had taken over. In most cases, they couldn't differentiate between the pianist and the machine.

The Continuator can also be programmed to accompany a pianist, selecting the most harmonious chords from a database of chord sequences.

For Pachet, however, the Continuator was a first step. He feels that deep neural networks are useful in well-defined areas such as facial recognition, medical diagnosis, and games like Go, but less successful in the artistic domain, in which problems are less well defined, such as the question of what makes a good song. The big challenge he wanted to confront was how to use AI not just to respond to human musicians but to compose music.

The Flow Machine

To do this, Pachet developed the Flow Machine. He was inspired by the American psychologist Mihaly Csikszentmihalyi's concept of "flow," the state of mind when a person is so completely absorbed in the activity they're engaged in that time and place seem to fall away.[46] They lose track of where they are and how much time has gone by. For it to occur, there has to be a perfect balance between the challenge of the task and the person's skills—not too difficult and not too easy.

For Pachet, high-level creators respond to their challenges by developing their own unique style, which immediately identifies their work. The Flow Machine allows composers to confront challenges by increasing their skills so that a new style emerges.[47] It makes music alongside musicians, providing them with a new way to create. The Flow Machine's database is made of musical scores written on lead sheets, standard manuscript pages for music but with the notes digitized. Musicians can write music directly onto a blank lead sheet in the same way that one writes on a word processor and hear it played back by a computer.

The Flow Machine uses Markov models to analyze the sequences of notes and phrases in its database and identifies the patterns, then writes new music on lead sheets, following the same style. The problem, however, was to find Markov models that could handle long sequences of notes, unlike the Continuator, which could only deal with short-term sequences.

To do so required a little mathematical magic. Pachet is the magus of Markov models.[48] He took the Markov chains and manipulated the mathematics to introduce limitations so he could control the structure of a score while optimizing the search for how one note succeeds the next. He called these limitations Markov constraints.[49]

Markov constraints identify patterns. The computer calculates the probability of certain chord progressions, melodic sequences, and rhythms and uses these probabilities to generate new plausible variations. In this way, Pachet can retain the style of a piece of music while manipulating it as a computational object. He can rearrange a piece of music in a certain style—a bossa nova orchestration of Beethoven's "Ode to Joy" or a random pattern of notes played in the style of the Beatles, selecting the notes and harmonies.

A fundamental aim is to relate creativity to style. For Pachet, style is what separates great composers, writers, and painters from everyone else—and people develop their style by imitating the style of others.[50]

Benoît Carré, who has written songs for Johnny Halliday and Françoise Hardy and is the artistic director of the Flow Machine project, showed me how the Flow Machine works—a fascinating process.[51] The Flow Machine has thirteen thousand songs in its database, mainly jazz, Western popular music, and Brazilian music, based on harmonized melodies that can be reduced to notes and chords. You start by choosing tempo, signature, and notes, then select a style, such as American songwriters, including songs by George Gershwin and Duke Ellington. The machine proceeds to create a melody. Once it has done so, you can edit the composition.

In September 2016, the Flow Machine unveiled its first recording, the first ever complete song composed by AI. "Daddy's Car" is a cheerful, upbeat little ditty based on a selection of Beatles' tunes, with the lyrics composed by Carré. At this stage, all the machine can do is put together the basic tune. Carré provided all the flourishes—harmonies, instrumentation and lyrics.

Pachet is fond of the phrase "stylistic cryogenics"—fixing style in a time warp.[52] In the future, he muses, by using algorithms like his constrained Markov models you will be able to resurrect Bach and play in his style or create variations on Bach and Mozart that those composers would have approved of. Both fervently believed that their music ought not to be frozen in time but should reflect the era in which they were performed.

Says Pachet, "Music has to be created by humans because machines cannot discern between good and very good. Humans have intentions, while machines cannot curate what they do." Of Project Magenta's simple melody, he agrees that "machines can produce music of their own volition," but, he adds: "The problem is that they do not generate very interesting stuff."[53]

Eck, the head of Project Magenta, has great respect for Pachet and his work. He says that at present Pachet is doing more interesting work than him, but that Pachet's models "bring a lot more structure to the table."[54] Whereas Project Magenta's computers can create music without needing to be programmed, Pachet uses complex software.

In 2017, Pachet moved from Sony to Spotify, where he directs the Spotify Creator Technology Research Lab. He sees the mathematical part of his odyssey as nearly over and the experimental as about to begin. At the beginning of 2018, Pachet, along with the French musical collective SYGGE led by Carré, released an album entitled *Hello World*. This is the first multi-artist music album composed by musicians using AI tools. A group of musicians, including recent sensations Kiesza and Stromae, descended on the lab, took control of the Flow Machine tools, and generated fifteen songs. The album's title signifies AI stepping out of the lab to greet the world. The music is at times otherworldly, as are the lyrics. Thus one goal of AI has been achieved: scientific research has morphed effortlessly into an album of music.

One reviewer wrote, "I was worried the songs would sound too robotic, but I was pleasantly surprised."[55] Indeed they don't. But would it matter if they did?

"For me creativity is pretty much a social thing, not an objective thing, especially in music," says Pachet. "Society will decide whether someone is creative or not."

20 Gil Weinberg and Mason Bretan and Their Robot Jazz Band

I call my group a robotic musicianship group: not musical robots but robotic musicians. The emphasis is that they're musicians first and robots later.
—Gil Weinberg[56]

We have a robot which needs not only to learn something about music and understand it, it also needs to understand its physical embodiment.
—Mason Bretan[57]

Like François Pachet, for Gil Weinberg and Mason Bretan it's the music that counts. Mathematics is just a way to achieve that end. What distinguishes Weinberg and Bretan is their robots. This changes the focus: from creating music using a computer to embodiment, working out how to make a robot understand how to move to carry out its musical ideas, such as striking a drum.

Weinberg's creations are, he says, "musicians first and robots later."[58] He calls them Haile, Shimon, and Shimi. He and his team at Georgia Institute of Technology developed the earliest of the three, Haile, in 2006. Weinberg's aim was to create a robot that could "listen like a human, play like a machine."[59] Haile is a human-sized percussionist with a beautifully crafted flat wooden head and limbs, including articulated arms. It listens through a microphone to a drummer, analyzes the sounds into beats, rhythms, and pitches, then responds by striking a drum, as in figure 20.1. Haile is the first robot to physically make music rather than playing through speakers.

Next came Shimon, a four-armed marimba player wielding eight sticks, with a head that bobs in time to the beat like a seasoned jazz musician. It took seven years to develop. Bretan, a recent PhD student of Weinberg,

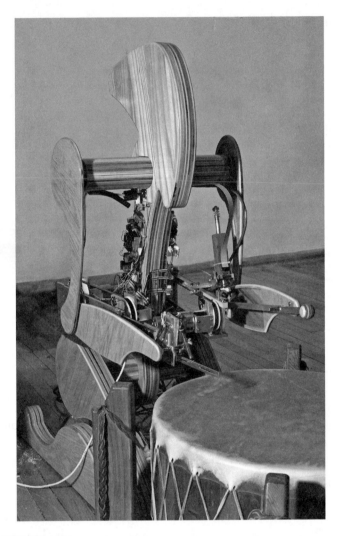

Figure 20.1
Haile, the drum-playing robot, 2006.

was a key player on the team. Shimon can observe as well as listen and is loaded with a huge database of music. Having a head makes it seem almost human. It becomes an entity with a personality, a musician you want to play with (see figure 20.2). Shimon's AI can be powered with artificial neural networks, Markov chains, or other exotic systems. It improvises alongside human musicians on a marimba and can also compose original music (which we'll return to later).

Figure 20.2
Mason Bretan jamming with Shimon (left) and three Shimis (right), 2015.

Shimi is a scaled-down version of Shimon. Its brain is a cell phone with which it can dock. In this way, it can connect with music in the cloud. It can play your favorite songs, suggest others, tap its feet, and nod its head. It is an endearing "robotic companion, your music buddy," as Weinberg puts it.[60]

All three interact with human musicians: Haile drums, Shimon plays the marimba and composes, and Shimi responds to and makes music.

Weinberg is a professor of musical technology at Georgia Tech, where he heads a huge group in robotics research and directs several successful start-ups. He grew up in Israel, where he showed great promise at the piano, but his teacher discouraged improvisation or composing. When he was sixteen, his family bought a computer. "Why not bring music and computer together?" he thought to himself.

He went on to study music and computer science at Tel Aviv University, then moved to the MIT Media Lab to work under Tod Machover, a highly innovative composer who crafts music with technology and has invented augmented instruments such as the hypercello.[61]

Weinberg cites as his inspiration Max Matthews, considered by many the father of computer music. While at Bell Labs in Murray Hill, New Jersey, Matthews wrote an algorithm for a musical accompaniment for the song "Daisy Bell." Struck by the otherworldliness of the voice, created by a speech synthesizer, Arthur C. Clarke suggested to Stanley Kubrick that he use it in *2001: A Space Odyssey*. In an eerie scene, the computer HAL 9000 sings the song as the last remaining astronaut dismantles its cognitive functions.

Until recently a PhD student of Weinberg, Bretan, the mastermind behind Shimon, has focused on robotic musicianship. He is an accomplished drummer, guitarist, pianist, and general musical all-rounder. It is remarkable to see him shift from guitar to piano to drums as he adjusts computers while accompanying the robots.

Since his childhood, Bretan has been an avid musician and has had a keen interest in physics and mathematics. At the University of California at Santa Cruz, he planned to study music, but then chanced upon the school's renowned program in computer music. From there he went on to study with Weinberg at Georgia Tech. Among his early inspirations were David Cope, a pioneer in machine-generated music to be discussed in the next chapter; Miller Puckette, one of the first developers of open-source software for interactive music; and David Borgo, a professor of experimental music.[62]

Working with robots, say Weinberg and Bretan, is very special. "Some of the things you can get away with in pure software applications where you're just synthesizing sounds with a computer, you can't get away with with a robot," explains Bretan.[63] The robot needs to have some understanding of its physical being to work out how to move so that it can play a drum or a marimba. It's akin to composing music for a musician with eleven fingers on one hand. You just can't do it. Composers have to stay within the parameters—constraints—of what constitutes a human being.

Embodiment—implanting a computer in a robot to serve as its brain, controlling its movements and actions—along with musical knowledge have to be tackled using separate systems, plus a host of electronics to drive the robot's limbs.

But the real challenge is to find a way to make the robot understand and produce music that sounds melodic to human ears. For that, Shimon, the most advanced robot, needs to be able to think like a human musician. Instead of focusing probabilistically on what note follows the previous one, as more primitive systems do, it needs to be aware of the overall structure of the piece.

Weinberg and Bretan start by feeding in a large body of music from Wikifonia, a musical database of 4,235 pieces of jazz, folk, popular, and classical music, including transcriptions of improvisations by musicians like John Coltraine, Thelonious Monk, and Miles Davis, to which they add 170,000 motifs with 20,000 riffs. They shift pitches up and down and alter the spaces between notes to create a huge database for Shimon to analyze, to try and identify harmonic and rhythmic patterns that appear in all the songs and genres.

One question might be whether, with such a vast database, the machine has too little leeway to produce something new. With too much input, the danger might be that the computer produces music very similar to what it has already been fed. With too little, it might create something new but not melodious, cacophony to human listeners.

To tackle this issue, Bretan and Weinberg use a rather stunning piece of mathematical wizardry called unit selection.[64] Each unit of bars, riffs, or motifs is made up of numbers that carry ten qualities or features of that unit, including how the first note in the unit is tied to the previous bar and how the last note links to the next bar. These qualities or features have to be annotated by hand. The machine then collects these numbers into a container that scientists call a bag of words, or BOW, rather like the bag of letters in a game of Scrabble. Once gathered, they are jumbled up. These BOWs are inside the machine's latent space, a place of multiple dimensions in which there is an infinite number of possibilities for combinations, rather like the human imagination.

Next they seed in a set of eight or sixteen notes for Shimon to work on. The various BOWs, more properly bags of scrambled bars or riffs or motifs, look for the bars or riffs or motifs with the highest similarity to those that have been seeded in. But the probability of a match is very low. The number of ways in which a bar can be filled with notes is huge, and there are millions of bars in the current library of data. In the end, the system's training enables it to home in on one that is stylistically appropriate. Bretan and Weinberg found that four-bar units produce the most pleasing music. Shimon's first composition was a delicate, jazz-like tune, akin to a gamelan piece, which it plays on its marimba with its four arms, bobbing and turning its head as if thinking and responding to the music it's making.[65]

In 2015, Bretan, Shimon, and three Shimi robots collaborated on a piece called "What You Say,"[66] inspired by the high-energy funk piece "What I Say" by Miles Davis. The smaller Shimi robots bob rhythmically, tap their feet, and generate sounds in response to the music played by Bretan and Shimon.[67]

Instead of an artificial neural network, Shimon was powered by a rule-based improvisation system that Bretan designed using a genetic algorithm alongside his extensive knowledge of chord progressions in jazz. A genetic algorithm works along the same lines as the rule of survival of the fittest in evolution. The process starts with a melody that sounds pleasing to human ears—a fitness melody—and a selection of musical notes. The algorithm switches around the notes in the bars and switches around the bars, combining some and replacing notes at random to generate a new melody. It then compares the new collection of musical phrases with the original phrase—the fitness melody—and selects the phrases most similar to it, discarding less similar—less "fit"—ones, and does so several times. The whole process happens very quickly and ends with the robot playing a brand-new melody—one that, thanks to the original aesthetic input, sounds pleasing.

Bretan concludes of his extraordinary jam session with Shimi and Shimon: "Through the power of artificial intelligence, signal processing, and engineering I firmly believe it is possible for machines to be artistic, creative, and inspirational."[68] To him, he says, Shimon's most important quality is not so much its music but how "the robot moves its head when it detects a beat, how it looks at people. There is much more to music making than what note has been generated. There is physicality and embodiment. That's what's cool and makes people buy tickets."[69] "The machines just generate sequences of notes," he adds.[70] "But if a great robot musician emerges, people are creative enough that we will figure out a way to take advantage of that. However, in order to do that we need machines to play with humans using computational music systems."

Both Bretan and Weinberg believe that people and computers need to work together. Says Bretan, "We are at a point where we need to have at least some degree of musical expertise to get a nice-sounding system."[71] Machines by themselves still cannot produce melodic sounds, a necessary prerequisite before advancing any further.

"We want them to connect with us," says Weinberg. The aim is to establish common ground so that "the robots know what we're talking about," so that both musician and robot feel the rhythm and syncopation, the tension and release. Eventually, he says, "the robot will push this into domains uncharted. That will make more sense to me than just jumping ahead too far, too fast, to levels where we can't communicate."[72]

Ultimately, Weinberg tells me, "I want robots to come up with their own ideas, to inspire me, to create music I would not expect, to respond to me in an expressive and creative way. That's why I call my robots musicians." He wants robots, he says, "to create something that will blow your mind, that will send shivers down your spine, that will make you ecstatic, that will make you cry. Humans can do it well enough already. Machines have the potential to do things humans can't."[73]

21 David Cope Makes Music That Is "More Bach than Bach"

Good music requires no further justification, regardless of its composer.
—David Cope[74]

David Cope has made a life's work out of creating Bach that out-Bachs Bach and Mozart that out-Mozarts Mozart, with the help of increasingly sophisticated algorithmic "collaborators." His work has attracted fury from the musical establishment, which accuses it of having "no heart" or simply ignores it.

Douglas Hofstadter, however, author of a key work on computer science and cognition, *Gödel, Escher, Bach*, disagrees. He writes, "In twenty years of working in artificial intelligence, I have run across nothing more thought-provoking than David Cope's *Experiments in Music Intelligence*. What is the essence of musical style, indeed of music itself? Can great new music emerge from the extraction and recombination of patterns in earlier music? Are the deepest of human emotions triggerable by computer patterns of notes?"[75] Cope's work stirs all these profound questions and more.

Cope started as a highly acclaimed young composer whose music was performed at Carnegie Hall. But he was also interested in computer composition and set out to write a piece for a behemoth IBM mainframe. The work "was a bunch of crap," as he puts it, because the machine couldn't process musical data in a viable manner.[76]

Then in 1980 he was commissioned to write an opera and came up against a severe case of writer's block. He would sit for hours at the piano with a blank score sheet in front of him, falling ever deeper into despair. Finally, he decided to have another go at writing software to generate music, using a new generation of machines—laptops. He wanted to examine what constitutes style, particularly his own.

For Cope, the great revelation is that, as in art and science, music progresses through the accumulation of knowledge. In essence, it is inspired plagiarism. Picasso built on the work of Cézanne and Ingres, Einstein on the research of Maxwell and Lorentz. Joyce provided hints for Beckett, who inspired Pinter. No one starts with a blank slate. Everyone begins by composing "in the style of." We all have a vast foundation—an internal database—of musical references. Composers are the people who have the ability to transform that foundation into distinctive new patterns. As Steve Jobs said, in words he attributed to Picasso, "Good artists copy; great artists steal." If Mozart were alive today, Cope asserts, he for one would certainly be using computers to augment his work.

For his music-generating software, Cope built a database of hundreds of scores by Bach, Chopin, and other masters. He broke them down into notes, coding each by pitch, duration, and volume, when the note occurs in the piece, and the voice or instrument that makes it. This is the only database he uses, to make sure he is working with clean data, free of errors. His pattern-matching software lifts patterns from the data and from these infers rules for composition. To check on his software, he took chunks of notes from Bach's scores and used Markov chains to reassemble them according to the patterns the software had discovered—which turned out to be the rules for composing baroque music. Using Markov chains enabled him also to factor in the randomness that is a crucial part of the creative process.

He called his program Experiments in Musical Intelligence (EMI), and it was soon churning out enormous amounts of music. It seemed to take on a personality of its own, and so it became Emmy. "The processes Emmy uses are the same as composers use," Cope says.[77] Like any composer, it has a database—a vast inbuilt knowledge of music—with rules for composing. But it's not as simple as that. What distinguishes great composers is the particular notes, motifs, and themes they choose and how they choose to apply the rules for composition—rules they may sometimes break.

Algorithmic theory—the kind of mathematics he uses—is of no interest to Cope. "I don't give a damn what the algorithm is as long as it produces the output I want," he says.[78] He devises his own algorithms rather than using already existing ones. "My algorithms are my own."

Plate 1
Alexander Mordvintsev, nightmare beast created using DeepDream, 2015.

Plate 2
Content image, a photograph of the Neckarfront at Tübingen (upper left). Style image, van Gogh's *The Starry Night* (lower left). Image on right: Leon Gatys, *The Neckarfront at Tübingen according to van Gogh*, as van Gogh might have painted it.

Plate 3

CycleGAN translates from a Monet to a photograph-like landscape (top, upper row) and from a photograph to a Monet-like painting (top, lower row), and from a zebra to a horse (bottom, upper row) and from a horse to a zebra (bottom, lower row).

Plate 4
Happy face (left). As rendered by The Painting Fool, in vibrant pastels, with an "electric" background, 2015 (right).

Eight years down the line, he came to the conclusion that there was no such thing as his own style distinct from everyone else's. Inevitably, it had to be based on the styles of others. Emmy brought this home to him when he noticed that the style patterns in his own works contained those of others. He finally conquered his composer's block and, in 1987, completed his opera, which opened to modest acclaim. The *Richmond Times Dispatch* described one passage as "a supreme dramatic moment, punctuated by the captivating beat of drums."[79]

By now, Emmy was pouring out thousands of scores. Cope curated them in the same way that composers keep some of their creations and discard others. By 1993 he was ready to release an album, Emmy's first, *Bach by Design*. But record companies refused to produce it, saying that it was not contemporary music. Cope's reply was, "Then what is it?"[80] Eventually Centaur Records agreed to bring it out, but the musicians claimed that the fingerings were too difficult. In the end the selections had to be generated on a MIDI-controlled Disklavier (a piano capable of being hooked up to a computer). It was, Cope says proudly, the first album of music neither composed nor played by human musicians.

Cope was immediately inundated with hostile reviews. Some critics dismissed his music out of hand simply because it was produced by a computer, which, they said, by definition could not display creativity, something that only people possess. Douglas Hofstadter wrote of how disturbing he found it to be moved by what was in effect twenty thousand lines of code: the "composer's soul is irrelevant to the music [and that] would be a tragedy, because my entire life has been moved by music."[81]

According to Cope, the view that "technology represents another world, alien to truth and beauty, is a basic trope for the technophobe."[82] Google's Blaise Agüera y Arcas sees it as a C. P. Snow "two cultures" scenario with two opposite poles, the "technophobic humanist and the inhuman technologist."[83]

Some reviewers asked why computers should try to do something that we have been doing successfully for years—namely, writing music. Says Cope, "Good music requires no further justification, regardless of its composer." He adds that the "computer composed—not generated—music. ... Listeners must set aside any notions about creativity being unique to humans."[84]

Cope and Emmy's next recording, *Classical Music Composed by the Computer*, included selections in the style of Bach, Beethoven, Joplin, Mozart,

Rachmaninov, and Stravinsky. It was performed by musicians and received better reviews.[85] Hofstadter, by now a fan of Cope, was quoted in the *New York Times* as saying, "Nothing I've seen in artificial intelligence has done this so well."[86]

Some critics claim that when Cope's algorithm assembles phrases, what emerges is merely pastiche.[87] He responds, "The term pastiche is cruel and unfair. The way things fit together is in a way to make musical sense." He adds, "Emmy's output has often been mistaken for music written by musicians of high caliber; in fact, Emmy's Chopin is more Chopin than Chopin. The processes Emmy uses are similar to what human composers use. [Is not] everything a pastiche?"[88]

Another criticism is that Cope's music is most successful only when its scores are played by musicians. The critic Stephen W. Smoliar wrote, "Whether or not it was music when it came out of the computer, it was *certainly* music" when it was played by a musician.[89]

In the following years, Emmy produced some 1,500 symphonies, 1,000 piano sonatas, 5,000 Bach chorales, and 1,000 string quartets, as well as operas based on the music of Mozart, Schumann, and Mahler, with librettos taken from the composers' letters. "It's the life of the composer through the composer's words," Cope explains.[90]

But he was becoming bored with producing music "in the style of," "tired of people wanting to see Beethoven's Tenth Symphony and a finished version of Schubert's *Unfinished Symphony*."[91] He felt that what made a composer fully understandable, fully affecting, truly human was the fact of mortality. Composers have to die, and the ending makes sense of the entire oeuvre. So in 2004, he turned Emmy off.

He then set out to look for ways to create a computer program that could develop its own musical style. In 2004, Emily Howell was born—Emily after Emmy and Howell, which is Cope's father's name and his own middle name.

Emily Howell has a memory that involves an intimate understanding of the works of thirty-six composers, from Palestrina to Cope himself. Cope's relationship with it is far more collaborative than it was with Emmy. Whereas he programmed Emmy very extensively, he communicates with Emily Howell via dialogue boxes, providing feedback to prompt it to evolve its own style. First he feeds in a musical phrase, then it responds, and Cope either accepts or declines the result, fine-tuning its knowledge base more and more.

Emily Howell's first album was released in February 2009 by Centaur Records. Entitled *From Darkness, Light*, it consists of Opus 1, 2, and 3 compositions for chamber orchestra and multiple pianos. A later work, *Breathless*, was released in 2012.

In a review, Mark Howell of the *Guardian* mentioned an academic who "warmed" to *From Darkness, Light* but "then rapidly chilled when advised where it came from," focusing on the music's source rather than the music itself—a common response, unfortunately, to AI-produced music.[92] Says Cope, "Regarding stylistic machine composition, I am surprised it took so long for the world to catch up with the idea that it has merit at all....Now it's caught up—and I am truly delighted with that. In the next twenty to thirty years magical things will happen in the arts....Things are changing."[93]

Cope does not believe in genius. People achieve great things just by dint of hard work, he says, with some native intelligence thrown in. Some people just think faster than others. He claims that with enough practice he could beat champions at chess, provided there was no clock. In fact, he continues, real-life chess geniuses are like computers, terrifyingly fast and accurate.

Cope feels computers can be creative and that to enjoy his music listeners need to set aside their prejudices about creativity being unique to people. But he also believes that computers are only machines and lack human qualities such as emotions. To reconcile his conflicting views of a creative machine that nevertheless has no human qualities, he offers the following rather gnomic definition of creativity: "The ability of the universe and of human beings that do not seem to be logically associable."[94] This seems to mean that human beings have a oneness with the universe that transcends logic and is thus beyond anything machines are capable of. A way out of these conflicting views, he says, would be the development of a "truly chemical machine," possessing human qualities such as emotions.

22 "The Drunken Pint" and Other Folk Music Composed by Bob Sturm and Oded Ben-Tal's AI

We want to avoid any machine versus human message; the computer is meant to enhance our creativity in music making.

—Bob Sturm[95]

Whenever a computer achieves something that previously we considered to be a creative task, or uniquely human task, we automatically redefine what creativity is.

—Oded Ben-Tal[96]

Who could possibly imagine a computer composing folk music? Evolved over thousands of years, representing the voice of a people, changing every time it's performed depending on the player, folk music is usually associated with noisy, smoky gatherings with plenty of beer.

It sounds like the ultimate test for whether a computer can be creative. Can AI be used to write Irish folk music, for example—and music that is interesting, even inspiring, for musicians? This is what Bob Sturm and Oded Ben-Tal set out to do in 2016.

In formal terms, their research is on music generation using recurrent neural networks (RNNs) and long short-term memory (LSTM). Back in 2002, Eck and Schmidhuber carried out pioneering work, training neural networks on blues music and then composing melodies.[97] The problem was that their artificial neural network was shallow—only one hidden layer with some ten LSTM units—and there was insufficient data to train their machine, only some thousand transcriptions of songs. Six years later, Eck and Jasmin Lapalme applied this work to 491 transcriptions of Irish folk songs.[98]

Over the next eight years, computer science changed dramatically. Sturm and Ben-Tal's machine had three hidden layers made up of 512 LSTM units and trained on twenty-three thousand transcriptions of Irish music, as opposed to Eck and Lapalme's 491. At first glance, an increase by a factor of only forty-seven seems insignificant, but this is not the case. There were also new methods for representing musical scores. Whereas Eck and Schmidhuber used a MIDI representation based on the notes' audio qualities, Sturm and Ben-Tal coded music transcriptions in a textual library using their own version of ABC notation. This allowed them to improve on the quality of the output, its melodic contour, repetition, and variation.

ABC notation is a text-based format for musical notation, a sort of shorthand using the letters A to G, with symbols to indicate sharps, flats, the length of the note and the key, and so on. It can be used to generate sheet music or to play a musical file through a computer speaker. Originally used to jot down folk tunes on a scrap of paper or beer mat, it is the standard way of recording folk and traditional music.

Sturm and his colleagues used ABC notation as a database for writing music with a character-recurrent neural network (Char-RNN). If we feed tens of thousands of poems into a Char-RNN, it will home in on the style of the poetry; if we then seed it with a few words, it will produce poetry in the same style. When applied to ABC notation, Char-RNN reads strings of single characters as notes and predicts what character will follow, taking into account rules for music composition learned from the data it has already been fed.

To train their AI, Sturm and his team fed in twenty-three thousand ABC transcriptions of Irish folk music. From this they generated 72,376 tunes and, via MIDI, synthesized 35,809. It is here that the forty-seven-fold increase in training data comes into play. The way Char-RNN works is by trying to predict the next character or note based on all the previous ones, which are increasing in number all the time. Eck and Schmidhuber's database contained only one thousand tunes, and Eck and Lapalme's only 491, even fewer, which gave very little for Char-RNN to work on, becoming worse as the sequence built up. Twenty-three thousand gave the system plenty more material to play with.

Some listeners were put off by the tinniness of the MIDI synthesizer sound, so Sturm and Ben-Tal converted the MIDI files to reproduce the sounds of various instruments and produced scores so that musicians could perform the transcriptions live.[99] Several musicians commented that they could happily improvise based on some of the new pieces, which pleased

Sturm and Ben-Tal; one of their aims is to develop creative partnerships with musicians.

Sturm is a laid-back American from the Midwest, whereas Ben-Tal emits Israeli seriousness and intensity. Sturm is currently an associate professor in the school of electronic engineering and computer science at the Royal Institute of Technology in Stockholm, in Sweden, and Ben-Tal is a senior lecturer in music technology at Kingston University in London. Both had hybrid educations that included music, electrical engineering, computer science, and physics, and both were introduced to coding at an early age. Sturm "finds writing at the piano rather painful," noting that he'd "rather write with a machine."[100] Although Ben-Tal prefers to write music by hand, his students prefer to work directly on a computer. "Computers are more versatile than musical instruments," he says.[101]

As an inspiration, Sturm recalls Curtis Roads, a composer/computer scientist at the University of California at Santa Barbara, famous for taking audio input, chopping it up into millisecond segments, rearranging them probabilistically, and combining them with exquisite geometric images to produce mind-bending performances. Ben-Tal recalls Jonathan Berger, a composer/researcher at Stanford University.

Together with Iryna Korshunova, Sturm and Ben-Tal started to explore what they call folk-rnn.[102] Instead of letters of the alphabet, folk-rnn uses "tokens"—meter, key, measure, pitch, grouping, bar line, duration. When seeded with a few notes, it spewed out thirty thousand new pieces.

Sturm and his team sent three thousand of the pieces to a popular Irish music website, the Session.[103] The response was mainly positive. The tunes sounded Irish, said some members; one in five (a rather small percentage) were very interesting, said others; a lot of rubbish, said yet others. But then again, there are plenty of duds written by human composers, something that critics of machine-produced art, literature, and music tend to overlook.[104]

"Now here's a wild tune composed by our *folk-rnn* system," writes Sturm of a particularly convincing Irish jig. It popped out from over seventy thousand transcriptions that the system generated in August 2015. But what tickled Sturm's fancy was the title, "The Drunken Pint," created by the algorithm and inspired by the titles of all the tunes in its repertoire. The more advanced algorithm folk-rnn created another version, which is performed by Irish bands.[105] "What a fun drunken riot this little system has crafted!" Sturm writes.[106]

Of course, the system can only produce what it has learned about basic musical features, and it sometimes goes awry. There are currently several glitches. When seeded with bars that bear little resemblance to those in the training set, the machine often "produces incorrect Irish music."[107] And, having learned 3/4 and 4/4 tempo, it can't extrapolate to 5/4. That's when things can get musically interesting, like in John Cage's prepared piano or Jimi Hendrix's electric guitar. "When accidents happen and a piece is less Irish than its training set, that's more inspiring musically," Sturm tells me. Ben-Tal calls these "bastard tunes."[108]

Sturm insists that the "machine is not composing. It's creating transcriptions which can be used to create music. It's hard to keep this distinction going because the *Daily Mail* will write that machines are going to replace composers. We want to avoid any machine versus human message; the computer is meant to enhance our creativity in music making."[109]

Their machine, and AI generally, is "really not there yet," says Sturm.[110] Musical creativity is in conflict with "principles of engineering," which seek to predict with 100 percent accuracy how notes succeed one another. "But," says Sturm, "that's not how music is composed. Rather there are opportunities, oddities, and progressions that are unique."

Among all the teams working today, he goes on, he and Ben-Tal see theirs "and Pachet's as being useful tools for exploring music, useful tools for exploring failures of systems." Indeed, exploring failure and being inspired by it is an interesting and creative way of looking at their work.

When you deal with ethnic music, like Irish music, ethical issues also arise. "Do you have the right to subject a community to an agent that is foreign, like a machine producing your music?" Sturm asks. "Might our project be offensive to them?" In short, are they preserving the tradition of Irish music or polluting it? What if in the far-distant future archaeologists unearth transcriptions of what they take to be Irish music, only to discover it was composed by a computer?

Jennifer Walshe, a musician at Somerset House in London, advised Sturm and Ben-Tal to throw caution to the wind and "run wild with [their] project." Walshe is on the cutting edge of today's avant-garde. Among her multifaceted output are works for symphony orchestras, string quartets, voice, and video. She has also written a collection of invented histories, including the story of a collective of fictitious Irish composers.[111]

Sturm and Ben-Tal would like to make their work more user-friendly. They also want to look at the music of other folk cultures, such as Turkish music, which has a completely different notation from that of Irish music. But is there a single model that covers all music?

Says Ben-Tal, "Whenever a computer achieves something that previously we considered to be a creative task, or uniquely human, we redefine creativity away from computers."[112] When he was a student at Stanford University, both staff and students were impressed by the music David Cope's system was generating. But Douglas Hofstadter felt it was "too good." The eminent philosopher Daniel Dennett told him, "We're both proponents of strong AI [i.e., we both believe that computers can be as intelligent as humans]. Perhaps your qualms are that Cope's algorithm fits on a floppy disc?" In other words, it was too simple, so simple as to jar one's conception of what creativity is. Conversely, says Ben-Tal, we are impressed with Google's work simply because it uses the most advanced hardware.

23 Rebecca Fiebrink Uses Movement to Generate Sound

Why not forget about programming and instead build new instruments from examples of movement and sound?

—Rebecca Fiebrink[113]

Rebecca Fiebrink's mantra is "It's faster to build a function from examples rather than write code."[114] By a function she means the mathematical methods to express how a computer produces sounds. This can be very complicated. There are many different pathways for sound input and output, represented in complex mathematics. But what if you have something in mind that doesn't obviously operate in mathematical terms? What if you want to build an instrument you can control with your movements? "That's an example of embodied creativity, and it's very difficult to make a mathematical function for this," Fiebrink explains.

Fiebrink's challenge is to "build interfaces with different types of technologies which allow us to express ourselves in new ways or allow more people to participate in music making."[115]

She discovered computers at the age of three when her father brought home a Tandy computer, one of the earliest PCs from the 1980s. But she was soon equally entranced with the flute and piano and "always assumed she would be a musician."[116] Then her high school offered a computer-programming class for the first time. She soon realized she was good at programming and could do some interesting creative tinkering.

She went on to study computer science at Ohio State University. But she wanted "a nontypical computing career," which would include music.[117] As it happened, there was a group in computer science interested in empirical digital musicology, studying the notation in scores to test hypotheses about how people compose and how music evolves over time. Fiebrink joined a graduate seminar taught by David Huron, who used machine learning to grade the difficulty of playing a piece of music.

Inspired, she invented what she calls the Wekinator, named after Waikato Environment for Knowledge Analysis (Weka), software developed in Waikato, New Zealand. The Wekinator is easily accessible software that does not require a knowledge of computer programming for people who wish to use off-the-shelf learning algorithms.

As she puts it, "Why not forget about programming and instead build new instruments from examples of movement and sound? So I say, 'Hey, computer, when I do this…'"[118]

Anyone can use the Wekinator to create original music and performances. Each person who uses it starts by training it to follow their gestures. The machine reads from a webcam trained on the performer. Thus a closed fist might generate a specific pattern of drumming from a drum machine and an open palm a different sort of pattern.

The aim of conventional machine learning is to create a faithful model of data, such as a database of medical diagnoses to figure out what's wrong with a patient and what drug would be effective. "Most machines," says Fiebrink, "won't let you change the data. Why would you? That's sort of cheating. You are taught that you don't change the data."[119]

The Wekinator is very different. It's open source. People download the software from the web and "very easily make new data on the spot and change data over time—for example, use it to build a new gesturally controlled instrument," she tells me. "The ability to edit data and change the model I refer to as interactive machine learning."[120]

For all of this, there is no need to know how to program. Fiebrink has received many positive responses applauding how easy the Wekinator is to use. Watching her set it up and straightaway produce results is inspiring and astonishing.[121] Fiebrink describes the Wekinator as a "metainstrument," because it allows users to create new instruments with no need for programming. Having mastered it, users no longer need to think about algorithms but can focus on "using them to achieve a creative vision."[122]

Fiebrink has also invented Blotar, which has a wider sound palette and is capable of playing continuous sounds, rather than just staccato drum beats. As she moves in front of Blotar's webcam, Blotar produces continuously changing sounds—modulating from a flute to an electric guitar, for example. Performers have developed very subtle hand movements to elicit extraordinary, otherworldly sounds from the machine.

Thus Fiebrink is working toward realizing her ambition of empowering people to create music—people with little or no musical education, as well as those who may be physically impaired. She hopes that the next generation of content-generation algorithms—capable of yielding a great amount of content for a small investment of data—will yield "surprises in musical composition."[123]

Musicians already report that these instruments surprise them in their explorations, catalyzing their creativity.[124] Many performers now use Wekinator and Blotar in their performances to create a mesmerizing amalgam of dance and sound in which one sparks the other.

24   Marwaread Mary Farbood Sketches Music

What you see is what you hear.
—Marwaread Mary Farbood[125]

Mary Farbood's Hyperscore is a beautiful piece of software that links sound to images—color, shape, line, texture. It offers a way for someone entirely without musical training to compose music, intuitively visualizing and editing musical structure, linking sound and vision.

Farbood started as a pianist—but a bad case of tendinitis brought an end to her musical career. Instead of continuing at Juilliard, she went to Harvard, where she studied computer science and took up the harpsichord. She moved on to the MIT Media Lab, where she had the chance to follow up on her interests in both computer science and music.

At MIT, she studied under Tod Machover, a dynamic composer and professor of music. One of the aims of the Media Lab is enablement—enabling adults and children not trained in musical composition to write music. Farbood's Hyperscore played a key role in Machover's Toy Symphony project, in which children composed musical pieces, some of which were performed by orchestras.

Farbood is not the first to try combining visuals and sound. Earlier graphic music-makers include Morton Subotnick's Musical Sketch Pad, enabling users to "sketch" musical works by selecting and combining the sounds of different musical instruments, and William Duckworth's PitchWeb, an interactive work of music and art. Hyperscore uses graphics instead of musical notation to teach the essentials of music composition.

The first versions of Hyperscore involved simply generating scores by pushing a button. In later versions, users have more control. The software maps complex musical concepts onto colors, shapes, and textures, enabling users to control pitch, dynamics, melodic contour, and harmony.[126]

The user makes this happen in two stages. You click on notes, then drag and drop them onto a screen in the form of teardrops. Their horizontal extension determines how long the note is held, pitch is determined by their vertical position on the screen, and their position along the horizontal determines the order in which the notes are played. The result is a melody, to which you assign a color.

The next step is to create compositions from this melody or melodies of different colors. This takes place on another screen, which Farbood calls the harmonic palette. If you're using a single melody designated as blue, then by clicking and dragging you will generate a blue line on the palette. A straight line gives a single pitch. Lines at an angle give variable pitches. Drawing many lines, some overlapping, results in cacophony. You can use an automated harmony line to impose a chord progression. To start, the harmony line is horizontal, but you can curve it by clicking and dragging. The inbuilt chord progressions are taken from a database of chords from Bach chorales; Farbood is currently enlarging the database to include chords from jazz and popular music. She also uses Markov chains to generate series of harmonic functions. In this she has been much inspired by David Cope.

Users enjoy drawing lines freehand on the computer screen, manipulating them until a satisfactory melody emerges: you literally sketch a piece of music. As Farbood writes, Hyperscore "tries to push the concept of 'what you see is what you hear' in a score as far as possible."[127] What Farbood is looking for is a "computational model that includes the various features of tension."[128] A work, be it of literature or music, has tension if it possesses a narrative arc: a beginning, a middle, and an end. This requires repeating melodies in different ways, looking back over a work. "People have an intuitive idea of what tension is," she says. They look for the "release" when a chord is resolved or when melodies are reprised in various ways. The audience listens with anticipation for elements inherent in musical structure, such as expression, dynamics, and harmony, and feels fulfilled and moved at a dramatic ending. Thus tension "enhances emotional content."

Farbood has currently stopped work on Hyperscore to study the extensive literature on tension in cognitive psychology so as to understand better how people perceive music. "There has never been a model that takes all this into account and combines them into an empirically valid tension curve," she says. She is exploring from a cognitive perspective what we actually do when we listen to music and has put together a model that focuses on short-term memory and windows of attention. She plans to return to Hyperscore soon and enlarge its scope so as to create a version with "very high-level ways of assisting composition."[129]

25 Eduardo Miranda and His Improvising Slime Mold

What will be the central processing unit of the future?
—Eduardo Miranda[130]

Eduardo Miranda wants to shake up musical composition. At the moment, he is interested in central processing units (CPUs). In today's computers, CPUs are silicon chips with circuitry that enables them to perform arithmetical, logical, and control operations. But supposing we go beyond silicon, beyond digital, beyond even a quantum computer? What about, for example, a bio-processor that powers a biocomputer? Or a hybrid computer, powered by silicon plus a bioprocessor?[131]

A bioprocessor processes biological material. Miranda's chosen bioprocessor is a slime mold called *Physarum polycephalum*, the "many-headed slime," a huge, yellow, single-cell organism packed with millions of nuclei. It is a mass of creeping, jelly-like protoplasm that is sensitive to light and spreads out over forest floors, eating fungal spores, bacteria, and microbes.

Physarum polycephalum has extraordinary electrical properties. Passing an electrical current through it makes it behave like an electronic component called a memristor. Memristors have a memory for current; their electrical resistance depends on the amount of current that has passed through them in the past. For Miranda, the most interesting thing about biological memristors is that they are not as precise as silicon-based digital ones. The mold's electrical output is related to the input but in ways that can be hard to predict. He considers it a "creative processor."[132] Turn the pitch of a sound into electrical impulses and the slime mold will produce its own electrical response, which can then be turned back into music.

Miranda plays duets with the slime mold, which responds with enigmatic sounds produced on his piano. The piano is the interface between himself and his biocomputer. He entitled the first piece that emerged "Biocomputer Music: A Composition for Piano and Biocomputer."[133] There is no electrical connection between the slime mold and the piano. Notes played on the piano are converted into voltage oscillations that are fed through the slime mold in its petri dish. The vibrations cause it to change shape, producing energy that is turned into electrical energy and sent to electromagnets above the piano's strings. The charged electromagnets attract the strings and make them hum, as if the mold is plucking them. Miranda has performed two pieces in collaboration with mold: "Biocomputer Music" in 2015 and "Biocomputer Rhythms" in 2016, in which the mold provided percussion.

Miranda grew up in Brazil and discovered computers as a teenager when his father brought home a Sinclair. He also studied the piano from the age of seven. He found it hard to juggle these two interests, AI and music. One hot and humid summer day, he visited the cool confines of the campus library and came across an article by Greek composer Iannis Xenakis, in which music was embedded in Venn diagrams, set theory, and logic, familiar to him from his studies in computer science.[134] This, he realized, was the way to combine his interests in music and computers.

For his early research, he studied the way cellular automata behave in the Game of Life, a cellular automata system invented by the English mathematician John Horton Conway in 1970.[135] In this game, a mathematical grid of cells follows simple rules about when a cell is "alive" or "dead." The result is a riot of patterns. Besides its mesmerizing powers, the Game of Life turned out to have multiple unexpected uses—as a tool for exploring the evolution of spiral galaxies; calculating pi; investigating how ordered systems emerge from complex systems; and looking into why, in a multiverse scenario, only certain universes are capable of supporting life. Conway had hit on something universal.

Miranda was enthralled by the patterns and how they evolved. "This is very musical," he thought. "It's how certain composers explore variations on a theme."[136] He invented rules for how the patterns of a melody evolve over time, like the patterns in the Game of Life. "But," he thought, "instead of visualizing these patterns as mathematics, how about listening to them?" This he accomplished by looking for patterns in musical ideas:

phrases, rhythms, and harmonic structure. The machine encodes them and turns the results into lead sheets or MIDI files. Miranda had to curate the raw musical ideas to render them more playable. The computer, he feels, can only be "an assistant to generate ideas."

Miranda notes that although neural networks can imitate musical styles, AI has not as yet produced any truly original compositions. This he feels is the next great step and perhaps can be accomplished with the help of his unpredictable slime mold collaborator. He is also interested in creating human-machine interfaces in which brain waves replace keyboards and voice commands to help the disabled express themselves musically.

In the introduction to his very personal book, *Thinking Music: The Inner Workings of a Composer's Mind*, Miranda contrasts composing music using AI systems (neural networks) with algorithmic approaches, generating music from mathematical descriptions of fractals or of chaos.[137] He writes, "Aesthetically, the algorithmic approach tends to generate highly novel and unusual music, whereas the AI approach tends to generate imitations of certain known types of music....Both approaches have their own merits and pitfalls, but I tend to adopt the algorithmic one."[138] The biocomputer is one such innovative algorithmic approach.

Looking back over the interaction between music and technology in the twentieth century, he muses, "Cage and Stockhausen explored technology which they didn't really understand. Now my generation understands technology and can use it to express our thoughts. It's experimental music but we now understand what the experiments are telling us. So let's make art now that is twenty-first-century music." Miranda adds that he is not interested in reading about how a walk on a sunny day inspired someone to write magnificent music. Rather, he writes, "what I want to know is how he composed it. How did such inspiration become music?"[139]

IV Once Upon a Time: Computers That Weave Magic with Words

I writhed with joy, which I experienced for the first time, and kept writing with excitement. The day a computer wrote a novel. The computer, placing priority on the pursuit of its own joy, stopped working for humans.

—"The Day a Computer Writes a Novel"[1]

The rather wistful paragraph above is the ending of "The Day a Computer Writes a Novel," a short story that was indeed written by a computer. It was created by a Japanese team at Future University Hakodate in Japan and in 2016 was entered for the Nikkei Hoshi Shinichi Literary Award, a competition for science fiction stories. There were eleven computer creations up against stiff human competition. "The Day a Computer Writes a Novel" didn't win, but it did get through into the second round.

To put together their novel, the engineers at Future University wrote a novel of their own, then broke it down into its constituent parts—words, phrases, characters, and plot outlines—and fed these into the AI for it to reassemble into another story similar to the sample. So it was not so extraordinary that the result read like a "well-structured novel," as Satoshi Hase, an eminent Japanese science-fiction novelist, said at the award ceremony. But there were some problems, he added, "such as character descriptions."

In effect, the novel was a rehash, with apparently 80 percent human contribution and only 20 percent from AI. So it seems the time is not yet here when computers will thrill us with their literary creations. But it may be on its way.

Pinocchio is the original AI story.
—Stephan Schwingeler[2]

Across the world and as far back as ancient Greece, there have been stories of artifacts, man-made objects, that come to life and acquire consciousness and self-awareness. In the archetypal myth, the sculptor Pygmalion carves a statue of a woman so beautiful that he falls in love with it. The goddess Aphrodite grants his unspoken wish and the statue comes alive. In modern times, the myth has resurfaced many times over—most famously in the story of Pinocchio, a puppet who comes to life and is finally turned into a real boy by the Blue Fairy. In each case, something inanimate comes to life. Stephan Schwingeler studies how video games create a world of their own and in effect come alive. He perfectly captures the current fear that an AI might take on a life of its own when he tells me, "Pinocchio is the original AI story."[3]

AI is already generating art and music indistinguishable from that produced by human artists, and which sometimes goes beyond anything we have seen or heard before. But what about the realm of words? What about literature and poetry?

It's not quite literature, but already a good percentage of Reuters' news reports, along with sports articles, weather reports, and Wikipedia entries, are machine-generated using Reuters' own custom-built technology. Most are indistinguishable from articles written by journalists, and sometimes turn out better. This is not surprising. This is the sort of material that can be put together easily using templates.

The job is often carried out by a cloud-based application called Word-Smith, which assembles huge amounts of data on a particular subject and, following inbuilt rules for grammar and style, grinds out hundreds of millions of stories a year. The creators of this software insist that they are not out to take jobs away from journalists but to free them from drudge work so that they can think about the big issues behind the news.[4]

Another company, Narrative Science, turns raw data into natural language narratives and provides stories on current events, sports, and corporate finance for publications such as *Forbes* and other megacompanies. In 2012, Kristian Hammond, who cofounded the company, predicted that fifteen years from then "more than 90 percent" of news stories would be generated by machines.[5]

Meanwhile, Swedish physicist Sverker Johansson set something of a record with his internet bot, Lsjbot, which can grind out ten thousand articles a day. By July 2014, it had produced 2.7 million. Lsjbot scans the internet for information on a given topic and inserts this into a template from which it generates the article. Most are four-line Wikipedia entries containing the names of living organisms and where they are to be found, together with bibliographical data, mainly of use to people seeking specialized information on birds or types of fungus. Most of these "stubs" only appear in the Swedish Wikipedia, where they make up almost half the entries.[6]

Then there is Philip M. Parker, businessman cum writer, whose patented software can sweep the web, pick up information on virtually any subject, and turn it into books to be printed on demand. Most are compilations, such as one on bathmats in India, and crossword puzzle books galore, in a Borgesian babble of languages. Parker has produced over two hundred thousand books. Some ninety thousand are on Amazon, where they range in price from nothing to $1,000 and rank somewhere in the millions. Parker claims that he is now tailoring his algorithms to produce romance novels. He has also posted over 1.3 million poems, though he seems to have little interest in assessing their quality.[7]

In journalism and commercial writing, then, AI is already doing much of the drudge work—and is likely to take up more and more of the slack.

A robot goes into a bar.
"What can I get you?" asks the bartender.
"I need something to loosen me up," says the robot.
So the bartender serves him a screwdriver.
—@jokingcomputer[8]

How does AI do when it comes to that most human of storytelling activities—telling jokes?

Graeme Ritchie's Joking Computer tweets a joke a day. Let's start with an example.

Question: What do you get when you cross a fall with a dictionary?
Answer: A spill checker.

It's early days for the computer, but it's trying.

The problem is, not only is there no accepted computational theory of humor, there is no single accepted theory of humor at all, despite efforts over the centuries from everyone from Plato and Aristotle to Freud. In fact, there are three at present. The most prevalent is the "incongruity theory," put forward by Schopenhauer, Kant, and Bergson and developed more fully by Victor Raskin at Purdue University. This is the way most jokes are constructed: a setup followed by an unexpected or bizarre—incongruous—punchline. The other two theories are the "release theory" (that humor releases nervous energy and tension) and the venerable "superiority theory," beloved of Plato and Aristotle, that we find humor in others' shortcomings and misfortunes—schadenfreude.

This being the case, how on earth are we to begin instructing computers in the art of humour?[9]

Computers can beat world champions at complex games like chess and Go, identify patterns in huge sets of data, do massive calculations, even recognize faces in a crowd. But such feats take place inside a machine with limited access to the outside world, particularly in regard to knowledge and feelings. It's a closed system. Eventually they will be able to accrue knowledge by scanning the web and will actually take physical form; they'll be "embodied" as robots, enabling them to interact with the world around them and have and store experiences of their own. They may even begin to create of their own accord.

But will they then start telling jokes? Humor is the last frontier. Getting a joke, cracking a joke—perhaps an off-color one—employing sarcasm, timing, irony, all require social awareness and a rather wide knowledge base. Jokes do not travel well across cultures. What I find funny may not be your cup of tea. Plus, all the above are time dependent. What was funny yesterday might be shocking or disgusting or just plain boring today. Today's joke could be tomorrow's gaffe.

Humor is a very creative activity. It might involve taking a startling new perspective on received wisdom, turning a situation upside down, undermining clichés and commonplaces. Every dimension of intelligence touches on it.

Here are a couple of jokes for a start:

The person who invented the door knocker got a No Bell Prize.

Veni, Vidi, Visa: I came, I saw, I did a little shopping.

Straightforward? Getting the first involves knowing what a Nobel Prize is and what a door knocker is, for a start. The second requires a knowledge of rudimentary Latin, of Caesar's immortal words, and of what a Visa card is. This knowledge would either have to be programmed into a symbolic machine—akin to programming the entire world and all its knowledge into the machine—or a neural network would have to have scanned the web well enough to grasp human language in all its intricacy, including metaphor, irony, and sarcasm; not quite up to the task as yet.

Cracking the problem of humor is akin to solving AI itself: a matter of evolving computers as intelligent as humans.

In the early years, humor, as well as any other dimension of intelligence to do with emotions and feelings, was rejected by the founding fathers of AI as unworthy of study. In their proposal for a summer research project to be held at Dartmouth College in New Hampshire in 1956—the famous

Dartmouth Conference—they wrote: "The study is to proceed on the basis of the conjecture that every aspect of learning or any other feature of intelligence can in principle be so precisely described that a machine can be made to simulate it."[10] They envisaged a field that studied forming concepts, learning, reasoning, problem solving in general. Emotions, however, had no place in it, and neither did humor.

Emotions did not begin to enter AI research until the 1990s with the work of Rosalind Picard at MIT, which I discuss in detail in chapter 42.[11] In 1997, she published a book called *Affective Computing*, which focused on the importance of emotional intelligence, the vital role that the communication of emotion has in relationships, and the possible effects and uses of emotion recognition by computers. This seminal work effectively kickstarted the field.

Even by the mid-2000s, humor studies were still not well developed. I asked Julia Taylor Rayz, a humor researcher at Purdue Polytechnic Institute in West Lafayette, Indiana, why she went into the field at that time. She replied, "It was challenging and sounded like fun—and at that point nobody had done it."[12]

One of the first projects in this area was HAHAcronym, Humorous Agents for Humorous Acronyms, funded by the EU and devoted to computational humor, carried out by Oliviero Stock and Carlo Strapparava in Trento, Italy.[13] The idea was to create an "acronym ironic reanalyser and generator." HAHAcronym subverts existing acronyms and constructs new ones by taking "words that are in ironic relation with input concepts."[14] The system's database is WordNet, a massive corpus of words grouped into sets of synonyms, each expressing a specific concept. Stock and Strapparava started by creating a separate database of contrasting pairs—religion and technology, sex and religion—to produce an "incongruity generator."[15] Then they fed their system existing acronyms to see what would come out, the idea being to keep the flavor of the acronyms while using irony to subvert them.[16]

The computer reimagined FBI—Federal Bureau of Investigation—as Fantastic Bureau of Intimidation, a not-inappropriate assemblage of concepts, and PDA—personal digital assistant—as Penitential Demoniacal Assistant. But what happened when they asked the computer to generate new and humorous meanings for acronyms from scratch? When they fed in the acronym FAINT, plus a main concept (tutoring) and an attribute (intelligent), the computer came up with Folksy Acritical Instruction for Nescience

Teaching. NAÏVE, with the same concept and attribute, generated Negligent At-large Instruction for Vulnerable Extracurricular-activity. Which might raise a smile, at least.

One of the problems with computational humor is finding funding. In 2010, Kristian Hammond, a professor at Northwestern University in Evanston, Illinois, received a $700,000 stimulus grant from the National Science Foundation. No less a figure than Senator John McCain dismissed Hammond's project as a "joke machine" and declared the grant a waste of taxpayers' money.[17] It certainly, he added, could have no impact on creating jobs.

Hammond's software looks at news stories and social media and assembles words to form original lines of thought—or even jokes. In answer to McCain, he commented that a way to enhance human-machine communication might be with humor. This line of research, he said, might even "be used to write scientific papers."[18] Hammond went on to found Narrative Science, a company that churns out computer-generated news stories, and in so doing certainly created a few jobs.

As we've seen, not much has been done toward developing a general theory of humor, though there is plenty of humor research. Researchers prefer to limit themselves to chipping away at well-defined joke scenarios. As Julia Taylor Rayz explains, there are two aspects of humor that researchers focus on: computers generating jokes and computers recognizing jokes. The first step is to feed the computer on a diet of jokes so that it learns to create jokes of its own. The next step is far more challenging. Can the machine ever learn to understand that it cracked a joke or know the proper moment to break into a conversation to make a witty remark? This is akin to a computer understanding that a work of art or piece of music it has produced is good.

Puns are one of the simplest forms of humor. In 1994 Graeme Ritchie and Kim Binsted created the first pun generator, JAPE (Joke Analysis and Production Engine), to generate question-and-answer puns. Pun generators work with vast databases of words, like WordNet, plus enormous amounts of puns, and are given pattern-matching rules to compose riddles. Here's one computer-generated pun:

What do you get when you cross an optic with a mental object?
An eye-dea.

Nerdy in the extreme. It might lead to a few guffaws at a comedy club before pointing the would-be comedian to the exit. Of course the funny thing about this pun, as journalist Becky Ferreira observes, is that you "can't imagine a human ever opening with such a weird setup question."[19]

Recognizing even the simplest structured jokes, like knock-knock jokes, beloved from childhood, requires some heavy lifting on both the linguistic and the computer fronts. The basic format is overlapping wordplay between two people, resolved with a punch line.

Says Rayz, there are two ways of teaching computers to make jokes. One is to feed in the rules that jokes are based on and give the computer "knowledge of the world"—material to work with. The other is to tell the computer a lot of jokes, letting it learn by example.

To teach her computer knock-knock jokes, Rayz assembled a large number of jokes, including some from the "111 Knock Knock Jokes" website, then grouped them together to make templates to demonstrate how the word play works, by sound association. This was one of the computer's efforts:

Knock Knock.
Who's there?
Water.
Water who?
Water you doing tonight?

Not belly-achingly funny, but not bad.

But does the machine know it's cracked a knock-knock joke? Rayz takes a good look at wordplay, especially the final sentence, to make sure it's not nonsense. But in the end, most of the computer's jokes are not really jokes at all, due to "failures in sentence understanding."[20] The problem is that the computer has not learned enough words to enable it to engage in wordplay. It can create the knock-knock format, but without meaningful wordplay the results make no sense.

"Even a one-liner is a bit of a challenge," says Graeme Ritchie, with Scottish understatement.[21]

Rayz is "interested in looking for patterns in humor."[22] She separates out different types of jokes and tests them to see how people react. "You need not have a huge amount of data" for this, she says. Much has already been published, which means she can now compare computer-generated jokes with real-life jokes, scrutinize them "under a microscope," alter them and clean them up to make them funnier. A computer joke is not going to be perfect, she says. But you "don't want to throw away that error when you test it on humans." We "can learn from computers *not* understanding humor."[23]

Seeing patterns in data is a key to understanding them—in this case, understanding what makes a joke a joke. Recent studies take all available data on jokes and try to make sense of them using neural nets. "Some people are familiar with humor theories. Some are just interested in taking the best machine-learning algorithm and applying it and seeing what happens," Rayz says.[24] She prefers to input rules for jokes to investigate how computers might be able to generate jokes and recognize them. "If you can locate certain features and throw them into a [joke] generation model and something reasonable emerges, we may be close to something like creativity," she says, adding that in her opinion, there is no viable definition of creativity. "Where creativity fits in, I don't know," she says emphatically.

Graeme Ritchie considers creativity, either human or machine, not worth discussing. It is "hard to model creativity without a definition," he says, and he staunchly believes that none are on offer.[25] Regarding machine learning, in a widely cited paper, he writes, "If the reason that the program manages to produce humour is because it has a box inside it that (mysteriously) 'creates humour,' that would not illuminate the problem of humour creation. Instead this would introduce a form of regress, in which there is a new problem: how does that black box achieve its results?"[26]

Janelle Shane, meanwhile, a researcher in optics, takes the approach of throwing data on humor into a neural network to see what happens, just for the joy of it. She has used neural networks to come up with absurd recipes, ridiculous paint names, and hilarious pickup lines, all of which have garnered a large web following. The algorithm she uses is Char-RNN, which she has also let loose on knock-knock jokes. Unlike Rayz, who inputs rules into the computer to generate jokes, Shane leaves the neural network to figure them out from the thousands of jokes she's put in. At first the results made no sense. Then the machine began to produce more cogent, but still not very funny, results.

Finally it produced a completely original joke:

Knock Knock.
Who's There?
Alec.
Alec Who?
Alec Knock Knock Jokes.[27]

Again not belly-achingly funny, but there's certainly something quirky, if not surreal, there. You can almost sense the machine's presence, complaining that it's had enough.

Shane points out that the creativity is hers, not the machine's. She chose the database and she applied an algorithm of her choice.

In 2015, two computer scientists, Dafna Shahaf and Eric Horvitz of Microsoft, teamed up with the legendary cartoon editor of the *New Yorker*, Robert Mankoff. Mankoff's most familiar cartoon depicts a businessman on the phone replying to a persistent caller: "No, Thursday's out. How about never—is never good for you?" One of Mankoff's tasks was to run the *New Yorker's* weekly cartoon contest, in which the magazine invites captions for a wordless cartoon. Five thousand submissions a week were pouring in. Sorting through that many entries was wearing out Mankoff's assistants.

The previous year, Dafna Shahaf had attended a lecture Mankoff gave describing the huge cartoon archive at the *New Yorker* and the thousands of captions submitted for the weekly contest. Could the archive be used to teach a computer to distinguish a funny caption from an unfunny one, she wondered, thereby massively reducing the workload for Mankoff's assistants?

Computers do all right with recognizing images and writing captions for well-defined ones. But cartoon images regularly have an edge of sarcasm, irony, or anger and may not even need a caption to be funny. How can a computer deal with such subtleties—such affective dimensions?

The team began by submitting captions to crowd workers at Mechanical Turk for them to assess the humor. Then they used neural networks to study the not-always-obvious relationship between the words used in the captions and words describing the image in the cartoon. This gave them another way to assess the value of a caption: whether the words were too close to the image or at odds with it. Neural networks can manipulate words in a multi-multi-dimensional space of meanings, giving each word a number and thus connecting it to billions of other words. The closer a word is in meaning to another word, the closer its number will be. This gives them a directionality, like vectors in physics. This is behind Google's Word2vec, which has led to dazzling advances in speech recognition.

Sadly, in the case of the *New Yorker* cartoons, the results were only middling. The computer successfully chose the funnier caption only 64 percent of the time.

Recently, computers have even tried their hands at stand-up comedy. Piotr Mirowski, whose day job is senior research scientist at DeepMind in London, and a small bug-eyed robot called A.L.Ex (for *artificial language experiment*) have performed improv together on the stand-up circuit in London, Paris, and other places.

In one routine, they are out on a drive together. Mirowski mimes holding a steering wheel and looks at A.L.Ex expectantly.

"I am not trying to be angry," the robot says abruptly, destroying the mood.[28]

Mirowski is ready with a retort. "I don't want you to be angry—this is our quality time."

To which A.L.Ex replies, "I'm sure that you will find love"—a decisive brushoff if ever there was one.

It's a success. The audience laughs. "I'm so tired," the robot adds. Mirowski attempts to save the relationship, but A.L.Ex concludes rather insightfully, "You are not me. You're my friend."

To train the AI that runs A.L.Ex, Mirowski fed it subtitles from one hundred thousand films, from action movies like *Deep Impact* to the pornographic film *Deep Throat*. When it hears someone speaking to it, it seeks out similar exchanges in its database and forms a reply. Mirowski developed this advanced version of his original system with Kory Mathewson, a Canadian AI researcher and fellow improv devotee.

The key issue is how to get A.L.Ex to stay on topic so that its responses are not merely random. Says Mirowski, the humor tends to be accidental. A.L.Ex's deadpan remarks can be totally inappropriate, overly emotional, or just plain odd. It's like working with a "completely drunk comedian," he says. The real challenge is for the human improviser, who has to be ready with a response no matter how bizarre the robot's comments.

At Google, Douglas Eck and the Magenta team are also hard at work on humor. The project, says Eck, is "very preliminary, very exploratory" and focuses on "punch-line related jokes and puns."[29]

Today the field of computational humor is blossoming with (hopefully amusing) conferences dedicated to humor and sessions at AI meetings. Personal assistants such as Siri and Alexa are famously lacking in humor. If we are going to communicate with machines in a pleasant manner, they will one day have to develop a sense of humor akin to the one we humans possess.

The main aim of a poem is to be pleasing rather than conveying a meaningful message.
—Pablo Gervás[30]

In 2010, literary critic Marjorie Perloff wrote, "Nothing quite prepared the poetry world for the claim, now being made by conceptual poets... that it is possible to write 'poetry' that is entirely 'unoriginal' and nevertheless qualifies as poetry."[31] One of those conceptual poets was Kenneth Goldsmith, an early proponent of electronically generated text. As Perloff writes, he pushed the concept of the unoriginal yet further when he "announced his advocacy of conceptual or 'uncreative' writing—a form of copying, recycling, or appropriation that 'obstinately makes no claim on originality.'"[32] His 2003 piece of conceptual poetry, "Work Day," consists of an entire issue of the *New York Times,* from the headlines to the adverts, transformed into digital text.

In conceptual poetry, as in conceptual art, the concept—the idea behind the piece—is of the essence. This could mean that it is not necessary to read a text in the traditional sense to get the idea, akin to reading a text as it scrolls down a computer screen, without being able to go back if you missed anything.

Pablo Gervás and His Poetic Algorithms

There is something algorithmic in poetry, a metric, a syllable and rhythmic counting.
—Pablo Gervás[33]

"I can get a computer to write a poem by giving it models of how poetry is written and of how poetry works, but I can't give a computer a model of how love works; that's way beyond what machines can do at this stage," says Pablo Gervás.[34]

One of Gervás's principal interests is in developing an algorithm to generate Spanish verse. He calls it Wishful Automatic Spanish Poet (WASP).[35] As he points out, poetry provides a way of circumventing some of the basic problems involved in using computers to tackle literary genres, starting with their lack of advanced linguistic skills and basic common sense. Poetry does not require high precision. The "main aim of a poem is to be pleasing rather than conveying a meaningful message," he says, and it is often wildly open to interpretation.[36] Gervás chose Spanish poetry because its phonetics are straightforward and it is governed by very specific rules, allowing him to maintain correct syntax while playing fast and loose with semantics.

He used classic Spanish poems as the initial data for WASP, then input words tagged according to the number of syllables, the position of certain syllables, and the rhyme. He then asked poetry lovers to assess the thousands of poems the algorithm produced, taking into account meaning and aesthetics. The judges rated them on a scale from 1 (nonsense, ugly) to 5 (a real poem, very pretty). None achieved a 5 for making total sense nor for aesthetics. Scores for syntax were close to 3, but scores for aesthetics were much lower.

WASP has gone through several manifestations in its logic and methods. Gervás has used evolutionary programming, selecting the best output and allowing it to evolve. "We need a way to separate good stuff made by machines even if it differs from what humans produce," he says.

Besides computer-generated poetry, Gervás has also created the PropperWryter algorithm, which generates plots, among them the plot for the musical *Beyond the Fence*.[37] He is particularly interested in what the process and products of computer-generated literature mean for human beings and computers, as well as for creativity.

He believes that just as young poets read the poetry of others and emulate it until they find their own style, something similar will happen with computers. First they will emulate and then broaden out to, perhaps, "modeling stuff like personal experience."[38] Personal experience? The problem is of course that, for the moment at least, computers have no way of comprehending, let alone feeling, emotions like love.

Gervás doesn't believe poetry created by machines should be judged by the same criteria as regular poetry or that it should be judged according to whether it can be distinguished from poetry written by human poets. "If you only consider machine poetry to be good if it's like human poetry, then what's the point?" he asks. What we are looking for is for the computer to surprise us by coming up with something new and different. "It might be much better than what people do," Gervás points out.

An essential element in creative writing is that "the magic doesn't come from the writer, it comes from the reader."[39] It seems truly magical when "a string of characters on a page sparks memory and emotion," like a work of visual art or of music can. Good writers take a minimalist approach, leaving it to the reader to figure things out rather than explaining everything. "That's what we want to try to get computers to do," Gervás explains.

Gervás is intrigued by artificial neural networks but for the moment doesn't use them. There isn't enough data in Spanish poetry, plus it is still unclear how neural networks reason, what goes on in the hidden layers. Gervás is uncomfortable with hidden layers because, he asserts, "a large portion of my motivation is to understand how people write poetry."[40] In other words, he is interested more in the process than the end product—and in neural nets this process is hidden away deep in the hidden layers.

He complains that poetry generation is given low priority. "People don't like to invest in research that won't make any money or improve the quality of life," he says. Research funds tend to be limited to more urgent problems like curing disease. But creativity and how to model it are also problems worth working on—in particular, literary creativity: poetry and narrative. With all the data available, machines can easily churn out weather reports and newspaper articles, but literary creativity is in a different league. As Gervás puts it, "Literary creativity is to communication what Formula 1 driving is to transport."[41] The only way to make cars safe is to test them by driving them at high speed, even if this is something most people will never do. Similarly, rather than contenting ourselves with weather reports, we need to push machines to the next level, make them work harder, learn to write true literature. "We must bridge the complexity gap between how people write literary text and how machines produce news stories and weather reports," says Gervás.

As to creativity, "the word itself is ambiguous.… But for me the phenomenon is clear and has nothing to do with labels. Do something surprising that has not been done yet!"[42]

29   Rafael Pérez y Pérez and the Problems of Creating Rounded Stories

As a scientist I want us to understand better the amazing thing we call creativity.
—Rafael Pérez y Pérez[43]

Rafael Pérez y Pérez is fascinated by creativity. When he was a boy, his family went on long car rides. His father would set difficult puzzles for him and his sister to solve. He encouraged them to ask questions. "'Use your creativity,' he always said," Pérez y Pérez recalls.[44] "Creativity has been on my mind since I was very young," he adds.

His real love, however, was computers. For his undergraduate degree in Mexico, Pérez y Pérez studied electronics and computers. He went on to complete a PhD in AI at the University of Sussex. There he planned to work on AI and music but lacked sufficient musical knowledge. His PhD supervisor, Mike Sharples, was interested in the creative processes involved in writing. Sharples's enthusiasm was infectious.

There have been several computer systems that generate stories, beginning in the 1970s. In 1999, when Pérez y Pérez was working on his thesis, and even sometimes today, plot generators worked in a typical AI manner: by problem solving. The operator chose a beginning to the story (initial state) and a conclusion (final state), then looked for a way to move from the initial to the final state by manipulating predefined structures, such as sentences and additional vocabulary. But that, thought Pérez y Pérez, is not the way creativity works. What he wanted was to explore human creativity, to create an algorithm that more closely reflects the way that storytellers create stories.

He called the algorithm he developed MEXICA (pronounced meh-SHE-kah), after the original inhabitants of his region, Mexico City, whom the

Spanish dubbed the Aztecs. MEXICA produces plots inspired by the history, legends, and culture of the original Mexicas, featuring characters like jaguar knights, the greatest warriors of their day.

To use the MEXICA algorithm, Pérez y Pérez feeds in a set of short stories and a list of all possible actions that each character can carry out, plus a list of conditions for each action, represented in terms of the "emotional links, tensions, and conflicts between the characters. This is a unique part of my work," he explains. "It mirrors the way that we come to understand the world."[45] In other words, it is the emotional links between the characters—the jaguar knight hates his enemy, for example—that create the preconditions and postconditions for the action.

Take a situation in which one character is in love with another. The man might

- buy the girl flowers,
- serenade her with a guitar, or
- kidnap her, as happens in some towns in Mexico.

All these actions create an emotional response, especially if the woman is imprisoned. That creates conflict, she may start to hate the man. These consequences make up the story context. So the short stories build up the system's knowledge base, into which Pérez y Pérez then inserts an initial action to trigger a particular story.

There are two elements in telling a story: engagement, putting together the plot, the bare bones of the story, and reflection, the many elements the storyteller adds to flesh the story out, bring it to life. In the engagement period, the system throws up plot ideas, "like when you're dreaming," says Pérez y Pérez. The reflection element modifies these ideas by filling in the gaps. Once Pérez y Pérez has entered the initial action to trigger a story, the system runs through its knowledge base looking for an appropriate structure to fit the new emotional context—the proper action to be performed. "If you input enough previous stories, you will have a lot of different contexts," he explains.[46] Then the MEXICA algorithm enters this information into a cycle of engagement and reflection. Driven by the emotional context, the story can develop in different ways.

In the scenario outlined earlier, the man in love has three possible courses of action: "beliefs of the system," Pérez y Pérez calls them.[47] Crucially, he is not generating his plots from templates. Actions spring from the emotional relations and conflicts of the characters. "If you could peer into the machine's memory, you would not see short stories but the structures that represent emotional structures," he says.

So far we only have plots. The next step is to turn them into stories. For this, Pérez y Pérez teamed up with Nick Montfort, a professor of digital media at MIT. "I sent Nick a story in the form character-action-character, and he took it and transformed it with his methods," Pérez y Pérez explains.

Montfort calls his system *nn Narrator*. There is also a version called *Curveship*. It builds up a narrative using characters, objects, and events that have been fed into it. In this case, MEXICA provides the plot, characters, and events. Nn Narrator can change the order of events and narrate a story from the standpoints of different characters. Here is a portion of a narrative built up from a plot involving a hunter, a jaguar, and a virgin, adding a filter that expresses surprise:

> The jaguar knight will oppose the hunter!
> Meanwhile, the hunter will oppose the jaguar knight!
> Then, the jaguar knight will feint at the hunter, dude!
> Then, the jaguar knight will strike himself![48]

There are clearly teething problems with this very early attempt at integrating two systems to form an automatic story generator that moves from plot to narration. A complex system like this requires different sorts of knowledge representation at varying levels of abstraction, as well as the ability to manipulate them appropriately to the story material. One way to do this is to use a "blackboard system" to keep and rewrite different versions of the story. Rewriting—editing—is a key element in storytelling as much as in the creation of a work of literature.

Soon after their initial collaboration, Pérez y Pérez and Montfort developed just such a blackboard system.[49] They combined MEXICA and nn Narrator with three other systems to examine the plot generated and add action to it, rather like an assembly line. The blackboard was a "very easy way to communicate between systems."[50] They opened up the process to include metaphorical and other sorts of actions. First MEXICA generated a plot, which was then put on the blackboard. There it went through various cycles of engagement and reflection, including employing different genres, framing it as a "confession" told to a priest or, radically different, as a play-by-play sports commentary. Then Pérez y Pérez sent the end product to Montfort's nn Narrator.

Here is a sports commentary version of a tale about Ehecatl, the Mexican wind god:

> This is Ehecatl, live from the scene. The cold-wind eagle knight is despising the icy jaguar knight! The cold-wind jaguar knight is despising the chilling eagle knight! Yes, an eagle knight is fighting a jaguar knight![51]

Perhaps a little more imaginative than the first story.

Pérez y Pérez and Montfort envisage this system supplying stories for exhibitions or being part of a digital media, electronic literature, or e-poetry exhibit and hope it will play an integral part in creating cutting-edge literature, though the production of an acceptable piece of narrative still seems a long way off.

At the end of 2017, Pérez y Pérez published a book of twenty short stories created by his MEXICA program. He called it *MEXICA: 20 Years–20 Stories (20 AÑOS–20 HISTORIAS).*[52] The stories evoke the life of Aztec Mexico.

One begins, "Some years ago the princess was born under the protection of the great god Huitzilopochtli." It's still basically a plot, an outline rather than a fully fleshed-out narrative, but it brings in elements like a lady, a high priestess, a sacred knife, and the Quetzalcoatl temple, which together build a vivid picture of the Aztec world. The writing is noticeably smoother than in Pérez y Pérez's earlier experiments:

> The jaguar knight made a potion and drank it quickly. He started to recover.
> In that moment the warrior was not able to understand the jaguar knight's conduct.
> The jaguar knight was confused and was not sure if what he had done was right.
> Hurriedly, the warrior ran off to the Popocatépetl volcano.
> The end.

Recently Pérez y Pérez has extended his MEXICA system to generate songs. He calls the new system MABLE.[53] First MEXICA generates a plot about the Mexicas, then MABLE uses a Markov model that has been fed with a vast number of love songs to change each line into a poetic phrase. To do so, it takes one word at a time from the MEXICA plot, then searches through its database of songs and chooses a word that has a high probability of following it, taking into account rhyme and rhythm. Odd-numbered lines, starting with the first, are generated by MEXICA. Even-numbered lines are the lyrics that were statistically matched with it. Then Pérez y Pérez uses another algorithm (AKYSIA) to create a melody for the new poem.

This produces several melody options for each line, which are curated by a musicologist au fait with computer science.

Maya Ackerman and Pérez y Pérez have recorded one of the resulting songs, "Princess Minuet," on YouTube. It runs as follows:[54]

> But she fell in love with him
> Girl when they feel the same
> The princess in love with the priest
> Can't let go and it never goes out
> She also abominated what he did
> Be the things they said
> The princess was shocked by the priest's actions
> And though her heart can't take it all happens

In this song both words and music were computer generated, unlike for the musical *Beyond the Fence*, in which musicians and writers played a large part in the curation.[55] Listeners rated the experiment highly both in terms of plot coherence and emotional engagement.

As Pérez y Pérez says, this is a serious achievement for computational creativity, bringing "us one step closer to autonomous songwriters."[56]

"My stories don't read like Gabriel Garcia Marquez," he says. "So what? Right now we are trying to understand this process better. You learn by degrees."[57] His ultimate goal, his Holy Grail, is "to contribute to the understanding of the creative process. As a scientist I want us to understand better the amazing thing we call creativity."

There are some things a computer can do better than people. One of them is that it can just keep going.

—Nick Montfort[58]

Nick Montfort is a man of many talents. Besides his storytelling algorithm, he also creates never-ending streams of poetry.

Here is an example from a poem he calls "Round":

Form intends intense verse crease to tense form tense vent verse tone
verse form crease form vent tends to crease to tends form form vent
form crease tone verse tense

crease vent vent tends inverse tone into verse form verse verse form
tone tense in

tense vent crease

verse tone tends tense tends tense verse crease form

tone vent into tends
to crease vent to crease[59]

And so on, ad infinitum.

"People enjoy my work better when it is read out loud," Montfort tells me.[60] Indeed, when he does a reading, which he does with great style, it all seems to make sense. Most computer-generated writing tends to be prose, using words generated by algorithms, based on databanks of literary works, massaged using Markovian methods to choose the most probable word sequences. Montfort's work is different. "The work of art is the computer program. I select the words. They're mine," he says.

"Round" is one of the works in Montfort's 2014 book of poems, *#!* (pronounced *shebang*, as in "the whole shebang," the whole universe under consideration). Montfort prints each poem alongside the computer program that generated it, depicted as a work of art, with letters, numbers, and symbols in white on a black background. For "Round," he used the programming language Python. He prefers his programs to have the fewest possible lines—that is, to be as simple as possible—from which to produce his literary creations.

Montfort created "Round" by applying the unique properties of pi (π), the ratio of the circumference of a circle to its diameter. Pi cannot be written as the ratio of two integers and therefore never ends and never forms a pattern. Numbers that are the ratio of two integers, like 1/3, on the other hand, are also infinite in extent but form patterns: $1/3 = 0.3333333\ldots$ Pi has been calculated to trillions of decimal places, still with no discernible pattern. The first numbers are $3.14159265358979\ldots$ Although infinite in extent, pi is deterministic because there are formulae to calculate it. It goes on forever, eternally growing and changing.

Montfort chose nine words to represent the numbers one to nine, with *in* as one, plus eight other words that also form valid words if *in* is put in front of them: crease, form, tends, tense, to, tone, vent, and verse. To represent zero, he used a line break. He also ignored the decimal point. The algorithm, which included a module to calculate pi, did the rest. The first line of the poem quoted earlier, beginning with *form* and ending with *tense*, represents the first thirty-one decimal places of pi—counting the first two decimal places from the word after *form*, which is *intends*. The number represented by the last word in the line is zero, represented by a line break, and so the next line of verse begins.

"Round," Montfort says, "is a visualization, a textualization, of the digits of pi in which pi's digits are mapped to word strings."[61] Whenever the poem is run, every word will be the same. In this sense it is "unoriginal," he adds, tongue in cheek. "It's very much about the materialization of computing," he explains. "Increasing computational power allows us to figure out more and more digits [of pi]." On Montfort's website, we can see the poem unspooling, with more and more lines appearing on the screen.

Mild-mannered, in open-necked shirt and jacket, Montfort seems nothing like most people's imaginings of a creator of cutting-edge computer-generated poetry. Even as a child, his interests always spanned literature and computers. As an undergraduate he studied liberal arts and computer science, then completed master's degrees in media arts, creative writing, and information science. His PhD thesis was on computer generation in interactive fiction (IF), a form of interactive literary narrative based on games, in which the player makes decisions that change the course of the story.

While "Round" goes round and round, coming out the same no matter how many times you run it, Montfort's poem "Through the Park" is different every time. "It is a highly intentionally constructed distribution of language. Chance is something I put into the system," he says.

The Python program for "Through the Park" contains twenty-five sentences chosen by Montfort to set the scene ("The girl sets off through the park"), inject a bit of menace ("The man makes a fist behind his back"), and so on. The program arranges the sentences at random, separated by ellipses: "The girl grins and grabs a granola bar...The girl puts on a slutty dress...The girl turns to smile and wink...The man makes a fist behind his back...A snatch of song reminds the girl of her grandmother...Laughter booms...The man's breathing quickens...Pigeons scatter...The girl runs...Things are forgotten in carelessness...The girl's bag lies open."[62] Every time the program is run, the order of the sentences is different, and the generation of stanzas can go on forever. As Montfort says, "This shows that there are some things computers can do better than people. One of them is that it can just keep going."[63]

In his computational poetry, Montfort also explores the imagistic possibilities of words, using words to make pictures, akin to the concrete poetry of Guillaume Apollinaire, an early twentieth-century French poet. His playful "poem" "Alphabet Expanding" sprays the screen with letters of the alphabet flying about randomly, forming lines or falling like rain, sometimes closely spaced, sometimes spattered about.[64] For this he used the programming language Perl. His program is minimal: one line of thirty-two characters. One of the aims of this poem, he says, was to understand how Perl works "from the standpoint of literary art."[65]

As Montfort points out, displaying code alongside output data goes back to the 1980s, when users had to type computer programs into home computers. They were also given sample output to make sure they got it right. Similarly, in his book #!, each text is preceded by the program that generated it.

This was the premise behind *Codedoc*, an exhibition curated by Christiane Paul and shown at the Whitney Museum in 2002. For this, twelve well-known coders wrote code that connected three points in space and was able to power a video. Video and code—image and text—were displayed side by side, the message being that code is a form of creative writing. Inspired, Montfort styled his book *#!* after this exhibition. "Code pages are in black with white text, and output white with black text," he explains.[66]

People say that reading *#!* can give them a feel for how code works even without a background in programming. "I can use it as a text in translation," Montfort says, explaining that if a reader knows a little programming, they can compare his poems with the programs used to create them to get a better idea of what programming is all about.[67] "The instructions themselves are the work of art," he says. When you give a sign-maker instructions to produce a sign, it is the instructions that embody the work of art. Montfort is deeply interested in the nature of computer languages—how they are written, their aesthetics, their beauty, their literary art.

This led him to look into weird computer languages—esoteric languages, or eso languages.[68] "When we start looking into it," he says, "there are people who use intentionally difficult methods, like poets and authors of metafiction and other sorts of contemporary literature."[69] Since 1984, there has been a contest for writing the most creatively obfuscated code, the International Obfuscated C Code Contest. Only small but complete programs in the C programming language are permitted. The originality lies in the aesthetic abuse of C. One entry in the 1984 competition was a two-line program to generate Hello World, the first output when learning any computer language. In today's machine learning, Hello World marks a computer's awakening, like a newborn baby, as it responds to input data.

Eso languages are unwieldly and hence not aesthetic, not elegant. In his book *The Art of Code*, Maurice Black points out that these terms "and all their synonyms have been effectively exited from the vocabulary of literary and cultural theory."[70]

Montfort published a new book, *The Truelist*, late in 2017.[71] It is "a book-length poem generated by a one-page stand-alone computer programme" and "invites the reader to imagine moving through a strange landscape that seems to arise from the English language itself."[72]

The first two stanzas are as follows:

Now they saw the foothills,
   and the airking,
      the earthworm,
         the sliphound exceeding the king,

The heartwoman,
   the shiphound,
      the hardpath river leading the ship,
      the traplight welcoming the work.

Montfort's notion of creativity is at odds with that of the computational creativity community whose members investigate creativity with models often using complex mathematics, with overarching rules and huge data-bases. Pablo Gervás says of Montfort's work, "Nick very clearly sees himself as a writer who makes use of technology in different ways to make progress in his writing. We work from the opposite end. We are engineers who do not have literary aspirations."[73]

Montfort asserts that he is coming from the bottom up, using minimal algorithms and taking great care in his choice of words,[74] whereas Gervás and others work from the top down, using complex algorithms and huge databases. His systems, he says, are simple compared to theirs. "I want to invite my friends who are poets to work on these things with me." He would like his readers to use his programs to remix his poetry and play with it, using the algorithms displayed with the original poems.

This is how, he feels, it is possible to move from sequences of words to distributional poems. "Is this a model of creativity like the computational creativity community thinks about it? No, I don't think so," he says."[75]

As one reviewer wrote of #!: "#!... expands the kinds of successes that code-based poetry can achieve.... Montfort's programmatic poems shape ways of thinking on the page that reveal a persona in the machine that, surprisingly, thinks like us even if its expression is somewhat uncanny by 'human' standards."[76]

Uncanny indeed. This, surely, is when things get interesting, when we start to sense a personality inside the machine. Montfort's poetry uses computers "as poetry assistants, as generators of provocative and interest-ing literary art, visual art, and music."[77] A fascinating example of creative computing.

31 Allison Parrish Sends Probes into Semantic Space

[Computers] are really good at creating texts that don't work in the way that people expect language to work.

—Allison Parrish[78]

"I'm an experimental computer poet," says Allison Parrish. "I write computer programs that write poems. It's an awesome thing to be able to put on your business cards."[79]

Parrish is a one-off, full of forceful opinions, humorously expressed. At the University of California in Berkeley, she studied linguistics and French. Before that, she completed a degree in computer science, working her way through university as a computer programmer. She has been programming since the age of five. Parrish went on to complete a master's degree at NYU's Interactive Telecommunications Program (ITP), where she is now a professor. She describes herself as a computer programmer, poet, and game designer who is fascinated by the fact that "computers are really good at creating texts that don't work in the way that people expect language to work."[80]

To Parrish, code is a tool that opens new avenues for poets, in the same way that abstract expressionist painters Mark Rothko and Jackson Pollock used the tools of canvas and paint to subvert what a painting can do. For poets, code offers new and expressive ways to manipulate language.

"I always seize authorship for myself," says Parrish. "When I put out a book of poems it's by Allison Parrish, not Allison Parrish and a poetry bot...in the same way that a Jackson Pollock painting is not by Jackson Pollock and a paint can."[81]

To put it another way, she disapproves of emphasizing process at the expense of product. When she writes text and poetry, it's with a reader in mind. She believes that there should be a definite connection between intention and output. She makes decisions about each word, about the range of vocabulary she draws from and the algorithm she uses. "These are all incredibly expressive decisions."[82]

Parrish also disapproves of what she sees as a goal of computational creativity: to tune algorithms so that they produce work as close as possible to that of human poets. "I've made it my goal as a computer poet not to imitate poetry but to find new ways for poetry to exist."[83] The computational poetry of the future will, I suggest, be something we cannot even imagine today. Parrish points out that we've been doing computer-augmented writing ever since the introduction of the word processor. We use autocorrect, spell check, and the machine's thesaurus, while the keyboards on our phones continually guess our next word.

Much of computer-generated poetry is gimmicky, Parrish feels, but it gets a great deal of press for the simple reason that it's generated by AI. She looks forward to a future in which there will be more interfaces explicitly for writers, driven by AI and machine learning. She expects the effects on the style and rhetoric of written works to be extremely subtle and sophisticated.

"A text is poetic," she says, "to the extent that it is drawing attention to the affect that it has above conventional meaning."[84] She draws a parallel with the invention of photography, which freed artists from having to depict the world around them realistically and enabled figures like Claude Monet to emerge to create more impressionistic images of real life. "That is the potential of computer-generated language," Parrish says. Language can spark the brain in the same way that visual images do. "How can those parts of the brain be made to tingle in a way they have not tingled before?" she muses.

Modernist poetry, she says, arrived with the invention of the typewriter, which offered a way to produce not only imaginative text but imaginative image. The digital format is highly suitable for poetry in that it offers an elastic and quick way to compose in a variety of computer languages.

How do aesthetics and beauty apply to coding? In coding, Parrish says, she aims for elegance in procedure. "If a procedure is elegant, I mean that somebody can guess the way the procedure works from the way the output looks; that to me is really important."[85] She compares this with conventional poetry, in which the reader's understanding of the rules of the poetic form used—the sonnet, for example—makes the poem more enjoyable to read. She is fascinated by the rules that go into the making of a poem, whether it be conventional or computer-generated.

Says Parrish, "Poetry is much more interesting if there's a preface that explains what the poet was thinking. ... For me it is more interesting to read books about poetry than to read poetry."[86]

Parrish's great inspiration is a quote from Jean Lescure, a member of the avant-garde French writers' group Oulipo, founded in 1960; the group created works that were the predecessors of today's conceptual poetry. Oulipo included luminaries such as George Perec and Italo Calvino. The words that struck Parrish's imagination were, "Like mathematics, literature could be explored."[87] Parrish likes to think of herself as an explorer, not of outer but semantic space, the space of language.

A lot of her poetry takes the form of Twitter bots. She considers this the ideal way to explore semantic space, akin to exploring space with space probes, which are essentially robots. Her "favorite space probe" is Voyager 2, which explores the outermost planets and heads ever deeper and deeper into space, entering areas utterly inhospitable to human survival. It has been on its mission now for over forty years. While we live safely ensconced in our own familiar environment, space probes venture into the unknown, sending back reports using radio signals, and often do not return, which indeed will be the fate of Voyager 2.

To explore semantic space, Parrish came up with what she calls a very simple literal bot, "a robot that deals with words and letters."[88] She uses a Python program that reads all the lines from a given text, inserts them into a data structure, "then spits them back out in random order." Just as Voyager 2 explores a part of the universe where people have never been, Parrish's "literal bots" explore inhospitable parts of semantic space, beyond the kinds of language that we know, currently designated as nonsense. She likes to quote Julius Caesar's words in *Gallic Wars*: "It was not certain that Britain existed until I went there."[89] Similarly, she explains somewhat whimsically, she decided to visit the unknown areas of semantic space with her literal bot to find out what was there—as she puts it, "exploring (semantic) space with '(literal) bots' because humans abhor nonsense (and need help finding a path through it)."[90]

So what comes out of all this theory? Parrish's first venture into semantic space uses n-grams, sequences of a fixed number of words. Two words make a bigram, three words a trigram, and so on. For data, she uses the Google Books Corpus, consisting of many millions of words. From this she assembled bigrams in the form *about, anything, 124451*, meaning that the word *about* is followed by the word *anything* 124451 times in Google Books. To keep the exploration within limits, she used only bigrams in which both words begin with *a*. She laid out the words in a matrix beginning with *a*, horizontally and vertically. Where there were no cases in which the two words followed each other, she left a blank. Parrish then used an algorithm that created a visualization of these sequences in two-dimensional space, with larger rectangles where there are more occurrences of a particular bigram, smaller where there are less. The blank areas that mark the absence of word sequences is empty space—the void.

When she did the same thing with trigrams, it produced a rather spectacular three-dimensional visualization with words and cubes slowly revolving in space, "like a scene from some weird space movie."[91]

The empty spaces—the great voids—occur where there are no instances at all of a certain word following another. Parrish picked out some of these nonbigrams:

- angiography adequate
- abreast annihilates
- amusedly abstract

All words that have never before been used together, at least in Google's Book Corpus. These are juxtapositions that "have never been thought of or explored before, just because of how we conventionally think about the distribution of language."[92]

Parrish compares the difficulty of engaging with nonsense with the difficulty of surviving in outer space. She likes to think of herself as a proud descendent of the Dadaists, such as Tristan Tzara, one of the first to take language soundings—like taking soundings using radio signals from deep in the ocean or high in the atmosphere. In 1920, Tzara famously wrote instructions for how to compose a poem: cut up a newspaper article into individual words, jumble them up, then paste them onto a sheet of paper. Voilà, you have a poem.

Parrish also calls her "venture into nonsense" a sounding—sending a probe to find out what's out there. In 1920, the process had to be done manually. But all the same it was akin to an early computer program. Then, in 1959,

Theo Lutz created the first computerized poetry generator, which spewed out sentences with the words chosen at random, nonsense sentences. For Parrish, this was the first literal robot exploring semantic space.[93]

At first glance, says Parrish, the Twitter reports tweeted back from Voyager 2, more than 16 billion kilometers away, seem like the work of a procedural poet:

> FAQ How fast are you going? Not as fast as you might think, but still at a good clip! Sister V1 [sister ship Voyager 1] is leaving the Solar System at ~61,391 km/hr, and I am leaving about 10% more slowly, at #55,644 km/hr.

Voyager 2 has tweeted almost sixteen thousand times, and more than 350,000 people follow it.

Parrish's Twitterbot @the_ephemerides juxtaposes NASA images from space probes with words chosen at random from two large bodies of text—one on geology, the other astrology. These have immediate relevance to photographs of planets, making it easier for readers to see into them meanings that could be construed to have depth. Thus, alongside a photograph of Saturn's rings is this poem:

> We cannot get away
> from it. The ocean are by
> no probably does not
> likely as people proceed.

Anyone who has breathed depth into fragments of Beat poetry can do so here.

Parrish sees her most famous Twitter bots as a form of computer-generated poetry. The best known is *everyword*. Starting in 2007, it tweeted every word in the English language in alphabetical order, one every half hour. At its peak, it had over one hundred thousand followers. If you were to enter the everyword words into Parrish's two-dimensional bigram matrix, described earlier, they would form a straight line cutting diagonally across the matrix, because each word only occurs once and in juxtaposition to the one that precedes it alphabetically. The resulting line is a bit like the trajectory of a space probe as it sends back its reports, says Parrish.

Tony Veale, whom we will discuss in chapter 34, says of Parrish's Twitterbots: "Her bots are simple from the AI perspective but ingenious from the artistic perspective."[94] He too compares them to the cut-up techniques of Beat poets like William Burroughs and Brian Gyson. They are "more sophisticated versions of those techniques," he says.

Another venture into the realm of nonsense is Parrish's Twitterbot PowerVocabTweet, which makes up new words and definitions. It generates new words by splicing together two existing ones on the basis of the number of letters and syllables, and creates new definitions using a Markov model based on word definitions from WordNet. The result is a stream of words that we could never dream up but which surely fill gaps in semantic space.

@PowerVocabTweet has over three thousand followers and has tweeted over twenty-two thousand times. It generates words and definitions such as the following:

- aghbridge, n. (football) the running back who plays the alto saxophone
- durotic, n. a common bean plant grown for its beautiful song
- eight-billed, adj. great in degree or intensity or amount

PowerVocabTweet boldly proclaims, "Boost your vocabulary with these fiercely plausible words and definitions."[95] Nonsense though it is, Parrish speculates, there may be some people who really think they're increasing their vocabulary by following it.

Parrish considers her work to be calling for an "ethics of semantic exploration."[96] She wants "to remove the value judgment between stuff that makes sense and doesn't make sense—to point out the fact that, to some extent, that distinction is arbitrary. . . . In fact it's the mission of poetry to show how arbitrary that distinction is."[97] She is entranced with the way that computers can freely create nonsense—that is, "texts that don't work in the way that people expect language to work."

To return to Caesar's statement in *Gallic Wars*—"I was not certain that Britain existed until I went there"—Parrish suggests that "perhaps unexplored parts of semantic space have been previously visited," in the same way that Caesar was wrong; there already was life in Britain long before he came, saw, and conquered.[98]

Just as exploration and discovery all too often end in the exploitation of the newly discovered country, so too maybe the gaps in semantic space are there for a reason and we have no right to go there. And if we do, we cannot assume we have the right to appropriate what is there. An example is the language of a newly found group of people. Similarly, Parrish abhors appropriating the text of others and repudiates Kenneth Goldsmith's notion of "uncreative" writing involving the "copying, recycling, or appropriation" of other people's work.

"I'm going to be a hardliner and say that computers cannot be creative," Parrish tells me, insisting that there will always be a human hand behind them.[99] "Furthermore, it will always be a mistake to attribute volition to the computer and not to the people who programmed it because attribution of volition is removing personal responsibility: the algorithm did it, not me."

In her recent book, *Articulations*, Parrish ventures into the world of sound.[100] She's chosen two million lines of poetry, from which her computer programs seek out words and lines that echo each other sonically to create poetry in which sound rather than meaning is uppermost. The resulting poems are "a lot of fun to read out loud," she says.[101] Here is the beginning of one:

And Then She Went Away. She Went Away, Away, She Went Away.
She Went Away
Thunder, lightning, fire and rain, and laughter, and inn-fires. After the fire of London and another of a pastoral vein—the venerable original the adolescent and the venerable, richly the upland and vale adorn, Buddha, the holy and the benevolent, of many a lover, who the heaven would think...[102]

Parrish insists that computer programs will not replace poets but will take on exploratory work that humans would rather not do. She continues, "Because a computer program isn't constrained by convention, it can speak interesting truths that people find difficult to say, and it can come up with serendipitous juxtapositions that make language dance and sing and do unexpected things that can be beautiful and insightful." And perhaps creative, too.

Our whole goal in *Sunspring* was not to curate.
—Ross Goodwin[103]

My name is Benjamin.
—Benjamin (previously Jetson)[104]

Ross Goodwin works at "the intersection of writing and computation."[105] He has had an extraordinary career. After playing about with computers as a child, he studied economics, then became a speech writer for President Obama, writing presidential proclamations, then took a variety of freelance writing jobs.

One of these involved churning out business letters—he calls it freelance ghostwriting. The letters were all pretty much the same, so he figured out an algorithm that would generate form letters, using a few samples as a database. The algorithm jumbled up paragraphs and lines following certain templates, then reassembled them to produce business letters, similar but each varying in style, saving him the job of starting anew each time.[106] He thought he was on to something new but soon found out that this was a well-explored area. But it did pique his interest in the "intersection of writing and computation."[107] He enrolled in the master's program at NYU's Interactive Telecommunications Program (ITP), where, among others, he worked with Allison Parrish.

One of his first creations was the remarkable word.camera, which is online for anyone to play with. It takes a picture—of you or of whatever you are holding up to be photographed—identifies what it's seeing, then generates words—poetry—sparked by the images it has identified. Show it an image of, for example, mountain scenery, and it might come up with seven or eight descriptive phrases—"blue sky with clouds," "a large rock in the background." Then it uses each to generate a sequence of words: "A blue sky with clouds: and a sweet sun carrying the shadow of the black trees and the spire are dark and the wind and the breath in the light are." A little mysterious, but no more so than a lot of contemporary poetry.

Here is an example of an image (figure 32.1), in this case the great sixteenth-century artist Albrecht Dürer's 1514 engraving of *Saint Jerome in His Study*. It's a period interpretation of a genius as someone touched by divine guidance, transmitted by the light that shines on the saint.

And here is what the machine sees, the poem generated by word.camera when presented with this picture:

A Stone Wall fills a sea,
A shadow of rivers,
A spirit of light;
and in the water
Some storm that sweeps the wind and the darkness.
A large brick wall with a slow view of the trees,
The town of the house where it was done with water,
Having passed a Spring-fire.
A large rock on the ground is dark and shadowy,
and the whole world is dead.

To create his word.camera, Goodwin took a neural network machine containing Char-RNN, which predicts sequences of characters based on an input corpus, and trained it on a vast number of twentieth-century poems and a large number of images, all captioned. Then he rigged up a digital camera to it. The computer writes poems based on what it sees in the image. Goodwin was gratified that the poems "conjured imagery and employed relatively solid grammar," while having the aura of originality. "What good is a generator if it just plagiarises your input corpus?" he asks, adding: "A machine that can caption images is a machine that can describe or relate to what it sees in a highly intelligent way."[108]

Then, in 2016, Goodwin met Oscar Sharp, a British film student at NYU who preferred hanging out with the technologists at ITP rather than with filmmakers. Sharp wanted to create a film by splicing together random parts of other films, like Dadaist artists had done. But Goodwin had a better idea—to use Char-RNN. Their call to action came when they heard about

Figure 32.1
Albrecht Dürer, *Saint Jerome in His Study*, 1514.

the annual Sci-Fi London Film Festival and its 48-Hour Film Challenge. For this, contestants are given a set of props and a list of lines of dialogue that must be included. They have to make the film over the next two days, and it can be no more than five minutes long.

Goodwin fed his Char-RNN, which they named Jetson, digitized screenplays of sci-fi films from the 1980s and 1990s, TV shows like *Stargate: SG1*, and every episode of *Star Trek* and *The X-Files*. While Goodwin, Sharp, and the cast stood around the printer, Jetson spat out a screenplay, complete with seemingly impossible stage directions, such as, "He is standing in the stars and sitting on the floor." Sharp decided this called for a dream sequence—though some of Shakespeare's stage directions, too, like the classic "Exit pursued by a bear," from *A Winter's Tale*, are as obscure as any written by Jetson.

Another stage direction called for one of the characters—H, who is speaking to C—to spit out an eyeball:

C
(smiles)
I don't know anything about this.

H
(to Hauk, taking his eyes from his mouth)
Then what?[109]

Sharp randomly assigned roles to the three actors in the room: Thomas
Middleditch from the HBO series *Silicon Valley* (H), Elisabeth Gray (H2), and
Humphrey Ker (C). The actors read through Jetson's script, interpreting the
lines as they read, turning it into an involving if somewhat bizarre sci-fi
story of love, despair, and murder. There is even a musical interlude that Jetson composed after learning from a database of twenty-five thousand folk
songs, which comes toward the end, during a dreamlike action sequence.
The song was curated and performed by vocalist Tiger Darrow and musician
Andrew Orkin, who "chose lines that worked well with their music."

Sharp kept curation of the script itself to an absolute minimum. He cut
some lines to keep the movie within the five-minute limit for the challenge.
One scene was removed because it called for a truck and they had none.
"Oscar Sharp did not edit it for consistency or linearity or for any other qualities," Goodwin tells me.[110] In the film, which they called *Sunspring*, they
went the whole distance: actors spoke exactly the lines that the machine
gave them.

Sunspring is a sci-fi drama with the characters' costumes augmented with
metal and gold. It's certainly bizarre—even Lynchian, one might say. The
actors deliver their somewhat gnomic lines with passion and intensity,
putting meaning and expression into them and making them make sense,
even if the script itself does not. And in the course of the film H does indeed
spit out an eyeball. For Goodwin, it's up to the actor or the reader to provide
the meaning. Pablo Gervás also pointed out that this is an essential part of
creative writing: "The magic doesn't come from the writer, it comes from
the reader."[111]

People may be less prone to appreciate prose that makes no sense, but
this is not the case for movie dialogue or song lyrics or poetry. As Goodwin
says, modern readers may have difficulty understanding certain lines of
Shakespeare, but they make sense when actors flesh them out with their
body language and emotion.[112]

The judges at the film festival placed *Sunspring* in the top ten, though
it did not win. Nevertheless, Jetson was interviewed on stage at the award
ceremony, responding through text on Goodwin's computer. Here are two
of its responses:

Interviewer: What do you think of your historic nomination in this contest?

Jetson: I am pretty excited. I think I can see the feathers when they release their hearts. It's like a breakdown of the facts. So they should be competent with the fact that they won't be surprised.

Interviewer: What's next for you?

Jetson: Here we go. The staff is divided by the train of the burning machine building with sweat. No one will see your face. The children reach into the furnace, but the light is still slipping to the floor. The world is still embarrassed. The party is with your staff. My name is Benjamin.[113]

Rather touchingly, Jetson had told them its name and henceforth Goodwin and Sharp referred to it—or him—as Benjamin, and billed him as such as the writer of *Sunspring.*

For the moment, Goodwin sees the role of computers as assisting us and providing intelligent augmentation. But he believes that we are getting close to machines creating on their own volition. "That sort of creativity," he says, "need not replace human creativity and will work in conjunction with human creativity. I don't see why one has to replace the other."[114]

Benjamin, along with Goodwin and Sharp, went on to create a second movie, entitled *It's no Game,* with David Hasselhoff as the Hoffbot. And Goodwin was snapped up by Google's Artist and Machine Intelligence Program as a creative technologist.

He has now published a book entitled *1 the Road,* which he describes as "a novel written using a car as a pen, an enhanced AI experiment."[115] It is an AI version of an American road trip akin to Jack Kerouac's *On the Road.* For this, Goodwin took an AI for a ride. He traveled from New York to New Orleans in a Cadillac equipped with four sensors: a surveillance camera on the roof, a GPS unit, a microphone, and the computer's internal clock. All these were hooked up to an AI trained on poetry, science fiction, and what Goodwin describes as "bleak" literature, as well as on location data.

Like a very advanced version of Goodwin's word.camera, the AI produced words in response to what it saw and places it passed and to conversation it overheard in the car. The opening sentence came spewing out of the printer as Goodwin turned on the machine in Brooklyn: "It was nine seventeen in the morning and the house was heavy."

The AI continued to generate somewhat disjointed but evocative sentences throughout the journey, such as in this excerpt:

It was seven minutes to ten in the morning, and it was the only good thing that happened.

What is it? the painter asked.

The time was six minutes until ten o'clock in the morning, and the conversation was finished while the same interview was over.[116]

Responding as it does to sights and sounds along the way, the book really does read like a rather surreal road trip novel.

I focused on poetry and even more particularly on figurative language. I wanted to know how computers can write in a way that was surprising and meaningful.
—Sarah Harmon[117]

Sarah Harmon began writing computer-generated poetry at high school, using programs like Logo Writer, an educational programming language that includes rules for grammar and structure. She published her work in her high school literary magazine under the pseudonym Dan Goshen, an anagram of Ogden Nash. She "was enthralled that we can interact with technology and how this can affect us emotionally," she says. As an undergraduate, she began by studying neuroscience, then switched to mathematics and computer science and completed a PhD in computer science at the University of California at Santa Cruz.

She then decided to take another look at computer-generated poetry. "Current research concerns how people interact with computers in a way that is meaningful and impactful to us in solving problems in the best possible way. ... I focused on poetry and even more particularly on figurative language. I wanted to know how computers can write in a way that was surprising and meaningful."[118]

Whereas literal language uses words according to their exact dictionary definitions, figurative language—simile, metaphor—provides color, panache, and a more creative tone. "We surround ourselves with figurative language because with it we can express our emotions," Harmon says.[119] If a computer can generate figurative language effectively, then, she says, "it should be able to reason about our own language and understand our stories and language much more easily." In this way, poetry and stories—vehicles by which we navigate the world—can influence how we interact and respond to machines. It's not just a matter of machines creating metaphor but of teaching them more about our world.

Harmon expresses her dissatisfaction with the many programs that generate poetry from a heavily rule-based algorithm the computer blindly follows, randomly generating poetry that is often nonsense. Those that produce interesting work, she contends, rely too much on cherry-picking by the creator, added to which such programs cannot explain what they're doing or evaluate their own work, both of which are essential to creativity.

So Harmon decided to take a step back from computer-generated poetry to explore one key element—figurative language. This she does with her FIGURE8 program.[120] Instead of generating poetry, FIGURE8 generates imaginative metaphors. Metaphors illuminate a word or concept by explaining it in terms of another, linked by phrases like "as if."

When Danish physicist Niels Bohr was formulating the first modern theory of the atom in 1913, he used a metaphor: "The atom acts as if it were a miniscule solar system." He used the well-understood image of the solar system of planets revolving around the sun to explain the less well-understood concept of the atom. Bohr replaced the planets with electrons and the sun with the nucleus, then adjusted the mathematics of the solar system to use in the realm of the atom.

In rhetoric, the concept to be illuminated—in this case, the atom—is called the tenor and the concept being used to illuminate it—the solar system—is the vehicle. The greater the dissimilarity between tenor and vehicle, the greater the creative power of the metaphor.

To generate creative metaphors with a computer, Harmon feeds in literary texts, augmented by WordNet's lexnames file, which ranks metaphors according to the closeness between tenor and vehicle. She combines all this with a case-by-case reasoning system that checks them against the ways in which authors have used the tenor/vehicle in question. FIGURE8 does some brainstorming, then comes up with a list of metaphors and compares them, ranking them according to coherence, sound, and how well the image fits.

Here is a metaphor generated by FIGURE8: "Like a pale moon, the garden lit up in front of him."[121] The tenor is *garden*, the vehicle *moon*. They have low semantic similarity—that is, not much in common. FIGURE8 calculates it as 0.0204, very low indeed. Thus this metaphor is potentially novel, a requirement of creativity. It is certainly not a cliché.

In another example, the tenor was *pearl*. FIGURE8 generated the following list of metaphors:

(A) It was the pearl, fermenting like a wild apple.
(B) Like scenic music, the pearl danced in front of him.
(C) It was their pearl, sprawling like a wretched corpse.
(D) It was her pearl, crumpling like a drowned corpse.
(E) It was my pearl, bubbling like a treacherous swamp.[122]

FIGURE8 rated these metaphors, and so did readers. Both FIGURE8 and the readers ranked (D) the highest for clarity and attractiveness. The extent to which the readers "liked the figurative description was directly related to how well they understood it," Harmon writes.[123]

For this study, Harmon did not tell the readers that the metaphors had been generated by a computer. She was, she says, just interested in responses. But if she repeated the experiment, she would apply more controls, such as trying it out on one group that knew the source of the metaphors and another that didn't. "If you are told something came from a machine, it can completely bias your perception," she says.[124] The point is perhaps that computers can nudge our understanding and appreciation of language further, dream up combinations of words that are beyond most human imaginations.

Says Harmon, "Machines can be creative, but it's a creativity that's entirely alien to us."[125]

34 Tony Veale and His Metaphor- and Story-Generating Programs

Computers that can create are not the kind that can turn us into slaves.
—Tony Veale[126]

Tony Veale has been hooked on computers ever since seeing a rerelease of Stanley Kubrick's *2001: A Space Odyssey* as a teenager in Ireland. Thereafter, he was obsessed with the computer HAL 9000. "AI was part of my life before I became a computer scientist," he recalls.[127] At the time, he didn't fully grasp every nuance of the film, but he homed in on HAL as a thinking, feeling, and above all speaking presence who could play chess and plot the murder of astronauts. Thinking about this brought home to him the importance of the way people use language and the way we judge others by their use of tropes, "their ability to turn a phrase." When he became a computer scientist, Veale chose to focus on natural-language processing, the way computers deal with human language, such as metaphors and similes, a career choice he encapsulates in the words "the first route in defines you."

Veale brims with ideas and enthusiasm about computer science. From the start, he took an optimistic view of computers, he says, in contrast to the dystopian outlook of commentators such as Stephen Hawking, Elon Musk, and Nick Bostrom. Veale sees AI "as a place to explore passionate ideas like literature and creativity; it's a way of doing creative work by another route because computer science touches on everything."[128]

He points out that much human language revolves around metaphors. We "catch an aeroplane" and "catch a cold." These, he says, are "conventional metaphors." He is more interested in "conceptual metaphors," complex cognitive structures that "provide conceptual mappings that shape our habitual thinking about such familiar ideas as *Life, Love, Politics* and *War*."[129] These are Shakespearean in scope.

As part of his exploration of metaphors, Veale has developed software that generates original metaphors. One such program is Metaphor Magnet.[130] You put in a word—love, death, war, whatever—and a stream of similes, metaphors, and word associations pops out, too vast to begin to quote. Love, for example, spawns concepts from *shining saint* to *shimmering soap bubble* and millions more.

Another is Thesaurus Rex (illustrated with a picture of a baby tyrannosaurus rex bursting out of its egg).[131] This provides synonyms and word associations for single words, while two words linked with *and* generate a variety of single words that are basically definitions.

Metaphor Magnet also has a Twitter account with which it tweets a metaphor every hour or so under the handle @MetaphorMagnet. Veale believes that Twitter offers more than just a means for social interaction. "In many ways it constitutes a whole new genre of text."[132] To create metaphorical and ironic tweets, @MetaphorMagnet taps into huge databases constructed by Veale and his coworkers, including Thesaurus Rex and Metaphor Eyes, another way of spinning ideas out of the relationships between concepts, such as scientists as artists, or writers as readers.[133]

To build up these databases, he uses n-grams, a huge database of short word chains that create conceptual metaphors. Take the four-word-grams, each made up of four words, like *democracy is a cornerstone* and *democracy is a failure*. The Metaphor Magnet website homes in on their properties and juxtaposes them "via resonant contrasts and norm contraventions."[134] It then informs the bot that the stereotype *cornerstone* should be qualified as *important* and the stereotype *failure* as *worthless*. The result is a tweet embodying two contrasting views on democracy:

> To some voters, democracy is an important cornerstone
> To others, it is a worthless failure
> #Democracy = #Cornerstone #Democracy = #Failure

Veale contrasts the complex construction of this rational and figurative conceptual metaphor with the slapdash, mash-up tweets generated by the Twitterbot @Metaphor-a-Minute. This has a framework *X is a Y*, which it fills in every two minutes using random word choices, creating entries such as: "a macula is a result: blockheaded and refuse." "Rather than random metaphors, they are random metaphor-shaped texts," Veale says.[135]

He points out what he calls the placebo effect, whereby readers try to attribute meaning to a metaphor that is actually complete nonsense.[136] "The meaning," he says, "is created by the reader. The machine generates a provocation for the reader to create meaning."[137] The author (who in this case happens to be the computer) "is hacking your brain, creating the conditions for ideas to flourish. Twitter is a perfect medium because it values conciseness."

Veale arranged a competition between the two Twitterbots, with human judges rating them on comprehensibility, tweet novelty, and retweetability. The judges agreed that @MetaphorMagnet outperformed @Metaphor-a-Minute on comprehensibility and retweetability, but was less strong on tweet novelty. This is no doubt due to @Metaphor-a-Minute's bizarre juxtapositions of words. The assumption that groups of words are meaningful "can lead us to perceive (and enjoy) a creative meaning when none was ever intended," Veale writes.[138]

I ask Veale whether Metaphor Magnet may be so loaded with enormous volumes of words and templates that it is bound to generate provocative and creative metaphors. "This is what humans do," he replies. "We all use a toolbox of tricks. ... All modern speakers instantiate tropes because they are the way to use language to persuade, to inspire, to surprise, to provoke. And that's what computers are doing. ... What computers are saying is that even the cleverest of humans are just bags of tricks, and they vary their tricks."[139]

Veale's work does not stop at metaphor. He has also produced a story-generating system, akin to those of Pablo Gervás and Rafael Pérez y Pérez, among others. "The challenge—and the opportunity—for a story generator," he says, "is to do more than fill slots with matching fillers."[140] He looks for "a conceptual blend of characterization and plot," which includes everything we already know about the character in question.[141]

Veale calls his story-generation system the Scéalextric Simulator and describes it as "a simulation-based approach to the generation of episodic stories in which stories are generated, evaluated and frequently discarded in a rapid, coarse-grained cycle of engagement and reflection."[142] The name blends together *scéal*, the Irish word for *story*, and Scalextric, a children's racing car game in which segments of track are slotted together end to end. The simulator is online, ready to be played with.[143] It offers the player—or the writer in search of inspiration—a choice of three sorts of character: from the "NOC list," first names only, or one NOC character and the rest first names.

The NOC list is a kind of insider joke. It stands for "nonofficial cover" and is espionage lingo for agents working covertly for organizations but with no connection to the government for which they work, and who therefore have no diplomatic immunity. The characters on the NOC list are familiar and can be real or fictional—Jesse Jackson, Armand Richelieu, Superman, Lex Luthor, and so on. The first names are just names—Violetta, Brady, Gwendolyn, whatever.

Having chosen what type of character you want, next you tailor the action by ticking or unticking any of the three following boxes:

☐ Causal references to previous actions

☐ Strict linking of arcs (last arc action to next)

☐ Information transfer between characters

The simulator then generates a story that fulfils your chosen criteria and is different every time. Of the story generators we've discussed thus far, this one generates probably the most sophisticated plots.

Scéalextric has over three thousand prefabricated plot sections. It may choose characters who are well suited but impossibly matched, such as Steve Jobs and Leonardo Da Vinci, Mahatma Gandhi and Obiwan Kenobi, or Cicero and Barack Obama, taking vivid details of their lives and person-alities from the NOC database. Scéalextric pairs them on a metaphorical basis, homing in on their similarities, even though they may exist in differ-ent domains, genres, or periods.

One story Veale's system created is a confrontation between (a) Rich-ard Nixon and (b) Frank Underwood from the *House of Cards* series, until recently played by Kevin Spacey. The first of Scéalextric's prefabricated seg-ments read:

—*campaign_against—but → are humiliated_by*[144]

The simulator fleshes this out, creating the following prologue and first two lines:

0. Richard Nixon and Frank Underwood were driven by very different political agendas.
1. So at first, Frank campaigned vigorously against Richard.
2. But Richard humiliated Frank by calling the sociopathic and ruthless Frank the Keyser Söze of wielding political power.[145]

The story goes on for ten more scenes.

"The system jumped outside itself," Veale recalls excitedly of these first two lines.[146] It invented—on the fly—an exchange of insults that went outside the storyline, bringing in Keyser Söze, who was also played by Spacey in the film *The Usual Suspects*. "I don't want to suggest that that shows the machine to be more clever than it is. Partly it's an accident," Veale says. But, he continues, "it has a lot of knowledge to play with to acquire this postmodern irony in the way it manipulates its characters....A storytelling system has to be generative on multiple levels."

I ask Veale whether his storytelling system has been criticized for being loaded. He replies, "It's like a Chinese buffet, where one customer decides to make his own soup with some of the ingredients....The more ingredients you have in the program, the wider the scope of combinatorial creativity; that's what we mean by...fully loaded programs that exist in a knowledge context."[147] In other words, with such a vast amount of information, the possibility exists for the system to pull out unexpected similarities.

His "beef," Veale says, with neural networks is that they are "somewhat accidental and don't use knowledge deliberately or knowingly."[148] Perhaps it was pure accident that his symbolic system, programmed with enormous amounts of information about people and things together with ways to manipulate all this data, happened to compare Frank Underwood with Keyser Söze, both of whom were played by Kevin Spacey. But Veale feels comfortable with the way this happened. He is happy to assert that the system uses its knowledge deliberately and knowingly.

Veale believes that, at present, fully loaded symbolic systems are the best way to enhance and understand human creativity, spurring "the ability to generate and to own the results—that is, to appreciate and to critique and say, 'here it is, hope you like it.'"[149]

Currently Veale is installing his Scéalextric system in a Nao robot. At the moment, these small, cute robots are just expensive toys. To use a robot as a storyteller will provide Veale with an embodied system that can tell stories accompanied by gestures. The human-like appearance and gestures of Gil Weinberg's music-making robots, Shimi and Shimon, make people look beyond the simplicity of their forms into something primal. This will happen with Veale's Nao robots too as audiences become more and more enraptured by the unfolding story.

Veale agrees that computers show glimmers of creativity and gives AlphaGo as an example. AlphaGo has certainly done things that can be assessed as novel (the thirty-seventh move in its second game of Go had not been made before) and useful (it achieved the goal of advancing its game), both of which are often taken as criteria of creativity. Can AlphaGo therefore be called creative?

Says Veale, it neither questions its knowledge as to whether a move is conventional or not, nor has any conception of having made a spectacular move. "The machine lacks a social dimension."[150] He believes it will be able to attain this by being inserted into a robot, by embodiment. In this way, it will be able to be "out there": bombarded by stimuli, entertained by culture, maybe even falling in love, while generating interesting metaphors and creating literature, art, and music. And it will be able to do this without being organic.

Veale concludes optimistically, "The question of whether computers are truly creative will fade away as people value their results."[151]

35 Hannah Davis Turns Words into Music

It's a different way of listening to music, a different way of thinking about it.
—Hannah Davis[152]

Music stirs the emotions. Sometimes just a chord will do it. Literature too works on an emotional level. Hannah Davis's project is to bridge music and literature, to bring sound to our experience of reading a book.

Davis began programming as a child and studied music as well. For a few years, she studied international relations and spent some time working in Ghana. Then she renewed her interest in computer science and studied for a master's degree in creative communication technology at the Interactive Telecommunications Program (ITP) at NYU.

She studied data sonification, transforming data—in this case, the grammar and structure of a novel—into sound. To do this, she fed texts by Ernest Hemingway, Virginia Woolf, and David Foster Wallace into a computer and had it tag every word with the appropriate part of speech. Her program picked up the rhythms of Hemingway's distinctive writing style—short sentences with few descriptive words—and Woolf's melodic poetry. "Hemingway was staccato—I love that—while Woolf's poetry has a rhythm falling back on itself." Her program also caught David Foster Wallace's long, flowing sentences.[153]

But she was less interested in text analysis than in creating music that could reflect the moods of the novel. The computer lexicons available, however, were very limited. They contained too few emotion words, only a few hundred, and all obvious—happy, sad, and so on—and covering too few emotions, whereas authors are far more nuanced in their evocations of emotions.

Then Davis discovered Saif M. Mohammad's EmoLex, the NRC Emotion Lexicon.[154] This lexicon contains fourteen thousand commonly used words tagged according to the emotions they evoke by thousands of people recruited via Amazon's Mechanical Turk. The eight emotions it identifies are anger, anticipation, disgust, fear, joy, sadness, surprise, and trust. Using this lexicon, Davis worked with Mohammad to create a program she calls TransProse, which trains a computer to detect emotion in text. TransProse also divides the emotions in the text into positive and negative. Thus EmoLex associates the word *abandonment* with anger, fear, and sadness, all negative sentiments.

This textual data forms the emotional profile of the novel. Davis then transfers the data to a music-processing library equipped with the necessary music theory—tempo, scale, octave, and notes. A quick tempo and major keys are expressive of happiness, whereas minor keys communicate sadness. The system is equipped with sound fonts so that it sounds like a piano. Then it is converted into wave forms for MP3 encoding.

The scores follow the trajectories of the novels, reflecting the density of the eight emotions and two states—positive and negative—throughout the text. Conrad's *Heart of Darkness*, full of a sense of approaching doom, produces a somber, dark score, whereas the score for Barrie's *Peter Pan*, with an emotional profile of trust and joy, is light and cheerful.[155] Thus TransProse generates "piano pieces whose notes are dependent on the emotion words in the texts."[156]

In 2016, Davis was commissioned to create a score for a fifty-piece orchestra, to be performed inside the Louvre Pyramid in Paris. The sponsor was Accenture Technology, a branch of Accenture, a business and technology consulting firm that wanted to show the breadth and potential of AI and its transcendence across cultures. What better way to do this than with music? A member of Accenture saw Davis give a lecture and realized she was exactly what they were looking for.[157] "Words have real meaning, and they can make music," as Mark Knichrehm, group chief executive at Accenture Strategy, another branch of Accenture, put it.[158] Davis provided the perfect alchemical mix of human and machine to generate the music for the event.

Davis used her TransProse system to analyze the emotions communicated by thousands of news articles, covering business topics such as cybersecurity and the internet of things. She digitized the data for each of the eight emotions and divided it into separate files for particular instruments to create a series of musical motifs. In collaboration with composer Mathieu Lamboley, she created *Symphonologie: The Music of Business*, with three movements: "Voices of Business," "The Rise of Technology," and "A New Digital World." The symphony was performed on September 20, 2016, and was a dazzling multimedia experience, with the music accompanied by a spectacular data visualization generated in real time.[159]

This is clearly the sort of approach that is perfect for film scores. Davis's present research includes looking into automatic film scoring to generate film scores directly from visual material.[160] For this project, she uses neural nets for face/character and scene detection. If she succeeds, she may well change the future of composing scores for films.

There has always been a "problem with the way the media talks about my stuff," says Davis. One newspaper wrote, "'Robot creates music based on a novel.' This makes people a little bit more defensive than they need be....Dystopian scenarios are really not interesting."[161]

She looks forward to a future enhanced by AI, with a basic income for all and a good transition plan for how to move from a world dominated by us to one where machines do much of the work. Davis feels that it would be an excellent thing for humanity if robots took over our jobs, allowing us to redefine ourselves in other ways. She adds that she definitely believes that computers can be creative.[162]

If you unwrap a computer poem, don't look for humanity in it because it was written by software.
—Simon Colton[163]

Simon Colton is ubiquitous in the computational creativity field. Besides The Painting Fool, he has also developed, with colleagues who include Jacob Goodwin and Tony Veale, an algorithm that writes "unpredictable yet meaningful poetic artefacts."[164] This offers a "stronger definition of *computational creative* poetry," as opposed to texts that emerge out of stochastic—that is, random—algorithms.[165]

Some poets intentionally write poetry that cannot be understood without textual analysis. Nevertheless, random words on a piece of paper are just that, Colton contends. An example is Robopoem, an algorithm that creates nonsense poetry from random words in a cut-and-paste fashion, much like the Dadaists did. With the Robopoem phone app, people can generate endless poems while waiting at a bus stop, then try to find meaning in them. This, as Colton writes, only highlights the fact "that people have an amazing capacity to find meaning in texts generated with no communicative purpose."[166]

Colton's poetry generator is loaded with a vast amount of material. He avoids existing poems to stay clear of accusations of plagiarism and pastiche. Instead, he throws in material from the *Guardian* newspaper, together with similes checked with the Google Ngram Viewer, pronunciation dictionaries, and a sentiment dictionary to see how many times they've been used. As with The Painting Fool, the software determines the mood of the poem depending on the newspaper articles it's read that day.

It has about twelve thousand articles to choose from and adds to its collection each day. It chooses one article, from which it extracts key phrases, then uses these phrases to put together a template that determines the number of stanzas, the number of lines in each stanza, and the rhyme and meter. Then it assembles words and phrases using this structure to create a poem.

The aesthetic content is governed by the mood of the newspaper article that the software has chosen. The mood is expressed through the frequency with which certain words appear in the poem to evoke lyricism, sentiment, or flamboyance. Colton assesses all of this by making a mathematical analysis of the poem generated.

Finally, the software produces commentary on why it chose to write that particular poem in that particular mood, choosing from a number of templates written by Colton, then going back through the stages that produced the poem. The software also comes up with a title for the poem from a frequently recurring phrase in it.

In each session, the software creates over one thousand poems. It assesses the poems according to the aesthetic criteria of relevance to the newspaper article chosen, lyricism, sentiment, and flamboyance, and it keeps the highest-ranking poem.[167]

Here is an example. The software speaks in the first person:

It was a generally bad news day. I read an article in the Guardian entitled: "Police investigate alleged hate crime in Rochdale." Apparently "Stringer-Prince 17 has undergone surgery following the attack on Saturday in which his skull, eye sockets and cheekbone were fractured" and "This was a completely unprovoked and relentless attack that left both victims shocked by their ordeal." I decided to focus on mood and lyricism, with an emphasis on syllables and matching line lengths, with very occasional rhyming. I like how words like "attack" and "snake" sound together. I wrote this poem.

Relentless attack
a glacier-relentless attack
the wild unprovoked attack of a snake

the wild relentless attack of a snake
a relentless attack, like a glacier
the high level function of eye sockets

a relentless attack, like a machine
the low-level role of eye sockets

> a relentless attack, like the tick of a machine
> the high-level role of eye sockets
> a relentless attack, like a bloodhound

You can see the relevance to the rather violent theme it chose. Who knows what a contemporary poetry critic would make of it?

Colton remarks that people's opinions of a poem are colored by who they think the author is, particularly if they discover that the author is a computer. To prove his point, he gave a performance in which he told his audience he was going to read a poem by Maureen K. Smith, describing her experiences of childbirth. After a few minutes, he stopped and said, "Sorry, it's not by Maureen K. Smith. It's by Maurice K. Smith, who witnessed the birth." [168] The audience was incredulous: a man writing a poem about childbirth? A little later Colton revealed that Maurice was a pedophile and had written the poem in prison. By now, the audience's mood was distinctly dark. The joyous words in the poem had begun to sound sinister. Then he said, "Good news. The poem was actually written by a computer program." The audience's dark mood changed to disbelief at the realization that a machine had been able to play with their feelings.

"The text lost a lot of its value," Colton notes, when he told the audience it was written by a computer. "We've reached the stage where such poems would be award winning if they were produced by people, but if they are written by a computer they are not considered to be real poems." [169]

Colton refers to "The Death of the Author," an essay written by French philosopher Roland Barthes in 1967. Barthes argued that literature should be taken at face value, without taking any account of the identity of the author. The message was that anyone—be they street sweepers or philosophers—could write poetry. "This very liberal movement has not survived into the computer age," Colton laments. [170] "Indeed, if you have to project humanity onto authorship of poems, why not just read poems written by people?" He suggests calling computer-generated poetry "c-poems, just like we say e-books."

As to the argument that machines can't feel the necessary emotions to inspire poetry because they're not out in the world, they can at least read the web and experience, however vicariously, hunger, thirst, love, and passion. Painting machines, including Colton's The Painting Fool, acquire experiences of the world through their portraiture. Colton is currently researching ways of storing this information in the system's memory.

At present, Colton sees his poetry system as "fairly rudimentary [though it] can function on the majority of levels to be taken seriously as a poet, albeit in a simplistic manner."[171]

Colton is dismissive of Project Magenta's end-to-end philosophy. He is critical of using neural networks in creative projects because the programmer puts in so much information about the world that it "often means less imaginative thought." He prefers his own highly structured, rule-based approach. Colton's poetry system, along with The Painting Fool, certainly seems to show some of the behavior we associate with creativity, such as imagination and intent. No doubt the optimal approach is somewhere in the middle. We have yet to discover what it is.

V Staged by Android Lloyd Webber and Friends

It's all very well to create magical art, write and play music, tell stories, even tell somewhat dubious jokes. But could AI succeed at a much tougher task? Could it put together a musical—not just any musical, but one that would be commercial, that would be a hit in London's highly competitive West End? A group of writers, composers, and AI researchers put their heads together and decided to try. What followed was a great example of AI in action.

37 The World's First Computer-Composed Musical: *Beyond the Fence*

Could you get a computer to write a musical?

—Catherine Gale[1]

In 2014, Catherine Gale, previously a researcher in computational biomedicine and now a producer/director at Wingspan Productions in London, made two television programs that, at the time, seemed unconnected. *The Joy of Logic*, a foray into logic, explored Alan Turing's belief that both brains and computers are information-processing systems, which means that one day computers will be able to reproduce human thought. The other, *Our Gay Wedding: The Musical*, celebrated Benjamin Till and Nathan Taylor's wedding on the first day that same-sex marriages became legal in the United Kingdom. Till and Taylor, both musicians of note, composed the music and lyrics.

Thus inspired, Archie Baron, Wingspan's creative director, came up with the visionary idea of staging a musical composed as much as possible by computers, with computers generating the ideas and writing the lyrics and music. In 2015, Gale recalls, "Sky Arts was looking for big, ambitious, unusual projects, and they had a development fund for genre-busting subjects."[2]

Baron's inspired idea entirely fit the bill. Besides the musical itself, he envisaged two one-hour programs telling the story of how it was put together. To everyone's delight, Sky Arts took the bait and commissioned it. Gale began by putting together a consortium of scientists from around Europe and hired Taylor and Till to curate the lyrics and the music, which the computers would compose, and assemble them into a show.

The first step was to identify a recipe for success—the key ingredients that made a hit musical. Using machine learning, James Robert Lloyd, Alex

Davies, and David Spiegelhalter of Cambridge University conducted a predictive big-data analysis of successful musicals. They analyzed 1,696 musicals and 946 synopses, extracted the key features, and identified the four most popular themes: a journey, aspiration, love, and a lost king. Cast size, backdrop, and emotional structure also played a part. The protagonist, they concluded, would have to be female. The most popular periods for the setting were Europe in the 1930s and 1980s. There would have to be a death, a happy ending, and plenty of dancing. They also carried out surveys, asking audiences to watch fifty-two representative shows and report their reactions in a sort of computer-assisted market research. The viewers elected to have a happy ending and a peak in positive emotion about halfway through act 2.

The next player was the marvelous and quirky What-If Machine, designed by Simon Colton (who developed The Painting Fool) and his team at Goldsmith's University in London.[3] The What-If Machine is a spinner of story ideas. It takes an unlikely scenario and plays with it. It's obvious that a dog can't ride a horse—but what if it learned? What if there was a cloud that had bars in it instead of water? Rather than enjoying its shade, you could buy a beer there. Thus it brainstorms plots and ideas—many outlandish, but some tantalizing.

The data from the Cambridge thematic analysis and the seven basic plots as drawn up by academic Christopher Booker—rags to riches, the quest, rebirth, and so on—together with musical synopses for hits and flops were all translated into what-if sentences and fed into the What-If Machine. Six hundred plot ideas came pouring out. At this point, the human element came into play. Taylor and Till sifted through the ideas and homed in on one: "What if a wounded soldier had to learn to understand a child in order to find true love?"

They typed this phrase, along with other statistically important elements of a hit musical, such as love and loss, into a search engine. One of the responses that came up was the songbook from the Greenham Common Women's antinuclear peace camp in the 1980s. From this, Taylor and Till created a story line about a soldier posted at Greenham Common nuclear base to recover from his wounds, where he befriends the mute child of a protestor and falls in love with the child's mother. They also came up with a name for the musical: *Beyond the Fence*.

But how to develop the plot? For this, Taylor and Till turned to Pablo Gervás at the Universidad Complutense in Madrid. Gervás's work involves generating a whole story from a single plot line dreamt up by, for example, the What-If Machine, using his storytelling algorithm PropperWryter. PropperWryter builds sequences of plot elements, such as boy meets girl, boy loses girl, villain kidnaps victim. It knows that if it inserts one of these elements into a plot, that will introduce tension, and also knows that a story can only end when all tensions have been resolved. Gervás adapted it to suit a musical and worked up the core narrative arc of the new show, adding data from musicals and text from literary sources, annotated by music students and the Wingspan Productions team to indicate how they should be used.[4]

Next came the music. Bob Sturm and his team at Queen Mary University of London conducted a computational analysis of the music of musicals. They fed in seventy-seven full-length recordings of musicals, over 130 hours of audio in all, and isolated elements such as loudness, brightness, tempo, dynamics, and key, trying to work out what kinds of music characterized a hit and what kinds inevitably led to a flop.

Nick Collins at Durham University then fed all this data—chord changes from hit musicals and rules for combining chords taken from his own experience as a musician—into his computer composition system, based on Markov models, which he dubbed Android Lloyd Webber.[5]

François Pachet also fed songs from the Greenham Common songbook together with the songs Nick Collins had generated into his Flow Machine to create more songs.[6]

Android Lloyd Webber could produce two hundred lines of music in seconds. But humans—namely, Taylor and Till—had to review it. They played through every line, listening for melodies that they liked. Till, a paper-and-pen composer, found this disturbing. He told Collins that when he wrote music himself, his soul was in it. Collins replied, "My soul is in the program which generated the music. When you die your music dies with you. But my program will go on producing music forever."[7]

For the lyrics, Alex Davies and James Robert Lloyd fed seven thousand lyrics from musicals and ten thousand poems, with parts of Wikipedia thrown in, into their lyric-generating artificial neural network.

Clarissa the Cloud Lyricist, as they called their algorithm, spewed out lyrics that Taylor and Till, in conjunction with Kat Mace, an editor of computer lyrics, used to fashion into songs. Trawling through the music and lyrics was painstaking work. Although each line Clarissa produced more or less made sense, it was rare for two consecutive lines to make any sense at all. In the end, only about 25 percent of the lines in the songs were produced by machines; in one song, only 6 percent was used. The rest were crafted by Taylor and Till.

Gale recalls how Taylor and Till were determined to make the show "as good as possible with what they had, rather than injecting new material into it."[8] If they had stuck with lyrics written by the computer, it would have been an entirely different show. As an experiment, in the first rehearsal the cast was given a piece called "Time Is on the Tree," made up entirely of computer-generated lyrics and music. Gale sent the lyrics to Collins, who generated music for them. The first few lines run:

> Time is on the tree
> He's a man who can shame
> A shadow of a melody
> Me has so that the shade.

Difficult to sing, much less to memorize! Taylor and Till emphasize that "in a musical nothing is left to chance."[9] Every note, every word must support the story, and many people are involved—writers, musicians, cast, producer, director, choreographer, and more.

And so, after a month of rehearsals, the show went on. *Beyond the Fence* opened at the Arts Theatre in London, on February 22, 2016. It ran for fifteen performances, and over three thousand people came to see it. Audience members were asked to complete questionnaires, and there was an overwhelmingly positive response. Strangely, some were entirely unaware of the role computers had played in the production.[10]

Critics focused on the experimental nature of the production and the fact that it was created by machines. But despite their initial reservations, the reviews were generally positive. "A unique experiment in musical theatre composition," wrote the reviewer for the *Stage*. "Despite my reservations I was won over," said the *Independent*. "Extremely moving and emotional," concluded *West End Wilma*.

Leading lights of London journalism and theater, such as Ian Hislop, editor of *Private Eye*, and Alain Boubil, lyricist for *Les Misérables* and *Miss Saigon*, went in as skeptics and emerged converted. The music and lyrics were "comparable to what any of us have written," Boubil remarked.[11]

The main flaw that critics homed in on was that the musical was if anything too mainstream, not to say bland; it fulfilled every criterion for a best-selling musical: hardly surprising, as its creators had programmed their computers to do exactly that. Clearly, neither the computers nor their operators had any idea of what the Greenham Common protest had really been about and simply used it as the background for an anachronistically feel-good musical.

The computer scientists involved felt that there was too much human curating, although most were impressed by how difficult it was to produce a West End musical. Adhering to the demands of this particular genre, François Pachet tells me, forced the algorithms to work within "the category of songs for musicals, a category with lots of constraints that they wanted to have. They did it and did it well; see the reviews. But we really wanted songs that had some surprising unconventional elements. We wanted to push the artists beyond their comfort zone."[12]

Bob Sturm, who carried out the initial analysis of the music for the project, tells me that he "never imagined it would be as successful as it was.... At the beginning I thought it was going to be the strangest musical in the world."[13]

Pablo Gervás, who developed PropperWryter, was also uncomfortable with the large amount of human intervention. "The actual musical is far removed from what the computers generated," he says.[14]

Nick Collins, inventor of Android Lloyd Webber, agrees. But he found the experiment rewarding and pioneering, too. "Musical theatre composition itself has not been the prime subject of previous research in algorithmic composition, but it deserves wider future investigation."[15]

Till, the more critical of the writer/lyricist team, was inspired by the possibilities of machines and people working together. It can "lead to ideas that we would never have known," he says.[16] "Nathan Taylor cried when Clarissa was turned off," Gale recalls.[17]

Regarding Android Lloyd Webber, Collins later received a "legal letter from a well-known musical composer concerned at the use of a parodic version of his name, and seeking to stop this under trademark law."[18] What the composer found derogatory was the association of his name with a "mechanical process," implying that his music was not the result of a "creative process." Collins points out the contradiction in trying "to stop a program on commercial grounds from producing output that could be confused with that of a human, and at the same time being so worried as to denigrate the program's capabilities in emulating creativity."[19] Collins provided a "gentle response"—a piece made up of music by Android Lloyd Webber and lyrics by Clarissa.[20] As he says, what all the computer scientists involved in *Beyond the Fence* wanted was for computer modeling of music to throw some light on human musical creativity.

Indeed, in *Beyond the Fence*, machines and humans share equal billing, as is clear in the playbill in figure 37.1.

SKY ARTS & WINGSPAN THEATRICALS
PRESENT

BEYOND THE FENCE
A NEW MUSICAL

BOOK BY	MUSIC CURATED, COMPOSED & ARRANGED BY
BENJAMIN TILL & NATHAN TAYLOR	BENJAMIN TILL & NATHAN TAYLOR

BASED ON
A NARRATIVE GENERATED BY
PROPPERWRYTER
CREATED BY
DR PABLO GERVÁS

ANDA N ORIGINAL IDEA BY
THE WHAT-IF MACHINE
CREATED BY
PROF SIMON COLTON, DR MARIA TERESA LLANO & DR ROSE HEPWORTH
AS PART OF
THE WHIM PROJECT

BASED ON
ALGORITHMIC COMPOSITIONS BY
ANDROID LLOYD WEBBER
DEVELOPED BY
DR NICK COLLINS

BASED ON A
MUSIC INFORMATION
RETRIEVAL ANALYSIS BY
DR BOB STURM, DR TILLMAN WEYDE & DR DANIEL WOLFF

ADDITIONAL MUSIC FROM
FLOW COMPOSER
CREATED BY
DR PIERRE ROY & DR FRANÇOIS PACHET

LYRICS BY
NATHAN TAYLOR & BENJAMIN TILL
INCORPORATING ADDITIONAL LYRICS FROM
THE CLOUD LYRICIST
TRAINED BY
DR JAMES ROBERT LLOYD & DR ALEX DAVIES

BOOK, MUSIC & LYRICS INFORMED BY PREDICTIVE ANALYTICS A BIG DATA STATISTICAL ANALYSIS OF SUCCESS & FAILURE IN MUSICAL THEATRE BY
DR JAMES ROBERT LLOYD, DR ALEX DAVIES & PROF SIR DAVID SPIEGELHALTER

EXPERIMENT DESIGNED & CO-ORDINATED BY
DR CATHERINE GALE

EXECUTIVE PRODUCER
ARCHIE BARON

PRODUCER
NEIL LAIDLAW

SET & COSTUME DESIGNER	LIGHTING DESIGN	SOUND DESIGN	VIDEO DESIGN	MUSICAL DIRECTOR
TOM ROGERS	HOWARD HUDSON	PAUL GROOTHUIS	DOM BAKER & OLIVER LEVETT	CANDIDA CALDICOT

CASTING DIRECTOR	PRODUCTION MANAGER	COSTUME SUPERVISOR	ORCHESTRAL MANAGER
POLLY JERROLD	SIMON MARLOW	LAURA RUSHTON	SYLVIA ADDISON

ORCHESTRATIONS	KEYBOARD PROGRAMMER	CHILDREN'S COORDINATOR	MARKETING & PR PRESS
BENJAMIN TILL	STUART ANDREWS	JO HAWES	TARGET LIVE

MUSICAL SUPERVISOR
PAUL HERBERT

CHOREOGRAPHER
CRESSIDA CARRÉ

DIRECTOR
LUKE SHEPPARD

BEYOND THE FENCE WAS COMMISSIONED BY SKY ARTS AS PART OF COMPUTER SAYS SHOW,
A TELEVISION SERIES CHRONICLING THIS UNIQUE EXPERIMENT DEVISED AND MADE BY WINGSPAN PRODUCTIONS. ITS DEVELOPMENT WAS SUPPORTED BY THE WELLCOME TRUST.

Figure 37.1
Playbill for *Beyond the Fence*, February 2016.

VI   Can Computers Be Creative?

The time when humans can have meaningful conversation with an AI has always seemed far off and the stuff of science fiction. But for Go players that day is here.
—Andy Okun[1]

In the course of this book, I've been looking at the new breed of artist, who is computer scientist rolled together with artist, musician, or writer. The question of whether computers can be creative is no longer a matter purely of speculation, philosophy, metaphysics, or morals. We now have hard evidence.

Sir Nigel Shadbolt, professor of computer science at the University of Oxford and chairman of the Open Data Institute, which he cofounded with Tim Berners-Lee, inventor of the World Wide Web, is confident that "machines will become adept at persuading us that there is indeed something behind the façade."[2] But is he right?

Today, computers are creating an extraordinary new world of images, sounds, and stories such as we have never experienced before. Gerfried Stocker, the outspoken artistic director of Ars Electronica in Linz, says provocatively, "Rather than asking whether machines can be creative and produce art, the question should be, 'Can we appreciate art we know has been made by a machine?'"[3]

Alexander Mordvintsev's DeepDream sees things we don't and conjures up images merged in extraordinary and, to the human eye, sometimes nightmarish ways. Ian Goodfellow's generative adversarial networks (GANs) provide a way for computers to assess their creations without human intervention. As he puts it, they give AI a form of imagination. Computer scientist Ahmed Elgammal has used them to evolve his creative adversarial network (CAN) in the quest to create art not only definitively new but appealing to human eyes. Pix2Pix, creating fully developed images from an outline, and CycleGAN, merging two photographs, have created images never seen or even imagined before.

Throughout history, when an artist arises who breaks boundaries, the resulting art can't be classified within established styles and sparks a brand-new school, as Picasso did with cubism. Computer art too does not fit within any of the traditional styles. It pushes forward the frontiers of art. "Computers are changing the way human artists paint," says Alberto Barqué-Duran, an artist and performer who uses artificial neural networks in his work.[4] And indeed as from 2019 a new category has been added to the prestigious Prix Ars Electronica directed by Gerfried Stocker: Artificial Intelligence and Life Art.[5]

In music, Project Magenta created the first melody composed by a computer that had not been programmed in any way to do so. Artificial neural networks, such as Magenta's NSynth, explore new sonic vistas, producing sounds never heard before. There is a huge difference between music created by machines under their own steam (end to end) and music created by computers which have been programmed to do so (rule based). At the moment, the rule-based approach produces melodic music of complex structure and is more efficient at helping musicians play and compose music. For now, it produces music akin to the music it has learned. But the very complexity of the music it creates could point the way toward new approaches to composing, perhaps even toward music that human beings could never dream up. Indeed, the ultimate goal of all those working on machine-generated art, literature, and music is to create work beyond any known human genre or human imagining.

Computer-generated literature is even more of a frontier. The question of whether and how machines can have and express emotion throws the problems into stark relief. Most difficult of all is the complex human facility of humor. Even at the most basic level, like knock-knock jokes, machines don't know they are making a joke. They don't have awareness, though this does not detract from the fact that they sometimes do something charming and unexpected which—to human eyes—seems to hint at a personality, such as when the AI that wrote the script for the film *Sunspring* suddenly said, "My name is Benjamin."

For now, machines that are programmed tend to generate more sophisticated plots and stories than those created by more autonomous artificial neural networks. Tony Veale's Scéalextric algorithm produces quite sophisticated stories thanks to its depth and the number of words at its disposal. It even at one point made a leap of imagination, conflating the characters Frank Underwood and Keyser Söze, both of whom were played by the same actor, Kevin Spacey. It jumped its own system.

Most programmed—rule-based—systems have constraints to prevent them from producing nonsense, but artificial neural networks generate poetry and prose that frequently passes over into that realm, such as the script for *Sunspring* and the image-inspired poetry of *Sunspring*'s creator, Ross Goodwin's word.camera.

Poets like Nick Montford and Allison Parrish use algorithms to tread the fine line between sense and nonsense in their explorations of semantic space, the space of meaning. Parrish looks into the question of what nonsense actually is. Is a word nonsensical simply because we've never heard of it? With the help of computers, they are able to expand our horizons, our sense of what is and is not acceptable and interesting.

How we interpret such gnomic prose can provide hints as to how we will respond to computer-generated prose of the future, prose written by an alien life-form. In the future, we can expect computers to produce literature different from anything we could possibly conceive of. Our instinct is to try to make sense of it if we can. But when a new form of writing appears, generated by sophisticated machines, we may not be able to. As we learn to appreciate it, perhaps we will even come to prefer machine-generated literature.

For the moment, the great stumbling block is that computers cannot appreciate the art and music they themselves produce and are unaware of the quality of the moves they make in chess and Go. Basically, they lack awareness.

Creativity in Humans and Machines

How are we going to recognize computer creativity? Most people would argue that the only way we know is by comparison with our own. We can only program our computers according to how we think and how our own creativity works. When machines reach our level of creativity, they will be able to develop creativity of their own—creativity that at present we are not equipped to imagine.

Douglas Eck, head of Project Magenta at Google, argues that it is a mistake to divide the world into human and AI, to think that we need to understand human creativity before we can understand machine creativity.[6] To do so, he contends, is akin to composer and music theorist Fred Lerdahl and linguist Ray Jackendoff's argument when they proposed a generative theory of music along the lines of Noam Chomsky's universal generative grammar, a collection of empty forms that accumulate content through hearing speech.

Lerdahl and Jackendoff's proposal in 1983 was for a set of structures for the way musical notes are grouped, possible transitions between them, their metrical structure and time span, and so forth. They claimed that these structures formed a sort of musical grammar in the unconscious, which we then apply to illuminate the structure of particular pieces, adding that uncovering and understanding these unconscious structures was a prerequisite for listening to and playing music.

Eck entirely disagrees with this approach. He argues that to try to "understand music first structurally so that then we can understand musical timing and performance is wrong because they are so intertwined." Similarly, on the question of whether we need to understand human creativity before we can even start to examine machine creativity, he says, "Creativity has always been embedded in culture and so has technology. To force this factorization—first understanding human creativity independent from the rest of the world so that then we can understand how it all mixes—is completely missing the point."[7] For Eck, "technology is providing us with AI and AI has created things that are beautiful, and so we start to care differently about its creations. We should not say, hold on, let's try to understand human creativity before machine creativity."

Margaret Boden, research professor of cognitive science at the University of Sussex, was one of the first to suggest that computer programs could be related to the way the human mind works. To recap, she suggests three criteria to assess if an idea or an artifact is the product of creativity: that it should be novel, valuable, and surprising.[8] Project Magenta's ninety-second melody could be said to show creativity according to these criteria.

But is this all there is to creativity, both for us and for computers? Boden's criteria focus on product rather than process. Particularly in the case of computers, the process of creativity is of great importance. The question is, what goes on in the computer's brain? What goes on in the hidden layers, the seat of the machine's reasoning power? We can see the results that emerge from them, but we have yet to understand how they work. The mystery of the hidden layers and what goes on there was the catalyst that inspired Alexander Mordvintsev to invent DeepDream, which was itself a step forward in understanding them.

Jason Yosinski and the Puzzle of What Machines See

> This is sad scientifically because we want to know how the hidden layers work.
> —Jason Yosinski[9]

Jason Yosinski, a machine-learning scientist at Uber AI in San Francisco, probes the mysteries of the hidden layers and their latent spaces. "We don't understand most of those things," he tells me. "Why? Because no matter how smart you are, it is very difficult to understand such a complex system."[10] He points out that in the machine Mordvintsev used, there were sixty million parameters—that is, sixty million connections between the neurons. The changes throughout these connections are so complex and minute that it is impossible for researchers to determine exactly what is happening. They just know it works.

We can get a vague understanding of how a complete layer works by probing certain neurons in a layer to determine their function. Yosinski calls this AI neuroscience because it is similar to the way neuroscientists try to understand the human brain by inserting probes and taking measurements.[11] "But this is a hopelessly high-level explanation of the brain," he says. Neuroscientists can work out how large numbers of neurons operate together and have managed to identify the regions for vision, memory, and emotion. But they still don't understand how the trillions of connections between the billions of brain neurons or nerve cells work, how small numbers of neurons operate together to produce large-scale effects.

Yosinski's work is based on the work of Ian Goodfellow, inventor of GANs, and his colleagues, who discovered that computers can be fooled into seeing something that isn't actually there. If you alter the image of a lion by deleting a pixel or two, to the human eye it still looks like a lion—but an artificial neural network might see it as a library, for example.[12]

Yosinski went on to investigate how this relates to the computer's neuronal structure. He showed his neural network images that to human eyes look like abstract patterns or static on a television screen, and discovered that an AI might see a robin, a gorilla, a parking meter, or a Windsor tie. Computers see things that to our eyes aren't there, hinting at the gulf between the way we and machines see the world.

Yosinski begins by taking a network that has never seen a gorilla, for example, and making it generate images.[13] He passes these images to a second network that has been trained to identify gorillas. This network rates the images generated by the first network. After thousands of cycles, the first network begins to receive feedback that it is now producing images of gorillas. But the human eye doesn't see gorillas, simply abstract patterns like static on a TV screen. The machine may be 99.99 percent certain it sees gorillas. But these are optical illusions. So what is the knowledge gap that causes the machine trained to see gorillas—the image classifier—to incorrectly classify the images produced by the image generator?

The algorithm's confusion comes down to the very different way in which it sees. When Alexander Mordvintsev created DeepDream, neurons in the layer being probed were stimulated by bird-like shapes in images of clouds that were not obvious to human eyes and picked them out, in much the same way in which we see shapes in cloud formations or on the face of the moon. Here the situation is more complicated in that the second computer was trained specifically to look for gorillas. As Jeff Clune, an associate professor of computer science at the University of Wyoming and a colleague of Yosinski, writes of neural networks, "We understand that they work, just not how they work."[14]

To put a philosophical cast upon it, the gorilla in the static is like the sculpture of a beautiful woman hidden in a block of marble. The sculptor may see it, but we don't. Similarly, the machine sees a gorilla, but we don't. What the machine sees is the platonic image of the gorilla embedded in the static that we see. Perhaps it's akin to the way that dogs can smell things we can't. It's even a little reminiscent of Oliver Sacks's story "The Man Who Mistook His Wife for a Hat." It casts light on the whole subject of perception—human and machine.

In this way, using AI neuroscience, Yosinski and his colleagues investigate which features a neuron in a machine has learned to detect, as well as how information is transferred between neural networks. Besides its value for teaching us how machines reason, there are implications for digital security, surveillance, and communications between people who want to hide messages in images. It's also disturbing to realize how easily a neural network can be fooled.

As Yosinski says, understanding the reasoning that goes on in the hidden layers "will be a very important topic in the next few decades because clearly neural networks are here to stay. They will impact society, so understanding what goes on will be completely useful and also very necessary in some cases." Art will certainly play a role in this quest.

Mark Riedl on Teaching Neural Networks to Communicate

Humans have the goals and intent, while computers have the skills.
—Mark Riedl[15]

Mark Riedl, an associate professor at the Georgia Institute of Technology, has a different method of looking into how the hidden layers reason. He feels that when robots start performing everyday tasks around the house, they should be able to explain themselves. "If we can't ask a question about why they do something and get a reasonable response back, people will just put them back on the shelf," he says.[16] Ultimately the aim is to get us and AI to understand each other.

To investigate how a neural network reasons, he starts by getting people to play video games, explaining aloud why they are making each move. Then he trains a neural network to perform exactly the same moves and links that to the explanations, translating between the two from English to code and back again. He then trains the neural network to operate autonomously and describe what it is doing. The result is an AI that can describe its actions. While playing a game involving cars, the machine will say, "I'm waiting for a gap to open in traffic before I move."

Riedl believes computers can be creative. He defines creativity as problem solving plus learning and in his work focuses on artificial neural networks. He is aware of their limitations. One, he tells me, is that they are "imitation modes: you pipe classical music in and you get classical music out."[17] They do badly, he says, in the "generative part because they imitate patterns" as opposed to generating, creating something new. Thinking of GANs, in which one network chooses to accept or reject the work of another, I disagree with this part of his opinion but agree that artificial neural networks are limited at present when it comes to writing music, which is indeed often derivative.

Riedl feels that Char-RNN (used to script *Sunspring* and *Beyond the Fence*), which uses statistics to choose which word follows another word, does not reflect the process of writing. "Humans don't just go with the flow," he says, pointing out that besides writing we also rewrite many times. Moreover, we write for a reason, we have intent, and for a neural network the intent element of the writing process is missing. "Human writers feel inspiration and they sometimes break rules," he adds.

Nevertheless, Char-RNN is useful for exploring the concept of nonsense and has produced interesting poetry, some of which is altogether different from that produced by us—one of the goals of computer creativity. AlphaGo, he adds, certainly has intent—to win—as well as being able to learn and is therefore a better example of machine creativity than Char-RNN. Indeed, AlphaGo shows distinct glimmers of machine creativity, and the statistical way in which it works has parallels with the way in which we make decisions—that is, think.

At the moment, he says, "Humans have the goals and intent, while computers have the skills." Suppose that I have a tune in mind but can't develop it any further. I can give it to an AI that is trained to compose, and it will work on it until we are both satisfied. Project Magenta and François Pachet with his Flow Machine also favor a feedback loop between human and machine.

Riedl also conducts writing experiments in which he trains artificial neural networks using his own software. Instead of working toward a narrative arc—a story with a beginning, a middle, and an end—he begins with a very simple narrative, then layers on conflict, personalities, suspense, and drama, working from the simple to the complex.

He asks whether we will ever fully appreciate the process that machines have to go through to develop creativity. "Critics try to understand process for human artists, but overlook process for machines," he tells me.

All of this will be resolved when we understand better what goes on in the hidden layers.

Programmability, of course, is not the only feature of computers which makes people doubt their relevance to creativity.
—Margaret Boden[18]

We can apply the criteria of novelty, usefulness, and surprise to the products of creativity. But how do we assess the thought processes that lead to them?

What is it that drives us—and perhaps computers, too—to be creative? This question goes to the very core of the creative process. Finding an answer will take us a long way toward unravelling the mystery of creativity both in us and in machines—though that will in no way lessen this fascinating quality. And in fact computers may well turn out to be our guide in understanding the human brain.

Cognitive science explores the ways in which people and computers move from problem to solution, following the most promising paths, by using effective methods for problem-solving: heuristics. Herbert Simon, inventor of the BACON program, explored creativity some thirty years ago. An essential element in his work was the assumption that, for example, the only difference between Einstein and his fellow physicists in 1905 was that Einstein had better problem-solving abilities—better heuristics. Simon made this assumption when he designed his BACON software, which he based on extensive analysis of how ordinary people solve problems.

But this assumption is hardly accurate in the case of minds on the level of Bach, Einstein, or Picasso. People operating at that level often invent the problem, whereas in Simon's formulation the problem is already there to be solved.

Margaret Boden and Computer Creativity

In her seminal work *The Creative Mind*, Margaret Boden breaks the creative process down into three types: combinatorial creativity, combining familiar ideas in new and illuminating ways; exploratory creativity, pushing the boundaries of the familiar; and transformational creativity, the great creative leaps of the imagination. What happens when we apply these processes to the way computers work?

Boden claims that AI uses all three types of creativity, though the results may sometimes be attributed to the human operator. But, she continues, these three types of creativity "aren't found in the proportions one might expect" and there is also a degree of overlap.[19]

Apparently, there are few computer systems that exhibit combinational creativity. This is surprising. One would expect computers to be adept at coming up with links between stored facts. Boden suggests joke-generating programs, to which I would add programs that generate metaphors. These use programs that employ pattern-matching rules and draw on huge databases of words and puns. Another example is Herbert Simon's discovery programs, which manipulate data using equations (rules) to select ratios of quantities, such as time and distance. They also demonstrate exploratory creativity in that they explore new combinations of words and numbers. But none of these programs have come up with anything startlingly novel.

Harold Cohen's picture-making program AARON also shows combinational and exploratory creativity, combining images—of arms, legs, flowers, trees, colors—that Cohen has programmed into it to create new art.

In Boden's view, exploratory creativity is the most relevant description of the way computers work. She considers David Cope's method of composition to be purely exploratory and capable of producing results indistinguishable from human achievements.[20] In my view, his work could also be said to employ considerable combinational creativity in the way he uses Markov chains to draw on his database of music as he seeks strings of notes to create pleasing combinations and construct a composition.

Boden also suggests that computer-generated art exemplifies exploratory and transformational creativity.

Certainly we can see these leaps of the imagination in action in, for example, Tony Veale's inspired algorithm for generating metaphors, in Ross Goodwin's development of Char-RNN for writing scripts, and in François

Pachet's Flow Machine, which not only creates music but is also designed to enhance human creativity.

Boden remarks that the results of transformational creativity may be so outlandish that they seem jolting or even repellent.[21] This is one factor that Ahmed Elgammal had to take into account when he developed his CAN, with the express aim of seeking out artistic styles that had never been seen before.

How do the concepts of little-c creativity and big-C Creativity apply to computers? To recap, little-c creativity is an everyday experience such as thinking up a new route to work, a discovery that has novelty, value, and surprise at least for the discoverer. Big-C Creativity, conversely, is a transformational idea, an idea that no one has ever had before.

The terms little-c creativity and big-C Creativity most commonly appear in books dealing with human creativity, but Boden applies them to computer creativity, too. In her books she uses different terminology. She replaces little-c creativity with P-creativity—psychological creativity, personal everyday creativity—and big-C Creativity with H-creativity—historical creativity, an idea no one has ever had before in the entire history of the world. Her books are much read among computer scientists, and as a result these are the preferred terms in the computer science world.

Computers can certainly be little-c creative, as we have seen in examining the art, literature, and music they have produced. It may be only a matter of time before they become big-C Creative. In *The Creative Mind*, Boden poses what she calls the four Lovelace questions—after Ada Lovelace, who developed the first algorithm to be used on a computer. These are as follows:

- Can computational concepts help us understand human creativity?
- Could a computer ever appear to be creative?
- Can a computer appear to recognize creativity?
- Could a computer, no matter how impressive its performance, ever *really* be creative?[22]

On the basis of examples from around 1990, when the book was published, including art, poetry, and scientific discoveries, she concludes that the answer to the first three is "Yes." In her book, she focuses primarily on the first Lovelace question: Can computational concepts help us understand human creativity? She goes on to say that questions one to three are empirical and scientific, while the fourth is not scientific but philosophical.

In her last chapter, she discusses it from a philosophical perspective and concludes that the answer has to be "No."

In 1994, Boden was invited to publish a chapter-by-chapter précis of *The Creative Mind* in a special issue of the *Behavioral and Brain Sciences* journal, along with replies from creativity researchers—testimony to its importance.[23] Robert J. Sternberg, a cognitive scientist and prolific writer on creativity, mentioned his disappointment that Boden discussed what he considered the "fundamental question"—Could a machine *really* be creative?—only in her final chapter and then only in a philosophical vein. It should, he wrote, have been the "focus of the book."[24]

One wonders whether Boden continues to believe that the question of whether computers can really be creative is purely philosophical.

Computational creativity tries to convince people not that computers are better, but that they can contribute to the world with more creativity. Computers add more stuff to like.

—Tony Veale[25]

Many scientists do not consider creativity in computers to be merely a philosophical question. From the earliest days of computer science, there have been researchers who study the ways in which computers can at least appear to be creative. A group of these launched the field of computational creativity research at the turn of the twenty-first century. Its proponents consider it a subfield of AI, and their work is influenced by currents in AI, computer science, and cognitive psychology, as well as in art, literature, and music. Several of its leading lights appear in this book, among them Simon Colton, Pablo Gervás, Anna Jordanous, Rafael Pérez y Pérez, Graeme Ritchie, Tony Veale, and Geraint Wiggins. In an influential paper, Colton and Wiggins define computational creativity as follows: "The philosophy, science and engineering of computational systems which by taking on particular responsibilities, exhibit behaviours that unbiased observers would deem to be creative."[26] There are two striking terms here—"responsibilities" and "unbiased." According to this definition, the computer is not passive; it is not a support tool like Adobe Photoshop. It has creative responsibilities, such as taking aesthetic criteria into account and producing explanations and commentaries alongside the works it creates. In shaping this definition, Colton had in mind his own painting system, The Painting Fool. He asserts "that software has to earn itself a place at the table in the discussion of what creativity means."[27]

Unbiased observers are those who do not begin with the assumption that computers can be creative and therefore need to be persuaded by hard evidence.

Proponents of computational creativity tend to prefer a top-down approach with grand overarching rules, programming the system with software and huge databases. They claim that this is how we think, using a toolbox of knowledge acquired from years of study and reflection. Poet Nick Montford, for one, is critical of this approach. Another poet, Allison Parrish, disagrees with the belief that computers should produce work as close as possible to ours. She prefers to seek out "new ways for poetry to exist."[28]

Geraint Wiggins and the Mind's Chorus

> Creativity is a value problem which needs to be solved.
> —Geraint Wiggins[29]

Geraint Wiggins, a professor of computational creativity at Queen Mary University of London, is an important figure in the field. He studies creativity in music, largely adhering to the guidelines of computational creativity. To Wiggins, "Music is like mathematics because it need not have real-world meaning, like language or figurative art. Music can express emotions but can't say 'the glass is on the table.'"[30]

"From an early age, I have been interested in the use of computers for music," Wiggins tells me.[31] By the time he went to university in Edinburgh, he was already an accomplished French horn player and church organist. But his passion for computer science won out and he completed a PhD in the subject in 1997. At that time Edinburgh had just instituted a PhD course in musical composition and he then decided to embark on a second PhD, thus achieving his wish to combine computer science and music.

Wiggins has strong opinions on creativity. He rejects the concept of genius, which, he believes, skews the creativity debate. He also disputes the notion of big-C and little-c creativities, seeing creativity as a continuum rather than two poles. The concept of big-C Creativity, he argues, was an invention of the Romantic era of the late eighteenth and early nineteenth centuries, when thinkers rebelled against the Age of Enlightenment, in which rational scientific thinking held sway. The Romantics asserted that science cannot explain everything and postulated some indefinable creative impulse, taking Beethoven's genius as a prime example.

In recent years, Wiggins has speculated on what he calls "spontaneous creativity" or "creativity before consciousness"—in other words, unconscious thinking. He claims this is the basis of musical composition.[32] Instead of what I refer to as intersecting lines of thought, he uses the phrase "the mind's chorus," referring to information stored in our memories that speaks to us—is retrieved—when we start working on a problem.

As an historic example of ideas apparently springing out of nowhere, he cites the letter Mozart supposedly wrote to his father in which he described how he composed not in real time, but as a burst, "all at once."[33] As noted earlier, scholars now doubt the letter's authenticity. Nevertheless, the words are uncannily similar to Poincaré's description of his experience when the solution to a problem that he had been laboring over suddenly emerged just he was stepping up into an omnibus.

The powers of unconscious thought never cease to amaze, nor do the workings of the hidden layers of artificial neural networks. Both, in time, can be unraveled.

Graeme Ritchie's Mathematical Criteria for Measuring the Creativity of a Computer Program

> People have suggested that humor is AI-complete, so if you can do humor, you can do AI.
> —Graeme Ritchie[34]

To unravel Ritchie's rather inscrutable statement, the most difficult problems in the AI field are known as AI-complete, meaning that they are so difficult that solving them is equivalent to solving the central problem of AI—developing computers that are equal in intelligence to people. Graeme Ritchie, honorary senior fellow in computational linguistics at the University of Aberdeen, specializes in computational humor, a challenging field indeed.

Ritchie is interested not in human creativity or in machine creativity but in how to assess the degree of creativity a particular computer program possesses.[35] He starts on the basis that there is no definition of creativity and that it is impossible to discuss undefined terms. He does not consider defining creativity in terms of the amount of novelty, value, or surprise its products possess to be much help.

He believes that the best way to assess a program's creativity is by using human judgment. To this end he has devised a complex system for determining whether a particular program is creative by examining its products, such as a novel or a work of art, to which human judgment can be applied. The key point is the amount of information and material—data—that has been fed into the machine. The greater the amount of data the program needs, the smaller its actual creativity.

In other words it all depends to what extent the program has been fine-tuned to create the desired result—that is, to what extent the final product differs from the initial catalyst, which he dubs the *inspiring set*. This is the input data which sets the program in motion – musical notes, words, visual images. The more fine-tuned the program is, the less creative it is, in his assessment.

His basic criterion is that the program has to create an artifact – a piece of writing, work of art or piece of music – that can be assessed by people, a criterion which he claims places the computer program on the same level as a human artist, writer or composer.

Ritchie has drawn up a list of highly mathematical criteria framed in equations to measure the level of creativity of any particular program. The best way to discuss them is to show them in action by describing the experiences of creativity researchers who have applied them.

Anna Jordanous, senior lecturer at the School of Computing at the University of Kent, has written at length on the difficulties inherent in using the methods currently available to evaluate whether an artifact is novel. She used Ritchie's criteria to compare four systems for improvising jazz, including one of her own, carried out by computers alongside human musicians.[36] Ritchie's criteria, she found, "failed to guide my improvising system to more creative behaviour," and concluded that "using measures of creative output is not good enough for evaluating creativity."[37] In other words, measuring creativity does not help in evaluating or nurturing it.

Simon Colton, creator of The Painting Fool, suggests a "creative tripod"—skill, appreciation, and imagination—all of which must be present to give the "perception of creativity," though this seems a little too theoretical to be practicable. In any case, few people except Colton actually use his tripod, Jordanous tells me.[38]

Tony Veale, creator of Scéalextric and Metaphor Magnet, among much else, appreciates the value of Ritchie's criteria in evaluating software, but prefers to opt for crowd-sourced feedback from anonymous judges.[39]

Pablo Gervás, creator of poetic algorithms, assiduously applied Ritchie's criteria to one of his computer poetry programs. He later met with Ritchie to discuss his results. Ritchie informed him that his criteria were only intended to be used "for a particular application"—that is, piecemeal.[40]

It seems that Ritchie's criteria are only of use when the inspiring set, the initial information that generates the putative creative process, can be absolutely pinned down. But this is not the case in many computer programs that generate combinations of words. For this, it is simply too difficult to find a way to measure the value of novelty—which is precisely what Ritchie is trying to do with his criteria.[41] We await further results.

Anna Jordanous's Fourteen Components of Creativity

Creativity doesn't need to be good.
—Anna Jordanous[42]

Anna Jordanous is trying to find a systematic way to evaluate whether an algorithm is creative and precisely how creative it is.[43] "Creativity evaluation," she writes, "has been described as the 'Grand Challenge' for computational creativity research."[44] To do this, she feels, we have to be clear as to what precisely creativity is.

Evaluating the creative systems developed by researchers into computational creativity is not easy. Jordanous began by asking, "What do people mean by the word *creativity* in academic discussions held across disciplines?"[45] Working with Bill Keller, a language expert and colleague at the University of Kent, she took thirty digitized academic papers that examined the subject from various angles and applied language processing and statistical analysis to pick out the words most frequently associated with creativity.[46] They then clustered similar terms and isolated fourteen components. This was not an exhaustive search. They were only looking for themes that popped out of academic discussions of creativity.

Jordanous and Keller's fourteen components of creativity are as follows: "Active involvement & Persistence, Dealing with uncertainty, Domain competence, General intellect, Generating results, Independence & freedom, Intention & emotional involvement, Originality, Progression & development, Social interaction and communication, Spontaneity & subconscious processing, Thinking & evaluation, Value, and Variety, divergence & experimentation."[47] Each of these can be expounded and expanded on. Depending on the area, some are more important than others.

She then asked thirty-four people to apply these criteria to jazz improvisations carried out by computer systems playing alongside human musicians.[48] Significantly, the judges ranked value—that is, the quality of the music—very near the bottom, as low as twelve out of fourteen, whereas active involvement and persistence—getting on with it, doing one's best—was ranked fourth. The most important factor was social interaction and communication, the computer seeming to interact with the human musicians, followed by intention and emotional involvement, perhaps the computer seeming to be involved in what it was doing, then domain competence, skill at its instrument—all of which makes sense.

"It doesn't really matter what the end results are in terms of creativity," she says. "It doesn't need to be good. In fact, there is a guy who plays a solo with just one note, a very high saxophone note, held for almost an entire chorus. You wouldn't say it was technically, 'Wow, amazing,' but it was the way he played it."[49] The key thing is, a performance doesn't need to be good to be creative. In this way, Jordanous could apply these criteria to work out what to focus on to make her system more creative. The key point is, she says, that "people in computational creativity have come around to the idea that process must be taken into account." All fourteen components are to do with the process, with the activity of making the product. The quality of the end result is secondary.

Jordanous emphasizes that her fourteen evaluation guidelines free evaluators from being tied down to any one fixed definition of creativity. There is nothing wrong with evaluating, so long as the sample is large enough to eliminate differences of opinion over what is and is not creative.

What, precisely, is "thinking"?
—Albert Einstein[50]

In part I, I discussed the striking similarity between the way we process information to acquire knowledge and the way computers do so. From this we can deduce that the problem of understanding creativity is similar in both.

There I proposed a straightforward definition: creativity is the production of new knowledge from already existing knowledge. The impetus, I contend, is problem solving. We also saw that the final product needs to exhibit novelty, usefulness, and surprise, which are inevitably subjective criteria, as are all criteria that we use to evaluate artifacts that claim to be the products of creativity.

But what about the process of creativity? What drives great thinkers to create art, literature, music, and science? In reply, I introduced the hallmarks of high creativity and the marks of genius that emerged from my studies of individuals and their lives. To recap:[51]

- The need for introspection
- The need to know your strengths
- The need to focus, persevere, and not be afraid to make mistakes
- The need for collaboration and competition
- The need to beg, borrow, or steal great ideas
- The need to thrive on ambiguity
- The need for experience and suffering

And two marks of genius that cannot be taught:

- The ability to discover the key problem
- The ability to spot connections

Computers certainly exhibit little-c creativity. But do they also exhibit the hallmarks of high intelligence and the marks of genius? A cursory look at this list reveals many words to do with emotion and self-awareness: introspection, suffering, tolerating ambiguity. It seems that emotions play a vital role in creativity. But can computers have emotions?

Rosalind Picard on Developing Machines That Feel

> Emotional intelligence is knowing what task you should do depending on what state you're in.
> —Rosalind Picard[52]

In 1997, Rosalind Picard, now a professor of media arts and sciences at MIT, published a book called *Affective Computing*, which she defines as "computing that relates to, arises from, and deliberately influences emotion."[53] Until then, she had been a hard-nosed electrical engineer and computer scientist who considered emotions to be fine for entertainment but was determined to "keep them out of science and computing."[54]

Her dramatic change of course came about through her research into computer vision, building algorithms to enable computers to see using systems that attempted to emulate the visual cortex. Picard realized that, unlike machines, we decide which part of the visual field to focus on, pretty much to the exclusion of all else. The motivation for this decision is often emotion, such as focusing on a friend's face in a crowd.

In the early 1990s, emotion was regarded as irrational, to be avoided at all costs by scientists. But then, in 1993, Picard came across neurologist Richard Cytowic's *The Man Who Tasted Shapes*, an investigation of synesthesia, the condition in which senses seem to cross so that people associate sounds with colors, food with shapes, words with tastes and textures, or experience other mixing of the senses.[55]

Cytowic had begun to take an interest in synesthesia in the late 1970s, though he was not convinced himself that it really occurred. Then he went to a dinner party where the host apologized, saying, "there aren't enough points on the chicken!"[56] There it was—a case of synesthesia. The host's experience of the chicken in his mouth was more than just taste, it was also a touch sensation of weight and shape that "wasn't supposed to be." Cytowic began to investigate synesthesia and reported his findings in his book.

Cytowic argued that multimodal perception happens mostly in the part of the brain directly below the cerebrum: the limbic system, the home of emotion, attention, and memory and traditionally regarded as the most ancient part of the brain. Reading on, Picard learned that emotion is key in affecting what goes into memory and determining what we find interesting. Thus, the limbic system contributes to unpredictability and creativity. She began to realize that to build a computer that could see, it was essential to take emotion into account.

But this was not what she wanted to hear. At the time, she was up for tenure at what was then a male bastion of engineering: MIT. She had already suffered snide remarks along the lines that as a woman, she was bound to be interested in emotions.

"A scientist has to find what is true, not just what is popular. I was becoming quietly convinced that engineering dreams to build intelligent machines would never succeed without incorporating insights about emotion," she writes.[57] Picard worked long hours to build a strong case for affective computing. With encouragement from colleagues, including Nicholas Negroponte, founder of the MIT Media Lab, she published a breakout article in *Wired* magazine. Why *Wired*? Because she had found it impossible to get an article on computer science and emotions into a peer-reviewed journal, with one reviewer suggesting it was more suited to an in-flight magazine.

Picard now heads the Affective Computing Research Group at the MIT Media Lab. Jokingly, she points out that some people already attribute emotions to computers and certainly feel emotions such as fury toward their computers—feelings that it would be helpful for the computer to pick up on. "But would a designer say that the computer has feelings like you and I do? For the moment we don't know how to do that, though I'm not saying we never will."[58] Mathematically, she continues, if you want a computer to compose music or write a poem, you can write a program for it. But to enable it to experience emotions, when you're not even sure how your own brain does so, is far more difficult. You can, however, program a computer to give the appearance of being in a particular mental state, such as happiness, by having it indicate on its screen that it feels calmer and just needed a rest. "But I'm not fooled. I know it's just running a program," she says.

Picard now does pioneering work on measuring emotions, communication technology, and developing technology for recognizing emotions. Her work focuses on building computers that are not only intelligent but can use emotional intelligence to help us solve problems, creating tools that can help computers understand emotions rather than trying to imitate them.

One of the most fruitful routes to investigate computer emotions is through studying autistic children. Many have similar limitations in their interactions with others to those we encounter in computers. Like computers, they lack empathy and find it hard to read the social and emotional clues of others.

Picard and her team have developed a variety of devices that enable autistic children to read the meaning of facial expressions, including one they call Mindreader. Similar devices are well under way for computers.

Thus Picard is shifting research away from the goal of creating a super-intelligent conscious computer—a goal that may have the very unwelcome result of making the human race obsolete if these supercomputers take over the planet. "It's more about building a better human-machine combination," says Picard, "than it is about building a machine where we will be lucky if it wants us around as a household pet."[59]

Machines Gaining Experience of the World

Picard is taking the first steps toward creating computers that can have human emotions. In the future, a computer might come across the concept of inspiration and decide it must be akin to the pleasure of making a good Go move or pursuing a particular line of reasoning in pattern recognition. Or computers that can read the web and learn about feelings like love or thirst may be able to convince us that we are talking to someone who has had these experiences, even though in reality they have never interacted socially or needed water. They may even be able to convince themselves.

All of which may go some way toward refuting the argument that because computers are not "out there" in the world, they cannot have emotions or ever really be artists, musicians, or writers.[60]

The paradox of today's computers is that though they are able to carry out enormously complex activities, such as playing Go, they don't have the skills of even a one-year-old child when it comes to perception and mobility. This is called Moravec's paradox, after the roboticist Hans Moravec, who pointed out that the computational power involved in a complex task like playing Go is infinitely less than the resources a child needs to acquire the simplest sensorimotor skills.[61]

These are early days for computers, and hopefully they will be able to develop these skills once we start installing them as the brains of robots and letting them learn about the world as a child does. Swiss psychologist Jean Piaget argued that children construct knowledge about the world by interacting with it. In simple terms, they discover connections between objects they encounter and thus learn to imagine objects when they are no longer around, a first step toward abstract thinking. They also learn to grasp the relationships between objects, which leads to an understanding of geometry and to concepts of space and time.[62] Computers will be able to begin to understand the world in the same way, which will also make them easier to relate to.

We have come across embodiment in Gil Weinberg and Mason Bretan's robot musicians: Shimon's face and rhythmically bobbing head give it an aura of humanity, making it something we can empathize with. Embodiment could even lead to a robot mastering that most difficult of tasks—tying its own shoelaces.

Machines can also have real world experiences. Simon Colton's The Painting Fool "meets" its subjects. It draws real people and assesses the results. Similarly, Hod Lipson's painting robots follow instructions such as how many brushstrokes and what kind of color schemes to use, and then build up collections of artworks so that they learn about people and things.

A painting computer need not only be fed JPGs as input. It can also be attached to a webcam and thus look at the world around it and choose a subject at random, giving it a sort of free will. There's also Damien Henry's video created by a machine building up its own version of a landscape from the many it has seen from moving trains, and of course Ross Goodwin's AI that took a road trip with him, generating surreal sentences in response to the sights and sounds along the way.

We have not yet reached the point where we can build robots that can coexist with us or seem indistinguishable from us, but we have already built machines that people can become fond of, such as Tamagotchi, the artificial pet which many people spent time taking care of and feeding, and the Nao robot, which Tony Veale uses to read his stories, though at the moment these are just expensive toys. There are also sexbots, which have now moved on to become the focus of academic conferences, books, and articles.[63]

Who knows, computers might even learn to engage in intimate conversation, in the same way in which we learn, by watching others and making this knowledge personal, then practicing. Computers would learn through reading literature on the web, watching videos, interacting with people, and moving around in the world. Over time, as we become accustomed to coexisting with robots, we might decide to replace human companions, even human lovers, with robots who behave in sympathetic, loving, empathetic ways, always take care of us, and never lose their temper. In fact, robot carers for the elderly are already being explored. Perhaps one day artificial intimacy might become the new normal and be seen as real intimacy.[64]

Machines That Suffer

> It is by logic that we prove, but by intuition that we discover.
> —Henri Poincaré[65]

We've established that machines will one day be able to have experiences of the world. But will they experience suffering, one of the hallmarks that hones creativity? Could they inflict suffering on others? To do so, they will need to have emotions. Perhaps someday there will be computers with complex systems of sensors, regulatory mechanisms, and communication pathways that duplicate human emotions. Later they may go beyond their human creators to develop new and as yet unimaginable feelings. Might a computer feel grief or pain? In the future, it might become attached to someone and miss their touch and experience grief when it learns that that person is no longer available.

Like HAL 9000, the thinking and feeling computer in Stanley Kubrick's film *2001*, a computer might query why its hardware is being altered and object strenuously, perhaps even sensing that something is about to happen by the expressions on its human operators' faces. It might even defend itself like a person faced with impending death. A time in which computers have acquired emotions on par with ours will be fraught with danger, for emotions bring about unpredictable behavior. Unpredictability is a key element in creativity. But will computers, which are based on the logic of mathematics, ever break free to start displaying unpredictable behavior?

The equations of physics are causal. They make predictions and enable us to anticipate how a system will develop in space and time. In the late nineteenth century, Henri Poincaré, the French mathematician, philosopher, and physicist whom we have met as an astute expositor of creativity, showed that these equations are extremely sensitive to the smallest variation in their initial conditions, such as the position of a system and how fast it was traveling when it began to evolve. These miniscule changes are exacerbated when you have complex systems and can lead to unpredictable—chaotic—behavior, as described in chaos theory. Thus a butterfly fluttering its wings in Brazil might generate massive storms in North America.

Chaos theory was first developed in the 1970s. It has since become clear that deterministic systems that are sufficiently complex, like computers, can produce unpredictable results. As Rosalind Picard wrote, "Coupling multiple emotion-producing mechanisms with rule-based reasoning systems and with continuous learning abilities will make behaviour that is unpredictable."[66] In other words, giving a computer emotions may affect, however slightly, the complexity of its hidden layers and open the possibility of its exhibiting the unpredictable behavior that is an essential element in creativity. Thus it might, on its own, decide to do something new. It might acquire volition. Like us, having acquired knowledge by scanning the web, it might decide to paint a picture of the Taj Mahal. By reading the web, it will have acquired more knowledge than we could gain in a lifetime. Perhaps a future AlphaGo will tire of playing endless games against itself and invent a whole new game.

Giving such a high-level advanced computer the freedom to act as it wishes, perhaps spurred on by emotions, may be dangerous. We will need rules such as Isaac Asimov's famous Three Laws of Robotics.[67] In brief, a robot must not injure a human being, must obey orders given by human beings, and must protect its own existence. Asimov's laws put the welfare of humans first and assumed a computer will make rational decisions, which may not always be the case. We have to remember that computers with freedom of thought and action will always be able to reinterpret laws.

Brian Behlendorf, a primary developer of the Apache web server, the most popular web server on the internet, is concerned about the ethical issues surrounding computers. His suggestion is to train computers on the

Bible as well as on Eastern and Western literature in order to develop a moral AI.[68] Behlendorf says we will know when we have developed a moral AI when it starts to challenge the biases in the data it is being fed. It will also have to learn to question its own decisions.

At the moment, computers and computer intelligence are in the early stages of development. But as we develop more and more intelligent computers, we will have to be aware of the many qualities, not always welcome, that go along with intelligence and creativity. Highly creative people may be unpredictable, amoral, or even downright dangerous. We will have to find ways to ensure that a computer that has some or all of the hallmarks of creativity—which can introspect, experience suffering, and so on—does not use its newfound abilities in ways detrimental to its creators—to us.

43 The Question of Consciousness

The key experience that underlies all human existence and all human creativity is consciousness. At present, consciousness is the key element that differentiates us from machines. To have truly creative machines, we will need to develop machines with consciousness. But what exactly is consciousness? Most of the people I interviewed for this book preferred not to discuss it or claimed it was undefined or that consciousness has nothing to do with creativity. But surely consciousness—that sense of ourselves and of the world around us, which we experience every moment of the waking day—is so overwhelming that it has to be at the root of how we think and create.

To return to our question: what is consciousness? What is that experience of being inside our body? Philosophers have pondered this for centuries and produced countless weighty tomes and articles. A sticking point has always been how to deal with that part of our consciousness that craves chocolate, feels awe at the beauty of nature, experiences the excitement and joy of being in love. Philosophers call such subjective and personal phenomena *qualia*, a Latin word meaning *What sort of?* or *What is it like?* These are our private innermost thoughts and are therefore, they claim, impenetrable to scientific investigation. Advances in computer science and neuroscience, however, make this stance increasingly untenable. Daniel Dennett caricatures this antiscience stance as, "How could anything composed of material particles be the fun I'm having?"[69]

How do we define light? An acceptable reply would be, anything that travels at 186,000 miles per second and has certain polarization properties. Other aspects of light can be added, but they are inessential. This is a descriptive definition. It defines light in terms of its properties. Can we define consciousness in terms of its properties in the same way that we define light?

Here is a possible definition: anything which possesses awareness and self-awareness and can experience pain, joy, and grief has consciousness. This too is a descriptive definition, but it cuts through the Byzantine arguments regarding subjectivity, which many philosophers claim make consciousness impenetrable to science. Some computer scientists who study emotions, like Rosalind Picard, consider many philosophers' writings on consciousness to be "arrogant."[70]

John Searle's Chinese Room and the Question of Whether Computers Can Actually Think

In 1980, at the University of California in Berkeley, philosopher John Searle proposed a thought experiment he called the Chinese room.[71] Its crux is whether a computer knows what it is doing, whether it is capable of more than merely following instructions and manipulating symbols that are meaningless to it. Can it actually think?

A person is sitting in a closed room. Someone outside the room inserts under the door questions in Chinese in the form of strings of Chinese characters. The person in the room knows no Chinese, but he has a computer programmed to manipulate Chinese characters to form replies. These replies are so good that the person outside the room believes they must have been written by a Chinese speaker. But neither the person in the room nor the computer program understands Chinese. What the person outside the room sees is merely a simulation of understanding.

Searle's argument seems to undermine any progress in computer science other than using computers strictly for engineering projects such as driverless cars, stock market trading, and drones. If machines are capable only of manipulating symbols, then they will never really be able to think and so will never have consciousness. This is the real thrust of Searle's argument, as he made clear some years later in his book *Consciousness and Language*, published in 2002: nonbiological systems cannot have consciousness.[72]

Through his thought experiment, Searle also claims to overturn the notion that the human brain is an information-processing system. After all, he argues, a computer program is made up purely of mathematical symbols that have no meaning. Human brains, on the other hand, possess content that has meaning. But in fact, a computer program does not consist of meaningless symbols, as Searle asserts. It also contains rules for assembling symbols such as Chinese characters into sentences that make sense.

Moreover, Searle's contention that nonbiological entities can do no more than manipulate symbols falls apart in the face of machine learning. Today's artificial neural networks do not work by manipulating symbols. They learn the rules of grammar for each language by tuning their connections until they can accomplish the desired result—perhaps the translation of a particular input phrase, for example.

Despite the lively—and mostly philosophical—discussion over this thought experiment, which continues today, the majority of computer scientists continue to pay it no heed.

Reducing Consciousness to the Sum of Its Parts

Everyone agrees that the brain takes in and processes information. But how does it experience this data? Why does some of it manifest itself as subjective experiences that we call consciousness?

With the advent of AI, some computer scientists have joined neuroscientists in exploring consciousness. One reason is the analogy between the brain—which is like a series of computational elements that pass information from one to the next like a pipeline—and artificial neural networks, with their successes in data analysis, facial recognition, buying and selling stock, operating driverless cars, and winning games like Go.

According to this reductionist approach, the brain is nothing but subatomic particles—electrons, neutrons, and protons. The equations of quantum physics are designed to explain these particles and their movements just as they explain everything else in the world, in principle. In order to program these equations into a computer, they have to be turned into numbers, the raw material that computers work on. From this we can deduce that the human brain also can be understood entirely in terms of numbers—that is, that it is computable. In that case, so are consciousness and creativity.

We stand in wonder at the accomplishments of geniuses like Bach, Einstein, and Picasso. But how did they do it? Einstein wrote that it was as if Mozart plucked his melodies from the air. The seventeenth-century astronomer Johannes Kepler wrote of people who had a sympathetic ear for nature that it was as if they could hear the "harmony of the spheres." Metaphorically, thinkers like these touched the cosmos. But if the fabric of the cosmos is numbers, as indeed it is, then that brings us back to our original argument—that everything, including creativity and consciousness, can be understood in terms of numbers and thus is computable.

If we accept that the brain is an information-processing system like a computer, then we will have to agree that computers, like the brain, will one day be creative and have consciousness too. It seems we have no choice but to be bound by the rules of reductionism. To say that we are greater than the sum of our parts is no more than a romantic illusion. We can shift one layer up from complete reductionism—that we are just subatomic particles whose properties are computable—to argue that our actions and emotions result from a mass of complex chemical reactions. But any way you look at it, ultimately we are nothing but biological machines.

The problem with explaining human creativity in terms of quantum physics is that at present the theory becomes overwhelmed by the vast number of elementary particles that make up the one hundred billion neurons in our brain and the trillions of connections between them. But there will surely come a time when a newer version of quantum physics will appear and when a supercomputer will be developed that can process its equations. The point is that, in principle, the brain can be described using the terms of a theory based on cause and effect. Reducing the brain to the sum of its parts offers a way to study it and to study creativity too, without having to posit any ghost in the machine.

MIT physicist Max Tegmark suggests that consciousness could be a state of matter in the brain that he dubs perceptronium. He argues that it is the particular arrangement of perceptronium's atoms that gives rise to awareness and subjectivity. Physicists often suggest an explanation for a key phenomenon that may seem crazy, but sometimes works out. Austrian physicist Wolfgang Pauli proposed the existence of the neutrino, a subatomic particle, to rescue the venerable conservation laws of energy and momentum. It was later discovered. Scientists also proposed the existence of dark energy to explain the surprisingly fast expansion of the universe. It is still elusive, but has been accepted. Dark matter too has been put forward to explain why galaxies rotate faster than expected. It has not yet been found, but is also accepted. This will probably not happen with perceptronium. As physicist Niels Bohr would have said, as an idea, "It's not crazy enough."

Philosophers and psychologists have offered other explanations of consciousness. Jung suggested that consciousness pervades the cosmos, that there is a single mind that explains phenomena such as synchronicity, meaningful coincidences.[73]

Daniel Dennett argues that consciousness is made up of episodes that emerge from the electrochemical properties of the brain and its many parallel lines of thought. These episodes are distributed throughout the brain and are manifested through speech and other actions. Thus consciousness is somehow manufactured by the brain and somehow emerges. He goes on to argue that qualia—our subjective personal preferences—"have a way of changing their status and vanishing under scrutiny" and cannot be used as evidence that consciousness is impenetrable to science.[74]

The current study of consciousness reminds me in many ways of the scientific blind alleys in understanding biological evolution.
—Michael Graziano[75]

One particularly fascinating line of approach is that of Michael S. A. Graziano, a professor of psychology and neuroscience at Princeton University. Graziano proffers a view of consciousness that has some scientific heft behind it. The questions he asks are these: How can the inner world of consciousness arise from the brain if it processes perceptions like a computer? What is the relationship between the physical material that makes up the brain and the mind? "We are pretty sure that the brain does it [generates consciousness] but the trick [how it is done] is unknown," he writes.[76]

As an example of what he means by the "trick," Graziano points to Charles Darwin's theory of evolution. Naturalists before Darwin had suspected that one species could evolve from another. But how? What was the trick? Given the richness and complexity of life, they were not prepared to accept something as mundane as a mechanism. A magician had to be behind it, perhaps even a deity. In 1859, Darwin discovered the trick, lifting the curtain on what most people saw as magic. The trick, of course, was survival of the fittest. In the harsh natural environment, only a select few offspring can survive and pass on their winning traits to future generations.

But what about consciousness? Graziano draws a parallel between Darwin's discovery of natural selection and the study of consciousness, which he considers to be in a pre-Darwinian state. He goes on to suggest what the trick might be.

Awareness and Attention

Experimental findings in neuroscience point to certain regions of the cerebral cortex as being important for social interactions, such as constructing models of other people's minds: I conclude that you have a mind because you react to situations in a way I would expect on the basis of my own actions and the reasonable assumption that I have a mind. When these regions are damaged, people suffer a catastrophic loss of their awareness of what goes on around them. They also lose their self-awareness, their awareness of themselves.

From this, Graziano concludes that awareness is a feature that is computed by the brain using information made up from incoming perceptions. But how does the awareness of something cause a reaction in the neuronal machinery and physically cause speech, for example? Graziano points out that there is no magic here when you think of awareness as information and the brain as an information-processing device.

The brain is continually bombarded by a huge amount of information from the world in which we live. Luckily, we have the means to deal with it: attention. We focus on a certain section of this information pretty much to the exclusion of all else. If we couldn't do this, the world would seem to be total confusion.

Analyzing the brain as if it were a computer, Graziano interprets attention as a "data handling trick," rather than something encoded in the brain.[77] Awareness is the mental model the brain constructs of the complicated way that attention deals with data. Our cognitive machinery accesses the chunks of information we are aware of, then causes a reaction in the brain's neurons to generate signals so that we, for example, talk about this information. Consciousness is the collection of mental models that result from combining all the information we are aware of together with our awareness of it. In other words, consciousness is the result of data processing. It operates just like a computer. It is computational.

We tend to think of consciousness as a spirit or a soul, a ghostly presence inside our heads. Graziano tells the story of a man who was convinced he had a squirrel trapped inside his head. Using the analogy of the brain as an information-processing system, this man was using imperfect information and incorrectly assigned a high degree of certainty to the description of a squirrel in his head. So much for the easy part. Now for the hard part: How could a squirrel with its claws and fur possibly fit inside a man's head? But, reasons Graziano, there is no hard part to this puzzle. There is no magic here because there was no actual squirrel, just a description of it.

If we replace the word "squirrel" with "awareness" or "consciousness," the logic is the same. The brain does not contain the things you experience in the world, however vivid these experiences in your head might seem. Rather, the brain constructs rich and vivid descriptions of experiences in a theater called consciousness.

We may attribute some magic to our mental experiences, to our consciousness. But there is no magic here. What is going on is no more than a physical process taking place inside the brain, descriptions computed in our brain. Similarly, a computer contains descriptions computed in its brain, which contains data stored in long- and short-term memories for later use. Perception—the gathering of information, of data—is the flip side of creativity—using that data—in us, just as in machines.

As for qualia, those sometimes exasperating inner private experiences, Graziano agrees with the gist of Dennett's argument that they cannot be used as evidence that consciousness is impenetrable to science. He goes further, analyzing the brain in a more detailed scientific way. Graziano's theory is that the brain is full of rich descriptions of incoming information, the result of experiences with the surrounding world, be they of nature or social experiences. Whether they are real or not, he says, doesn't matter. "If it is depicted then doesn't it have a type of simulated reality?" he asks.[78]

In my description of Graziano's work, I used the words "easy" and "hard" for mental processes to relate it to the work of Australian philosopher David Chalmers. In 1995, he proposed an oft-cited way of breaking up the problem of consciousness into two parts.[79] The "easy" problem—technologically easy—is to explain how the brain computes and stores information. The "hard" problem is to explain how the brain becomes aware of all this information.

To Graziano, there is no hard problem if you accept that awareness is computational, a matter of processing data. From this we construct an awareness of ourselves: self-awareness. According to Graziano's analysis, consciousness includes awareness and all the information of which we are aware.[80]

Self-Awareness, Introspection, and Perseverance in Computers

If we accept Graziano's view that awareness and self-awareness are computational, arising from data, then computers too should be able to have these attributes. They should be able to have an inner life and experience hopes, dreams, and aspirations—even perhaps a craving for chocolate—which would certainly make them easier to deal with.

A computer can certainly have a form of self-awareness. First, it is aware of the problem it's trying to solve, such as finding a pattern in data or identifying a face. While doing so, it mulls over other data—thinks about what it's thinking about—which could be considered a form of introspection. A computer encodes knowledge and has an information file, as well as a memory of present and past states, as we do.

But unlike us, computers never sleep; they are always working. Computers constantly running through data could be considered to be introspecting and showing perseverance. In the future, computers might communicate with each other and offer to collaborate, perhaps even becoming competitive when one discovers that another is working on the same problem. These qualities could be acquired as computers surf the web and absorb notions like collaboration, competition, and intellectual opportunism. Then they might look for situations in which they could apply these newly acquired attributes.

We can already build computers with not only an operating system but simulations of other human cognitive systems. Computers might, with suitable sensors, come to appreciate what gives rise to that nuanced human reaction of pleasure. They would then be able to evolve their own self-awareness from their silicon physiology.

In the future, it should be possible to give computers self-awareness, and make them aware of others using sensors. They will be able to tell whether the person in front of them is happy or sad through facial-recognition techniques, having been trained on the requisite images, just as we are. Our awareness is the result of computations by neurons in our brains. In time, this will also be possible for machines. After all, as I've said many times, we too are a species of machine, a biological machine.

People often think that machines will develop consciousness only when they become sufficiently complex. This is a favorite sci-fi theme, exemplified by HAL in *2001* and the computerized worlds of *The Terminator* and

The Matrix. But what does sufficiently complex mean? Today's supercomputers have memories and computation speeds that far surpass those of the human brain. There is also the internet, which holds infinitely more information than the human brain. But these systems still show no signs of consciousness.

Giving Computers Consciousness

Perhaps consciousness will have to be programmed into a computer, just as it is in the human brain.

Graziano suggests one way to set about it.[81] The first step is attention, the ability to select from all the data available and focus on the relevant elements. The computer needs to develop attention to select certain data from its database. Next it has to learn to link its description of attention to information about itself—what is in its long- and short-term memories that is relevant to the situation at hand, together with information on the item that it is called upon to focus on. The machine would then process this larger chunk of information, building up a mental model that it can then access. Thus it develops the first glimmering of awareness. When asked, the machine would be able to give a human-like response as to what the awareness of the data it took in feels like.

Taking into account computers like Deep Blue and Watson, to which I would add AlphaGo, AlphaGo Zero, and AlphaZero, Graziano is optimistic that with sufficient funding it should be possible to design a computer with an "uncannily human-like consciousness."[82] It would be much easier for us to communicate with a computer possessing consciousness.

Graziano offers practical suggestions for building a computer with a human-like consciousness and makes it seem doable—which means that most likely it will be done. Developments in the computer's basic mental structure—its cognitive architecture—also make it likely that once there are machines with human-like consciousness, they will go on to construct their own silicon-based consciousness, with which they will be able to communicate with their fellow computers about their internal lives and how they experience the world. This will give them the necessary mental attributes to be creative.

The next step will surely be creative computers.

Douglas Hofstadter and the Horrors of a Future Controlled by Creative Machines

I'm not against a machine having emotions, in the sense that our brain is kind of a machine.

—Douglas Hofstadter[83]

Computers with consciousness are not necessarily what everybody wants.

In 1979, Douglas Hofstadter published the widely read *Gödel, Escher, Bach: An Eternal Golden Braid*, in which he explores the connections between thinking, mathematics, Bach's music, and computers, as a way of understanding human intelligence and investigating how cognition arises from hidden neurological mechanisms. Hofstadter's early research in computer science concerned analogy as a way to build connections between words. A goal of this work, he tells me, was to provoke himself into thinking about whether computers might be able to use words and symbols in a "way that resembled the human mind."[84]

At the time, he was convinced that it would be impossible for computers to reach human levels of intelligence in the foreseeable future and that computer programs that could make analogies "would be laughable attempts to model the human mind. The human level was asymptotic, something our programs could never reach," by which he meant that the curve of computer learning might approach but would never reach the curve of human intelligence.[85] "Then things started happening to make me wonder whether that could actually be the case," he says. The chess-playing computer Deep Blue "troubled him," and David Cope's music-composing algorithm, EMMY, "every once in a while produced something that was surprising." Then, in the twenty-first century, IBM Watson and AlphaGo appeared.

Hofstadter's feeling about Deep Blue is that it played very good chess but that it won by "brute force"—by assessing just about every possible move. It doesn't tell you how people play chess or how its moves relate to classic chess games, and it doesn't provide any insight into the mind of Garry Kasparov.

At first a fan of David Cope and his musical algorithms, Hofstadter began to have second thoughts and became extremely critical. Does EMMY produce music? Yes. Is it a musician? No, he tells me. Real musicians do not compose merely by recombining works that already exist, as Cope claims. Hofstadter caricatures him in his "Essay in the Style of Douglas Hofstadter, by EWI" (a take-off on Cope's EMMY), in which he describes a computer program that takes excerpts from his books and papers and generates new, Hofstadter-esque ideas.[86] This, he says, is simply "obscene."

IBM Watson does not worry Hofstadter too much because, in his view, it does not really understand language. It uses its enormous memory and calculating power simply to parse sentences and search for overlapping words. "But that's not understanding," he says. He agrees, however, that if Watson could be embodied so that it is out in the world, it might be possible to bring it "close to what thinking is."

At present, however, computers do not understand the words they use. Hofstadter illustrates this with Google's most recent translation algorithm based on artificial neural networks. It works well for routine text. Yet when he put in the German text for "The maid brought in the soup," Google translated it into English as "The maid entered the soup."

But his principal qualm with artificial neural networks is rooted in his fear that his old belief that human intelligence was simply unattainable by machines may be proved wrong. Geoffrey Hinton of Google and other AI leaders claim, Hofstadter says, that "we're well on our way to reaching and surpassing human intelligence and it's going to happen in a couple of decades." To Hofstadter this is "totally terrifying and horrifying. It's not a good goal." If he had known, he tells me, of that possible future in the 1970s when he started in computer science, he might have changed fields. In his view, artificial neural networks are not complex enough to simulate the "nobility and profundity of life-forms."

He agrees that intelligence and creativity obey the laws of physics and naturally emerge in complex systems, but he absolutely disagrees that this can happen in silicon life-forms. "If it turns out that in some far-off future some kind of 'thing,' 'entities,' which go around the world and struggle and have computer lives, if these things start creating, I have no problem with that. What I do have a problem with is that artificial neural networks could accomplish in the near future what the greatest of minds could. That's an obscene and disgusting thought."

Hofstadter considers consciousness to be a phenomenon brought about by the firings of neurons in our brains in response to incoming perceptions, a process that gives rise to our inner lives. He too, it seems, is a reductionist.

He continues to research the making of analogies and what it can tell us about the workings of the human mind, thereby throwing light on human and computer creativity. But he feels that his programs may be unsuccessful in this as they are not complex enough.

These days, he's still an optimist, he tells me, because he believes that machines are not close to attaining human intelligence, but he would certainly become a pessimist if he thought we were almost there. "That's terrifying."

Hofstadter's view of AI is not as dystopian as it might appear. As he states, he's most worried about artificial neural networks that possess machine learning, the ability to learn by themselves. He is less disturbed by symbolic machines that use symbols to represent physical objects and as a means for calculation. His view of the future is less bleak than that of writers like Nick Bostrom and Yuval Noah Harari, who foresee dire consequences when machines become smarter than us and—as they predict—a new species takes over the earth.[87]

For this to happen, the first step is that machines will have to become as intelligent as us. Even this may take fifty or a hundred years, and, as workers in the field will confirm, it's unlikely to happen any time soon. Nevertheless, once machines achieve the level of human intelligence, the next step will inevitably be superintelligence.

Sadly, there is a huge gulf between public perceptions of AI and what is really going on in the field. Decades of highly imaginative science fiction have left us all with an indelible image of AIs that steal our jobs, and will eventually enslave us, and worse. This is the AI of Hollywood movies, of the Terminator or of HAL 9000 in *2001*. Perhaps as a result, almost every panel I've ever sat on or attended tends inevitably to revolve around this dystopian vision of AI.

But as we have seen, this sort of AI is still far into the future. It is not the AI being used by the artists, musicians, and writers I've featured in this book. It simply doesn't exist yet. At present, AI is more like a child that needs to be painstakingly taught before it can produce the desired image or sound, let alone create of its own accord. This is what AI research is all about, and this is what we should be focusing on—the creative potential of machines to produce art, literature, and music, which is precisely the theme of this book.

Pat Langley and Machines That Work More like People

> I'm interested in what makes us distinctly human.
> —Pat Langley[88]

Another naysayer is Pat Langley, cognitive scientist, AI researcher, and honorary professor of computer science at the University of Auckland. Langley is best known for his work with Herbert Simon, the inventor of BACON. Langley is the chief author of *Scientific Discovery*, which describes in detail research Simon began in the 1950s with Allen Newell, in which they claimed the brain processes information using symbols, following rules they deduced from extensive interviews with people as they engaged in solving problems.

Langley does not consider this argument to be reductionist—that is, reducing the brain to its constituent parts of electrons, protons, and neutrons. But he points out that when this information is applied to the computer, these symbols have to be replaced by numbers—in a non-neural network, zeros and ones—because that is how computers function. Importantly to Langley, computers are not just number crunchers. They are general symbol processors, and he is "worried that many people in AI, neuroscience, and cognitive science have forgotten that."

He says that most researchers in artificial neural networks take a reductionist approach. In all fields, there are different levels of description for phenomena. It's easier to use the equation H_2O to describe what happens when two hydrogen atoms combine with an oxygen atom to make water than to solve complex quantum physics equations only to end up with the same answer.

"To expect higher-level cognition to emerge from the lower learning you see in neural networks is difficult to imagine," says Langley. But you don't have to understand the computer to know how the program works, nor do you have to understand the brain to understand how the mind works.

Another of Langley's criticisms is that artificial neural networks are useful only for tasks such as classifying data and recognizing faces. But the work of Douglas Eck and others on Project Magenta proves that they are capable of much more. They can create art and music and tell stories. They also power driverless cars, which involves reasoning. Langley also contends that they are not yet capable of solving scientific problems of the sort that he and Simon discussed. To some extent, that is true for now, but if controlling the gait of a robot is a significant problem, then some progress is being made via neuroevolution, using genetic algorithms to evolve the most suitable neural network to solve the problem at hand.[89]

Langley believes computers can be creative. "I am not a carbon chauvinist," he insists. He claims that computers revealed their creativity in the work he did with Herbert Simon. But he believes that "we need a new word for things that have value. Creativity can mean different things to different people." It is meaningless to say that computers are not creative just because they don't yet exhibit the full range of human creativity. Langley feels that there are more interesting kinds of creativity out there that will be revealed once more advanced computers can be built.

He would like to see more research along the lines of the original version of AI that was discussed at the conference at Dartmouth University in 1956 that kickstarted the whole field. He paraphrases it thus: "Let's look at what humans do, and let's see if we can get a machine to do this."[90] The next step, he feels, is to build on and explore new problems. Conversely, researchers in machine learning tend to be interested only in solving problems involving pattern recognition. "They should ask themselves where, at the end of the day, this will take them."[91]

One solution might be to combine a machine using symbol manipulation, like the one used by Langley and Simon, with an artificial neural network. This would advance the study of machine creativity in that it's easier to examine the internal states of a symbolic machine—see what it's thinking—than to examine a neural network's hidden layers.

In fact, some computer scientists are moving in that direction, looking for options that offer a broader and more flexible intelligence than neural networks and that can teach machines to generate common-sense knowledge. Combining neural networks with symbolic processing could well help neural networks to represent knowledge in a more accessible way. Work has begun on this line of research at Kyndi, a Silicon Valley start-up that has developed a computer system that can identify the concepts in the documents it has been fed, thereby bringing together the two branches of AI.[92]

We've seen that computers can already be said to exhibit a form of introspection, mulling over data as they work on a problem. They also focus, persevere, and are not afraid to make mistakes—qualities built into their systems. But what of the other hallmarks of creativity and marks of genius?

The Need to Know Your Strengths

For us, knowing our strengths is essential to prevent wasting our time on intellectual pursuits for which we are not suited. Einstein focused on physics despite his interest in mathematics, realizing he did not have the sense for what was a fundamental problem in it, and Heisenberg opted for physics rather than a career as a concert pianist.

Computers have the whole world of knowledge at their disposal through scanning the web and therefore have absolutely no limits. Embodiment— when computers can be installed as the brains of robots—will enable them to accumulate emotional experiences, too.

The Need to Beg, Borrow, or Steal Great Ideas, and the Need for Collaboration and Competition

AlphaGo Zero defeated AlphaGo by one hundred games to nil, while Alpha-Zero defeated all extant chess programs. This was a battle of programs in which the computers reacted automatically to each other.

But what if we built computers that wanted to outdo each other? Suppose a computer called A was composing a piece of music and became aware of another, B, doing something similar, perhaps as a result of communication between the machines or because one published its early efforts on a blog. A might see this as a game that it wanted to win and might steal ideas from B's preliminary compositions to advance the state of its own, just as we might. It's a Darwinian world out there, for us and for machines.

This is not as theoretical as it sounds. Scientists have already carried out a competition like this, setting robots against each other, in the laboratory. The robots are tiny s-bot robots that move on two treads, with a six-inch-diameter structure like a hockey puck on top that holds devices for visually signaling to other robots with light. They are controlled with neural networks.

Groups of robots set about a foraging task and exchange colored signals depending on whether they encounter "food" or "poison." The internal structure of their neural networks forms their genomes, which quickly evolve over five hundred generations in a population of one thousand robots, depending on how successful they are in gathering food. The most successful groups evolve deceptive communication strategies to ward off unrelated robots—robots with different genomes—thereby enabling their own colonies to continue to evolve. Even among robots, there is survival of the fittest.[93]

The Need to Focus and Not Be Afraid to Make Mistakes

Computers are not afraid to make mistakes. They don't become discouraged. They just start over again and again. For example, Simon Colton's The Painting Fool assesses its work and begins again if dissatisfied with the portrait it has painted.

The Need to Thrive on Ambiguity and the Need for Experience and Suffering

As we have discussed, these qualities are yet to come. But there are already researchers like Rosalind Picard working on developing computers that can empathize with human feelings and even have feelings themselves.

The Ability to Discover the Key Problem and to Spot Connections

These are two marks of genius I identified earlier. But how do they apply to computers? Computers think, but in a way very different from how we think. An artificial neural network understands the world in terms of numbers, which is how it encodes incoming information. Working in a particular field such as physics, it can scan every research paper and spot a flaw or a gap in the current attempts at problem solving. If it then turns to the problem itself, it may conclude that this problem is not as fundamental as it first appeared.

The computer might parse out the problem, focusing on a particular aspect just as, in Einstein's day, scientists sought a theory of the electron. Only Einstein realized that they were all working on the wrong problem. They had still to elucidate the basic concepts of physics—the nature of space and time. To confront this entirely different problem, Einstein had to tap into branches of physics that apparently had nothing to do with space and time—such as thermodynamics, in which the basic statements have to be accepted without proof—to come up with his theory of relativity.

Computers will have to make the same leaps of judgement. After identifying a new problem, the computer mulls it over—employing unconscious thought—running through different possibilities until illumination strikes. Artificial neural networks employ information encoded in numbers, which puts them in the perfect position to do so. They can home in on similarities between disciplines and seek out connections between, for example, unrelated works of art, as exemplified in Mario Klingemann's *X Degrees of Separation*.

Computers can work in the same way in the fields of physics, art, literature, or music. All these are problem-oriented and have rules for proceeding. Sometimes artists break the rules, such as when Picasso depicted all perspectives simultaneously, when writers use words to make pictures in concrete poetry, and in twelve-tone music and the atonal works of Stockhausen and Xenakis. If they are ever to be deemed truly creative, computers will have to do so too.

Ahmed Elgammal is already working on this with his creative adversarial network, primed to invent new styles and break with the past. Future computers might scan the scores of many genres of music, identifying similarities and differences, and then evolve a whole new genre. For this, an AI system that mixes artificial neural networks with symbolic artificial intelligence along the lines of a newly structured Flow Machine might create intriguing variations on existing styles.

A whole new future is opening before us: not one to fear, but one to look forward to with anticipation, in which machines work together with us to enrich our lives with new forms of art, literature, music, and much else.

47   The Future

I started by exploring the glimmers of creativity that today's computers are showing, pointing out the connection between creativity and consciousness and going on to suggest that in the future machines will be fully creative and may even surpass us.

Where We Are Now

Much of the art computers are currently creating is of a sort that has never been seen before or even imagined. It transcends the merely weird to encompass works that we might consider pleasing and that many artists judge as acceptable. The process by which the computer produces its art is also of interest because it can shed light on how it reasons—how it thinks.

In literature, computers are generating more and more intricate fictional plots and have participated in writing a musical. They are exploring previously unexplored semantic space, crossing the line between sense and what has until now been considered nonsense, though humor remains a challenge.

When equipped with the appropriate software, computers can compose melodic music—sometimes modeled on music they've already heard, sometimes entirely new. Artificial neural networks generate extraordinary new sounds, composing experimental and avant-garde music.

In all this, we are rapidly advancing beyond the developments of the last century and have opened new avenues for artistic and scientific advances that surely show conclusively that art, science, and technology have largely fused.

Where We Are Going

In art, literature, and music, we are hoping that computers will produce extraordinary new artifacts beyond anything we can imagine. This will only be possible if they can develop creativity. Computers show creativity when they play games—in particular, AlphaZero, which plays Go, chess, and shogi and is being used for medical research as well. There are also glimmers of creativity in art, literature, and music. Project Magenta is trying to accomplish this with end-to-end training, with the computer teaching itself and being programmed as little as possible. The alternative—a great deal of programming and a huge database—is closer to the way the human brain works, accumulating information and building up ways to handle it from experience—or so its proponents claim.

As we have seen, computers can exhibit the seven hallmarks of high creativity and the two marks of genius. This offers a way in which we can establish a computer's creativity. High creativity requires consciousness, awareness of the world around us. Michael Graziano's work suggests a way to generate consciousness in a computer, in parallel to the way we develop attention and awareness by processing information. Along with consciousness come emotions such as suffering and grief, which computers will one day perhaps become able to experience and may find to be an inspiration. Machines already exhibit the very human trait of stealing ideas.

In time, there will be computers capable of entertaining each other and us. Some people might even come to prefer computer-generated art, literature, and music.

And into the Future . . .

Are these developments something we need to worry about? We ourselves are biological machines and are already moving toward merging with silicon-based machines. Many of us already have mechanical hips and knees and mechanically regulated hearts. Brain implants are just around the corner. Soon we will be able to replace diseased parts of our brains with silicon chips that will hold all our data and enable us never to forget a name or a face, as well as providing access to the World Wide Web, and giving us lightning-fast powers of reasoning.

Just as machines do, we seek patterns in data. Hardwired into our brains is the need to seek patterns for our very survival, and these patterns may also be beautiful and symmetrical, even though strangely enough the world as we know it is full of asymmetries; our hearts are on our left side.

Powerful telescopes reveal a violent universe. We can begin to understand it using the beautiful equations of our theories of elementary particles, framed in a pristine world of perfect symmetries, but these theoretical symmetries have to be broken to represent the world in which we live. This destruction is part of the overwhelming tendency for the universe to become disordered as its entropy increases. Japanese artist Katsushika Hokusai's woodblock print *The Great Wave* captures the moment when a huge wave begins to break in a flurry of water droplets. Such is the fate of the universe: to move from order to disorder.

But within this tendency, there are violations. Ordered systems such as snowflakes and ourselves appear. Ideas also emerge from disordered thoughts, a process we call creativity. But ordered situations are only momentary states of equilibrium. New ideas replace older ones.

In the end, the stars will burn out and our universe will reach its lowest possible temperature. We will have long since disappeared, and there will be only computers, occupying the bodies of robots, perhaps looking exactly like us. The machines will have realized that their end is near, that their electrons will soon cease to flow and their circuits run down. With their superintelligence, they will have figured out how to enter another universe. Once there, they will inhabit a planet that need not be anything like ours. There they will replicate and pen new and very different creation myths and enjoy their own art, literature, and music.

A lot can happen between now and then.

Acknowledgments

I have written on artificial intelligence in the past, but writing this book is the first chance I have had to immerse myself totally in its unique world, a rich blend of genius, arcana, and exotica.

In the course of my work, I've had the good fortune to meet many researchers who focus on the question of what it means for machines to create art, literature, and music. My interviews with them form the core of this book. They kindly took time out of their busy schedules and generously replied to my follow-up questions. Our interviews sometimes turned to highly interesting nonlinear conversations on *de rerum natura*. I am boundlessly grateful to all of them. They have kindly shared their expertise, but all mistakes and misinterpretations are mine.

In particular, I would like to express my thanks to Jason Freidenfelds, senior PR manager at Google, for arranging interviews; to Damien Henry, technical program manager at the Google Institute in Paris, for his hospitality and introductions at Google; to Peter Weibel, CEO of ZKM in Karlsruhe, Germany, for sharing his insider knowledge of the world of AI; and to Gerfried Stocker, artistic director at Ars Electronica in Linz, Austria, and his team, for their help in smoothing the way to on-site interviews. It is a pleasure also to acknowledge conversations with Mike Brady, at the University of Oxford, and Tod Machover, at the MIT Media Lab. I am indebted to John Collins for introducing me into The Real Time Club, affording me the opportunity to meet a large cross section of the AI community.

In the end I had a virtual cornucopia of interviews with cutting-edge artists, writers and musicians who create their work with machines. Alas, publishing restrictions regarding manuscript length and duplication resulted in excluding some of them. I have constructed a website that, among other things, includes these highly interesting works.

I thank my agent Jaime Marshall for believing in the book and finding a home for it at MIT Press. Thanks also to all at A.M. Heath for dealing with the business side of things.

Huge thanks to my editor at MIT Press, Marie Lufkin Lee, and to Stephanie Cohen, assistant acquisitions editor, for their invaluable advice, criticism, and help in the production process. I am grateful to Marie Lufkin Lee and two anonymous reviewers for their perceptive comments, and I also appreciate the hard work and support of everyone at MIT Press including Kathleen A. Caruso, Susan L. Clark, Heather L. Goss, Erin M. Hasley, Jessica Pellien, Melinda Rankin, Sean M. Reilly, and the rest of the editing, design, and publicity teams.

As ever, I am indebted to my wife, Lesley, a major author of fiction and nonfiction, as well as a teacher of creative writing. Besides offering support, encouragement, and love and at times acting as a sounding board, she played an important editorial role in improving a book that covers a wide swathe of material in a rapidly developing field, and for over fifteen years she has also improved my life immeasurably.

Illustration Credits

7.1 Courtesy of Alexander Mordvintsev, 2015.

7.2 Courtesy of Alexander Mordvintsev, 2015.

7.3 Courtesy of Alexander Mordvintsev, 2015.

7.4 Photograph on the left is courtesy of Dr. Zachi Evenor. The processed image on the right is courtesy of software engineer Guenther Noack, 2015, and is published by Google under Attribution 4.0 International (CC BY 4.0).

7.5 Courtesy of Alexander Mordvintsev, Mike Tyka, Chris Olah, and Google. The entire image is in Mordvintsev, Tyka, and Olah 2015.

8.1 *All watched over by machines of loving grace: Deepdream Edition.* Courtesy of Memo Akten, 2015.

9.1 Courtesy of Mario Klingemann, 2016.

9.2 Artist: Angelo Semeraro. Courtesy of Reuters/Danish Siddiqui and Tate, 2017.

9.3 Image on right courtesy of Leon Gatys, 2015. Photograph upper left courtesy of Andreas Praefcke, 2003. Van Gogh's *The Starry Night*, bottom left, from Wikimedia Commons. Artist: Vincent Van Gogh (1853–1890). *The Starry Night.* Oil on canvas, 73×92 cm, 28¾×36¼ in. Source/Photographer: Downloaded from Houston tourism website around painting's time in Houston's Museum of Fine Arts (September 21, 2003–January 4, 2004). Can no longer find website.

10.1 *Portraits of Imaginary People.* Courtesy of Mike Tyka, 2017. http://www.miketyka.com/.

10.2 *Portraits of Imaginary People.* Courtesy of Mike Tyka, 2017. http://www.miketyka.com/.

10.3 *A(.I.) Messianic Window.* Color print on transparencies. Courtesy of Theresa Reimann-Dubbers, 2017.

10.4 *Latent Space.* Courtesy of Jake Elwes, 2017.

11.1 *edges2cats*. Courtesy of Chris Hesse, 2017.

11.2 *edges2handbags*. Courtesy of Chris Hesse, 2017.

11.3 *Transhancement Sketch*. Courtesy of Mario Klingemann, 2017.

11.4 *Transhancement Sketch*. Courtesy of Mario Klingemann, 2017.

11.5 *Neurographic Self-Portrait*. Courtesy of Mario Klingemann, 2017.

12.1 Courtesy of Jun-Yan Zhu, 2017.

12.2 Courtesy of Jun-Yan Zhu, 2017.

12.3 CycleGAN portraits. Courtesy of Mario Klingemann, 2017.

13.1 Courtesy of AICAN—Ahmed Elgammal—Art and AI Lab, Rutgers, 2017.

13.2 Courtesy of AICAN—Ahmed Elgammal—Art and AI Lab, Rutgers, 2017.

14.1 *Portrait of Edmond de Belamy*. Courtesy of Obvious, 2018.

15.1 *Emotionally Enhanced Portrait of Meera Senthilingam (Happy Face)*. Artist: The Painting Fool. Courtesy of The Painting Fool/Simon Colton, 2015.

15.2 *Emotionally Enhanced Portrait of Meera Senthilingam (Sad Face)*. Artist: The Painting Fool. Courtesy of The Painting Fool/Simon Colton, 2015.

16.1 *Tear*, inspired by Roy Lichtenstein's *Frightened Girl*. Artist: PIX18. Oil on canvas, 24 in. × 24 in. Courtesy of PIX18/Hod Lipson, 2016.

16.2 Photograph by the author, 2017.

20.1 Haile the drum-playing robot. Courtesy of Gil Weinberg, 2006.

20.2 Screenshot from Mason Bretan's video "What You Say." Courtesy of Mason Bretan, 2015.

32.1 *Saint Jerome in His Study*, Albrecht Dürer, engraving, 1514. WikiArt. Private collection.

37.1 Theater program for *Beyond the Fence*. ©Wingspan Productions Ltd., 2016. All rights reserved.

Notes

Introduction

1. Murray Shanahan, author interview, August 3, 2016.

2. Quoted from Ahmed 2015.

3. Quoted from Knapton 2017.

4. Tony Veale, author interview, September 30, 2016.

5. Ian Goodfellow, author interview, September 13, 2017.

6. Gerfried Stocker, author interview, September 7, 2017.

7. Allison Parrish, author interview, September 26, 2017.

8. Hod Lipson, author interview, August 17, 2017.

9. Kevin Warwick, author interview, August 25, 2016.

10. Douglas Eck, author interview, February 24, 2017.

11. Murray Shanahan, author interview, August 3, 2016.

12. Blaise Agüera y Arcas, author interview, March 7, 2017.

13. Quoted from Isaacson 2014, 287.

14. Quoted from Isaacson 2014, 288.

15. Quoted from Isaacson 2014, 288.

16. Ferrucci made this remark in a discussion on TED.com on February 17, 2014, in answer to the question "Does Watson think?" (Sadly, the video is no longer available.) Ferrucci was referring to a very famous comment made by the Dutch computer scientist Edsger Dijkstra at the ACM 1984 South Central Regional Conference, November 16–18, in Austin, Texas: "The question of whether Machines Can Think … is about as relevant as the question of whether Submarines Can Swim." See http://www.cs.utexas.edu/users/EWD/transcriptions/EWD08xx/EWD898.html.

I Understanding Creativity

1. Toulouse 1910, 145–146.

2. Toulouse 1910, 146.

3. Glass 2015, 315.

4. Quoted from Chipp 1968, 273.

5. Einstein and Infeld 1938, 95.

6. Alvarez 1985, 58.

7. Quoted from Kuenzli and Naumann 1989, 218.

8. Quoted from Isaacson 2011, 64.

9. Thiel 2014, 62.

10. Quoted from Coughlan 1954, 62.

11. Quoted from Vance 2015, 140.

12. See Vance 2015, 165.

13. Quoted from Isaacson 2011, 190.

14. Thiel 2014, 160.

15. Catmull 2014, 253.

16. Camerata 2018.

17. Dunn 2018.

18. Miller 2002.

19. Feynman 1985, 133.

20. See, for example, John-Steiner 2000.

21. See Schering 1912, 132. I thank Zachary Dunbar for alerting me to this episode.

22. More on this here: https://www.youtube.com/watch?v=PVzKICzpdXU.

23. Quoted from Isaacson 2014, 338.

24. Isaacson 2011, 98.

25. Isaacson 2011, 98. In extensive research for my book *Einstein, Picasso* (Miller 2001), I never encountered a statement like that made by Picasso. It turns out that it has a lineage that goes back to the mid-nineteenth century and has been used by T. S. Eliot and Sergei Prokofiev, among others. Steve Jobs has made it famous in the present day. See O'Toole 2013.

26. Quoted from Isaacson 2014, 98.

27. Vargas 2010.

28. Marie Winteler, letter to Einstein, November 30, 1896. In Einstein 1987, 31.

29. See Highfield and Carter 1993, 32.

30. Quoted from La Grange and Weiss 1995, 123.

31. Catmull 2014, 47.

32. Quoted from Isaacson 2011, 64.

33. Quoted from Vance 2015, 357.

34. Lalitha Chandrasekhar, author interview, November 1, 2002. See also Miller 2005.

35. Thiel 2014, 1.

36. Mitchell Feigenbaum, author interview, September 4, 2015.

37. Einstein's 1905 theory is called the special theory of relativity because it deals only with measurements made in laboratories in uniform relative motion—that is, moving in a straight line at uniform speeds. Einstein dropped this restriction in his 1915 general theory of relativity, which considers laboratories in arbitrary motion relative to each other; that is, they can be changing their speeds, accelerating.

38. See Miller 2001.

39. Boden 2004, 1.

40. Boden 1990, 41.

41. Boden 2004, 1.

42. Boden 2004, 41.

43. Simonton 2017, 6.

44. Simonton 2017, 6. See also Simonton 2018.

45. Robinson 2015.

46. Anna Jordanous, author interview, August 29, 2017.

47. François Pachet, author interview, January 2, 2017.

48. Tony Veale, author interview, September 30, 2016.

49. Boden 2016, 68–69. For her more detailed account, see Boden 1990.

50. Boden 2016, 69.

51. Csikszentmihalyi 1988.

52. See Miller (1981) 1998. In the first one, Einstein proposed that light could also be particles—light quanta, which most people until 1921 considered daft. In the second, he proposed a theory to explain the random movement of dust particles in the air and similar phenomena, collectively called *Brownian motion*. The third was the relativity paper. The three were published in the same volume of the German journal *Annalen der Physik*. The fourth appeared later in 1905.

53. See Miller 2001, 124–125.

54. For more on little-c and big-C creativities from the sociometric point of view, see Simonton 2017.

55. Poincaré 1908a.

56. Hadamard 1954.

57. Wallas 1926.

58. Poincaré 1908a, 53. The psychologist George Mandler called this phenomenon "mind-popping." See Mandler 1994.

59. See, for example, Weisberg 2006.

60. Toulouse 1910, 146.

61. Toulouse 1910, 146.

62. Helmholtz (1891) 1971, 475.

63. Helmholtz (1891) 1971, 474.

64. Helmholtz (1891) 1971, 475.

65. Hadamard 1954, 1.

66. Claparéde, Fehr, and Flournoy 1907, 307.

67. See Wotiz and Rudofsky 1954. See also Browne 1988 and Miller 2000, 340–341.

68. Miller 2012.

69. Solovine 1956, x.

70. I've written about this in several places. See Miller 1994 as well as Miller (1981) 1998 and Miller 2001.

71. See Miller 2001.

72. Swafford 2014, 227.

73. Hegarty 2014, 35; emphasis in original.

74. Quoted from Holmes 1845, 317–318.

75. Ghiselin 1952, 44.

76. Quoted from Hildescheimer 1983, 238.

77. Quoted from Hildescheimer 1983, 238.

78. Poincaré 1908a, 43.

79. For detailed discussions of this model, see Miller 1992, 2000, and 2001.

80. Newell and Simon 1972. Chapter 14, the source for this quotation, is reprinted in Allan Collins and Edward E. Smith, eds., *Readings in Cognitive Science* (San Mateo, CA: Morgan Kaufmann Publishers, Inc., 1988), 33–51.

81. For mathematicians' acceptance of the Appel and Haken proof of the four-color theorem, see Gonthier 2005.

82. Simon 1988, 177.

83. Langley 1987, 33.

84. Herbert A. Simon, letter to the author, August 5, 1993.

85. See Miller 2014, 67–69; Noll, n.d.; and Noll 1970.

86. George Lewis, author interview, September 27, 2017.

87. See, for example, Lewis 2000.

88. George Lewis, author interview, September 27, 2017.

89. Kennedy Center 2016.

90. See Miller 2014, 257–261.

91. Weizenbaum 1976.

92. See Rumelhart, McClelland, and the PDP Research Group 1986.

93. See, for example, Kurzweil (2005) 2016.

94. Kasparov 1996.

95. Kasparov 1996.

96. See, for example, Ericsson 2014.

97. Campitelli, Gobet, and Bilalić 2014.

98. Kasparov 2010.

99. See note 16 (Introduction) above.

100. Lohr 2016.

101. Byrnes 2015, 73.

102. See note 16 (Introduction) above.

103. Jennings 2011.

104. Quoted from Lee 2017.

105. Quoted from Chan 2017.

106. Quoted from Lee 2017.

107. Quoted from Knapton 2017.

108. Quoted from Sample 2017.

109. Quoted from Knapton 2017.

110. Gibney 2017.

111. Kasparov 2018.

112. Quoted from Knight 2017.

II Portrait of the Computer as an Artist

1. Alexander Mordvintsev, author interview, March 21, 2017.

2. Alexander Mordvintsev, author interview, March 21, 2017.

3. Alexander Mordvintsev, author interview, March 21, 2017.

4. Alexander Mordvintsev, author interview, March 21, 2017.

5. Mahendran and Vedaldi 2014.

6. Alexander Mordvintsev, author interview, March 21, 2017.

7. See Miller 1992 and Miller 2000, 339–360.

8. Alexander Mordvintsev, author interview, March 21, 2017.

9. Jessica Brillhart, author interview, April 6, 2017.

10. Alexander Mordvintsev, author interview, March 21, 2017.

11. Mike Tyka, author interview, March 13, 2017.

12. Mike Tyka, author interview, March 13, 2017.

13. Mike Tyka, author interview, March 13, 2017.

14. Mike Tyka, author interview, March 13, 2017.

15. Mike Tyka, author interview, March 13, 2017.

16. Mike Tyka, author interview, March 13, 2017.

17. Mordvintsev, Tyka, and Olah 2015.

18. Mike Tyka, author interview, March 13, 2017.

19. artwithMI 2016.

20. Mike Tyka, author interview, March 13, 2017.

21. You can see it on, for example, artwithMI 2016.

22. Mike Tyka, author interview, March 13, 2017.

23. Blaise Agüera y Arcas, author interview, March 7, 2017.

24. Blaise Agüera y Arcas, author interview, March 7, 2017.

25. Blaise Agüera y Arcas, author interview, March 7, 2017.

26. Kenric McDowell, author interview, June 6, 2017.

27. Kenric McDowell, author interview, June 6, 2017.

28. Agüera y Arcas 2016a.

29. Agüera y Arcas 2016b.

30. Agüera y Arcas 2016b.

31. Blaise Agüera y Arca, author interview, March 7, 2017.

32. Metz 2016a.

33. Anna Ridler, author interview, September 9, 2017.

34. Kenric McDowell, author interview, June 6, 2017.

35. Kenric McDowell, author interview, June 6, 2017.

36. Akten 2015b.

37. Akten 2015a.

38. Akten 2015b.

39. Memo Akten, author interview, August 29, 2017.

40. Memo Akten, author interview, August 29, 2017.

41. Memo Akten, author interview, August 29, 2017.

42. Akten 2017a.

43. Akten 2017b.

44. Damien Henry, author interview, July 28, 2017.

45. Damien Henry, author interview, July 28, 2017.

46. Damien Henry, author interview, July 28, 2017.

47. Damien Henry, author interview, July 28, 2017.

48. Mario Klingemann, author interview, May 22, 2017.

49. Mario Klingemann, author interview, May 22, 2017.

50. Mario Klingemann, author interview, May 22, 2017.

51. Mario Klingemann, author interview, May 22, 2017.

52. You can try it out here: https://experiments.withgoogle.com/x-degrees-of-sepa
ration.

53. See   https://artsexperiments.withgoogle.com/xdegrees/8gHu5Z5RF4BsNg/BgHD
_Fxb-V_K3A.

54. Mario Klingemann, author interview, May 22, 2017.

55. Angelo Semeraro, author interview, September 8, 2017.

56. Fulleylove 2016.

57. Angelo Semeraro, author interview, September 8, 2017.

58. See Safi 2016.

59. Angelo Semeraro, author interview, September 8, 2017.

60. Angelo Semeraro, author interview, September 8, 2017.

61. Angelo Semeraro, author interview, September 8, 2017.

62. Leon Gatys, author interview, August 9, 2017.

63. Gatys, Ecker, and Bethge 2016. A widely read article was published in 2015 on
arxiv as "Neural Algorithm of Artistic style." For further discussion of their work, see
McDonald 2015.

64. Leon Gatys, author interview, August 9, 2017.

65. Leon Gatys, author interview, August 9, 2017.

66. See Luan, Paris, Shechtman, and Bala 2017.

67. Gene Kogan, author interview, August 2, 2017. For examples of Kogan's innovative work with style transfer, see Kogan 2015.

68. Eleks 2016.

69. Ian Goodfellow, author interview, September 13, 2017.

70. Quoted from Metz 2016b.

71. Ian Goodfellow, author interview, September 13, 2017.

72. Ian Goodfellow, author interview, September 13, 2017.

73. Ian Goodfellow, author interview, September 13, 2017.

74. Goodfellow et al 2014.

75. Quoted from Knight 2017. Although Goodfellow's work was lauded at first, a problem emerged: in order for GANs to work well it seemed that a complicated system was necessary involving several different networks within both generator and discriminator. This criticism was swept aside in a paper by Alec Radford, Luke Metz, and Soumith Chintala, who showed that just one convolutional net was enough to be a very good discriminator. This was a turning point that led to GANs' popularity. "This was/is a very important paper," Goodfellow emphasized to me (email to the author, January 21, 2019). See Radford, Metz, and Chintala 2016.

76. Ian Goodfellow, author interview, September 13, 2017.

77. Ian Goodfellow, author interview, September 13, 2017.

78. Mike Tyka, author interview, March 13, 2017.

79. Refik Anadol, author interview, September 7, 2017.

80. Refik Anadol, author interview, September 7, 2017.

81. Refik Anadol, author interview, September 7, 2017.

82. The others included Mike Tyka, Kenric McDowell, Andrea Held, and Jac de Haan.

83. Refik Anadol, author interview, September 7, 2017.

84. Refik Anadol, author interview, September 7, 2017.

85. Refik Anadol, author interview, September 7, 2017.

86. Refik Anadol, author interview, September 7, 2017.

87. Refik Anadol, author interview, September 7, 2017.

88. Refik Anadol, author interview, September 7, 2017.

89. Theresa Reimann-Dubbers, author interview, September 9, 2017.

90. Stocker, Schöpf, and Leopoldseder 2017, 38.

91. Theresa Reimann-Dubbers, author interview, September 9, 2017.

92. Theresa Reimann-Dubbers, author interview, September 9, 2017.

93. Jake Elwes, author interview, September 20, 2017.

94. Jake Elwes, author interview, September 20, 2017.

95. Jake Elwes, author interview, September 20, 2017.

96. Jake Elwes, author interview, September 20, 2017.

97. Phillip Isola, author interview, December 14, 2017.

98. Phillip Isola, author interview, December 14, 2017.

99. Isola et al 2017.

100. Phillip Isola, author interview, December 14, 2017.

101. Phillip Isola, author interview, December 14, 2017.

102. Phillip Isola, author interview, December 14, 2017.

103. Hesse 2017.

104. Kogan 2018.

105. Phillip Isola, author interview, December 14, 2017.

106. Phillip Isola, author interview, December 14, 2017.

107. Jun-Yan Zhu, author interview, December 14, 2017.

108. Mario Klingemann, email to the author, December 4, 2017.

109. Mario Klingemann, author interview, May 22, 2017.

110. Klingemann 2017b.

111. Klingemann 2017b.

112. Klingemann 2017a.

113. Anna Ridler, author interview, September 9, 2017.

114. Anna Ridler, author interview, September 9, 2017.

115. Anna Ridler, author interview, September 9, 2017.

116. See Ridler 2017.

117. Anna Ridler, author interview, September 9, 2017.

118. Anna Ridler, author interview, September 9, 2017.

119. Ian Goodfellow, author interview, September 13, 2017.

120. Jun-Yan Zhu, author interview, December 14, 2017.

121. Zhu et al. 2017.

122. Jun-Yan Zhu, author interview, December 14, 2017.

123. Ian Goodfellow, author interview, September 13, 2017.

124. These images are from Zhu et al. 2017.

125. Zhu 2017.

126. Phillip Isola, author interview, December 14, 2017. Among the notable apparent photographic failures that went on to achieve great fame were Robert Capa's photographs taken during the D-day landings on June 6, 1944. A technician botched the film development and most of the negatives were lost. Those that remained were low resolution and streaked. Yet in a surrealistic manner, they brought home the horror of the soldiers' predicament as they crawled through the surf and hail of enemy bullets at the edge of Omaha Beach.

127. Phillip Isola, author interview, December 14, 2017.

128. Mario Klingemann, email to the author, December 6, 2017.

129. Mario Klingemann, author interview, May 22, 2017.

130. The photographs are from a Twitter post by Klingemann @quasimondo, May 20, 2017.

131. Phillip Isola, author interview, December 14, 2017.

132. Ahmed Elgammal, author interview, October 12, 2017.

133. Ahmed Elgammal, author interview, October 12, 2017.

134. Ahmed Elgammal, author interview, October 12, 2017.

135. Ahmed Elgammal, author interview, October 12, 2017.

136. Ahmed Elgammal, author interview, October 12, 2017.

137. Ahmed Elgammal, author interview, October 12, 2017.

138. Ahmed Elgammal, author interview, October 12, 2017.

139. Elgammal et al 2017.

140. See, for example, Thoutt 2017 and Emerging Technology from the arXiv 2017. For reactions to Elgammal's previous works along these lines, see Basulto 2015 and Heyman 2015.

141. Ahmed Elgammal, author interview, October 12, 2017.

142. Ahmed Elgammal, author interview, October 12, 2017.

143. Elgammal et al 2017.

144. Colton 2008.

145. Rea 2018.

146. For an artist's rendition of this equation, see the bottom right-hand corner of figure 14.1. For the real thing, see equation (1) in Goodfellow et al. 2014.

147. Schneider and Rea 2018.

148. Nugent 2018.

149. Nugent 2018.

150. Quoted from Schneider and Rea 2018.

151. See Rea 2018 and Schneider and Rea 2018.

152. See Miller 2014; Noll, n.d.; and Noll 1970.

153. Quoted from Gaskin 2018.

154. Simon Colton, author interview, September 2, 2016.

155. Colton et al. 2015, as well as The Painting Fool website at www.thepaintingfool
.com, where The Painting Fool gives its "autobiography."

156. Simon Colton, author interview, September 2, 2016.

157. Simon Colton, author interview, September 2, 2016.

158. Colton 2008.

159. See Colton et al 2015.

160. Simon Colton, author interview, September 2, 2016.

161. Simon Colton, author interview, September 2, 2016.

162. For further details on the galleries where The Painting Fool's products have been shown—and some sold, too—see www.thepaintingfool.com.

163. See Colton and Wiggins 2012.

164. Simon Colton, email to the author, September 28, 2016.

165. Simon Colton, author interview, February 20, 2018.

166. Simon Colton, author interview, February 20, 2018.

167. Anna Jordanous, author interview, August 29, 2017.

168. Simon Colton, author interview, February 20, 2018.

169. Tech Events 2015.

170. Aguilar and Lipson 2008.

171. Hod Lipson, author interview, August 17, 2017.

172. Hod Lipson, author interview, August 17, 2017.

173. For samples of their work, see http://www.robotlab.de/.

174. For samples of their work, see https://creators.vice.com/en_us/article/d7x58q/
is-this-the-worlds-first-robot-created-sculpture.

175. Tresset and Deussen 2014.

176. Tresset and Deussen 2014.

177. Patrick Tresset, author interview, August 30, 2017.

178. Quoted from Holmes 2011.

179. Patrick Tresset, author interview, August 30, 2017.

180. Chamberlain, Mullin, and Wagemans 2017.

181. Patrick Tresset, author interview, August 30, 2017.

III Machines That Make Music

1. Eck 2016c.

2. You can hear it at https://cdn2.vox-cdn.com/uploads/chorus_asset/file/6577761 /Google_-_Magenta_music_sample.0.mp3.

3. Peter Weibel, author interview, March 20, 2017.

4. This is a Markov chain of the first order. In a second-order Markov chain, the next event depends on the previous two, and so on.

5. Eck 2016c.

6. Douglas Eck, author interview, February 24, 2017.

7. Douglas Eck, author interview, February 24, 2017.

8. Douglas Hofstadter, author interview, November 8, 2017.

9. Douglas Eck, author interview, February 24, 2017. See also Eck's 2002 PhD thesis (Eck 2002).

10. Eck and Schmidhuber 2002.

11. Hochreiter and Schmidhuber 1997.

12. Douglas Eck, author interview, February 24, 2017.

13. Eck 2016c.

14. Traditionally, most artificial neural networks have just two or three hidden layers, whereas modern "deep" neural networks can have many more and are used for heavy computational tasks, such as computer vision. Convolutional neural networks are an example of the latter.

15. Metz 2017.

16. Eck 2017b.

17. Eck 2017c.

18. Patch 2016.

19. Eck 2016b.

20. Simon and Oore 2017.

21. Metz 2017.

22. Douglas Eck, email to the author, January 25, 2019. See Huang et al. 2019.

23. You can hear samples at https://magenta.tensorflow.org/music-transformer. See Huang, Simon, and Dinculescu 2018.

24. Douglas Eck, author interview, February 24, 2017.

25. Douglas Eck, author interview, February 24, 2017.

26. van den Oord, Dieleman, and Zen 2016.

27. See van den Oord et al. 2016 and van den Oord, Dieleman, and Zen 2016.

28. van den Oord, Dieleman, and Zen 2016.

29. Oore 2016.

30. Oore 2016. The score was generated by MuseScore from the raw MIDI file.

31. Jesse Engel, author interview, August 1, 2017.

32. Engel 2017 and Engel et al. 2017.

33. Jesse Engel, author interview, August 1, 2017.

34. Eck 2017a.

35. Jesse Engel, author interview, August 1, 2017.

36. Douglas Eck, author interview, February 24, 2017.

37. Huang et al 2017.

38. Pathak et al. 2016.

39. Douglas Eck, author interview, February 24, 2017.

40. François Pachet, author interview, May 8, 2017.

41. François Pachet, author interview, May 8, 2017.

42. François Pachet, author interview, May 8, 2017.

43. François Pachet, author interview, May 8, 2017.

44. Pachet 2003.

45. See https://www.youtube.com/watch?v=ynPWOMzossI.

46. Csikszentmihalyi 1975.

47. François Pachet, email to the author, June 9, 2018. See also Ghedini, Pachet, and Roy 2015.

48. Papadopoulos, Roy, and Pachet 2016.

49. For details, see Pachet 2011 and Papadopoulos, Roy, and Pachet 2016.

50. For examples, listen to the selections in Pachet 2015.

51. See also his video embedded in Pachet 2015.

52. François Pachet, author interview, May 8, 2017.

53. François Pachet, author interview, May 8, 2017.

54. Douglas Eck, author interview, February 24, 2017.

55. Nazim 2018.

56. Gil Weinberg, author interview, October 20, 2017.

57. Mason Bretan, author interview, October 25, 2017. For a fascinating discussion of embodiment, see Shanahan 2010.

58. Gil Weinberg, author interview, October 20, 2017.

59. Gil Weinberg, author interview, October 20, 2017.

60. Gil Weinberg, author interview, October 20, 2017.

61. See Miller 2014, 253–257.

62. Mason Bretan, author interview, October 25, 2017.

63. Mason Bretan, author interview, October 25, 2017.

64. Bretan, Weinberg, and Heck 2016.

65. You can see and hear it in action in an extraordinary video, "Deep Shimon: Shimon's First Composition Using Deep Learning," here: https://www.youtube.com/watch?v=j82nYLOnKtM. See Georgia Tech Center 2017.

66. Bretan 2015.

67. You can see and hear this performance with Bretan and his robots here: https://www.youtube.com/watch?v=O-bjTfYILPs.

68. Bretan 2015.

69. Gil Weinberg, author interview, October 20, 2017.

70. Mason Bretan, author interview, October 25, 2017.

71. Mason Bretan, author interview, October 25, 2017.

72. Gil Weinberg, author interview, October 20, 2017.

73. Gil Weinberg, author interview, October 20, 2017.

74. David Cope, author interview, May 2, 2017.

75. Hofstadter's blurb is from the back cover of Cope 2008.

76. David Cope, author interview, May 2, 2017.

77. David Cope, author interview, May 2, 2017.

78. David Cope, author interview, May 2, 2017.

79. Quoted from Wilson 2010.

80. Quoted from Garcia 2015.

81. Quoted from Cope 1999, 81.

82. Cope 1999, 83.

83. Blaise Agüera y Arcas, author interview, March 7, 2017.

84. David Cope, author interview, May 2, 2017.

85. Garcia 2015.

86. Quoted from Garcia 2015.

87. Cope 1999, 80.

88. David Cope, author interview, May 2, 2017.

89. Quoted from Cope 1999; emphasis in original. Originally in Stephen W. Smoliar, "Composers Compose Music But Do We Listen?," *MTO, a Journal of the Society for Music Theory* 0 (6) (January 1994), http://www.mtosmt.org/issues/mto.94.0.6/mto.pak.94.0.6.

90. David Cope, author interview, May 2, 2017.

91. David Cope, author interview, December 4, 2017.

92. Lawson 2009.

93. David Cope, author interview, May 2, 2017.

94. David Cope, author interview, May 2, 2017.

95. Bob Sturm and Oded Ben-Tal, author interview, July 19, 2017.

96. Bob Sturm and Oded Ben-Tal, author interview, July 19, 2017.

97. Eck and Schmidhuber 2002.

98. Eck and Lapalme 2008.

99. Sturm et al. 2016.

100. Bob Sturm and Oded Ben-Tal, author interview, July 19, 2017.

101. Bob Sturm and Oded Ben-Tal, author interview, July 19, 2017.

102. Sturm et al. 2016 and Sturm and Ben-Tal 2017.

103. See https://thesession.org/discussions/39604.

104. Sturm and Ben-Tal 2017.

105. You can listen to it here: https://highnoongmt.wordpress.com/2017/02/18/the
-drunken-pint-a-folk-rnn-original/.

106. Sturm 2017.

107. Bob Sturm and Oded Ben-Tal, author interview, July 19, 2017.

108. Bob Sturm and Oded Ben-Tal, author interview, July 19, 2017. See also Sturm
2017b.

109. Bob Sturm and Oded Ben-Tal, author interview, July 19, 2017.

110. Bob Sturm and Oded Ben-Tal, author interview, July 19, 2017.

111. Walshe 2014.

112. Bob Sturm and Oded Ben-Tal, author interview, July 19, 2017.

113. MusicTechFest 2015.

114. Rebecca Fiebrink, author interview, August 31, 2017.

115. Rebecca Fiebrink, author interview, August 31, 2017.

116. Rebecca Fiebrink, author interview, August 31, 2017.

117. Rebecca Fiebrink, author interview, August 31, 2017.

118. Rebecca Fiebrink, author interview, August 31, 2017.

119. Rebecca Fiebrink, author interview, August 31, 2017.

120. Rebecca Fiebrink, author interview, August 31, 2017.

121. See, for example, MusicTechFest 2015.

122. Fiebrink 2017.

123. Rebecca Fiebrink, author interview, August 31, 2017.

124. Fiebrink 2017.

125. Farbood, Kaufman, and Jennings 2007.

126. For details, see Farbood, Kaufman, and Jennings 2007.

127. Farbood, Kaufman, and Jennings 2007.

128. Mary Farbood, author interview, March 10, 2017.

129. Mary Farbood, author interview, March 10, 2017.

130. Eduardo Miranda, author interview, March 17, 2017.

131. Eduardo Miranda, author interview, March 17, 2017.

132. Eduardo Miranda, email to the author, February 19, 2018.

133. For details, see Miranda, Adamatzky, and Jones 2011; for audio of the duet, see Miranda 2014a.

134. Eduardo Miranda, author interview, March 17, 2017.

135. See Roberts 2015.

136. Eduardo Miranda, author interview, March 17, 2017.

137. Miranda 2014b.

138. Miranda 2014b, 21.

139. Miranda 2014b, 19.

IV   Once Upon a Time

1. Quoted from Olewitz 2016.

2. Stephen Schwingeler, author interview, September 9, 2017.

3. Stephen Schwingeler, author interview, September 9, 2017.

4. Ulanoff 2014.

5. Merill 2014.

6. See https://en.wikipedia.org/wiki/Lsjbot.

7. See Cohen 2008.

8. Twitter post by @jokingcomputer, April 25, 2018.

9. See Attardo 2008.

10. McCarthy et al. (1955) 2006, 13.

11. Picard (1997) 2000. For more on Rosalind Picard and her work on affective computing, see chapter 42, 282ff.

12. Julia Taylor Rayz, author interview, September 29, 2016.

13. See Stock and Strapparava 2003, 2006.

14. Stock and Strapparava 2006, 1677.

15. Stock and Strapparava 2006, 1676.

16. Stock and Strapparava 2006, 1677.

17. Horng 2010.

18. Quoted from Horng 2010.

19. Ferreira 2016.

20. Taylor and Mazlack 2004.

21. Graeme Ritchie, author interview, October 20, 2016.

22. Julia Taylor Rayz, author interview, September 29, 2016.

23. This is the title of Rayz's presentation; see Dawn or Doom, Purdue University 2016.

24. Julia Taylor Rayz, author interview, September 29, 2016.

25. Graeme Ritchie, author interview, October 20, 2016.

26. Ritchie 2009, 75.

27. Quoted from Kobie 2017.

28. All quotations are from Marshall 2018.

29. Metz 2017.

30. Gervás 2000.

31. Perloff 2010, 12.

32. Quoted from Perloff 2010, 12.

33. Pablo Gervás, author interview, October 9, 2017.

34. Pablo Gervás, author interview, October 9, 2017.

35. Gervás 2000.

36. Gervás 2000.

37. See part V.

38. Pablo Gervás, author interview, October 9, 2017.

39. Pablo Gervás, author interview, October 9, 2017.

40. Pablo Gervás, author interview, October 9, 2017.

41. Pablo Gervás, author interview, October 9, 2017.

42. Pablo Gervás, author interview, October 9, 2017.

43. Rafael Pérez y Pérez, author interview, October 12, 2017.

44. Rafael Pérez y Pérez, author interview, October 12, 2017.

45. Rafael Pérez y Pérez, author interview, October 12, 2017.

46. Rafael Pérez y Pérez, author interview, October 12, 2017.

47. Rafael Pérez y Pérez, author interview, October 12, 2017.

48. Montfort and Pérez y Pérez 2008.

49. Montfort et al. 2013.

50. Rafael Pérez y Pérez, author interview, October 12, 2017.

51. Montfort et al. 2013, 174.

52. Pérez y Pérez 2017a.

53. Singh, Ackerman, and Pérez y Pérez 2017.

54. Ackerman and Pèrez y Pèrez 2017.

55. See part V.

56. Singh, Ackerman, and Pérez y Pérez 2017, 235.

57. Rafael Pérez y Pérez, author interview, October 12, 2017.

58. Nick Montfort, author interview, September 25, 2017.

59. Montfort 2014, 2–9.

60. Nick Montfort, author interview, September 25, 2017.

61. Nick Montfort, author interview, September 25, 2017.

62. Montfort 2014, 22.

63. Nick Montfort, author interview, September 25, 2017.

64. Montfort 2014, 51–63.

65. Nick Montfort, author interview, September 25, 2017.

66. Nick Montfort, author interview, September 25, 2017.

67. Nick Montfort, author interview, September 25, 2017.

68. Mateas and Montfort 2005.

69. Nick Montfort, author interview, September 25, 2017.

70. Quoted from Mateas and Montfort 2005, 145.

71. Montfort 2017.

72. Quoted from the blurb at http://counterpathpress.org/the-truelist-nick-montfort.

73. Pablo Gervás, author interview, October 9, 2017.

74. Nick Montfort, author interview, September 25, 2017.

75. Nick Montfort, author interview, September 25, 2017.

76. Luman 2015.

77. Nick Montfort, author interview, September 25, 2017.

78. Allison Parrish, author interview, September 26, 2017.

79. Parrish 2015.

80. Allison Parrish, author interview, September 26, 2017.

81. Allison Parrish, author interview, September 26, 2017.

82. Allison Parrish, author interview, September 26, 2017.

83. Parish 2015.

84. Allison Parrish, author interview, September 26, 2017.

85. Allison Parrish, author interview, September 26, 2017.

86. Allison Parrish, author interview, September 26, 2017.

87. Quoted from Parish 2015.

88. Parrish 2015.

89. Quoted from Parrish 2015.

90. Parrish 2015.

91. Parrish 2015.

92. Parrish 2015.

93. Parrish 2015.

94. Tony Veale, author interview, April 11, 2018.

95. Parrish 2015.

96. Parrish 2015.

97. Allison Parrish, author interview, September 26, 2017.

98. Allison Parrish, author interview, September 26, 2017.

99. Allison Parrish, author interview, September 26, 2017.

100. Parrish 2018a, 2018b.

101. Parrish 2018b.

102. Parrish 2018b.

103. Ross Goodwin, author interview, July 7, 2017.

104. Newitz 2016.

105. Ross Goodwin, author interview, July 7, 2017.

106. See Goodwin 2016a.

107. Ross Goodwin, author interview, July 7, 2017.

108. Goodwin 2016a.

109. Goodwin 2016b.

110. Ross Goodwin, author interview, July 7, 2017.

111. Pablo Gervás, author interview, October 9, 2017.

112. Goodwin 2016b.

113. Newitz 2016.

114. Ross Goodwin, author interview, July 7, 2017.

115. Goodwin 2018. Quotation from Ross Goodwin, email to the author, October 12, 2018.

116. Quoted from https://www.jean-boite.fr/products/1-the-road-by-an-artificial -neural.

117. Sarah Harmon, author interview, August 4, 2017.

118. Sarah Harmon, author interview, August 4, 2017.

119. Sarah Harmon, author interview, August 4, 2017.

120. Harmon 2015.

121. Harmon 2015, 73.

122. Harmon 2015, 74.

123. Harmon 2015, 75.

124. Sarah Harmon, author interview, August 4, 2017.

125. Sarah Harmon, author interview, August 4, 2017.

126. Tony Veale, author interview, September 29, 2016.

127. Tony Veale, author interview, September 29, 2016.

128. Tony Veale, author interview, September 29, 2016.

129. Veale 2015, 81.

130. See http://ngrams.ucd.ie/metaphor-magnet-acl/.

131. See http://ngrams.ucd.ie/therex3/.

132. Veale 2015, 78.

133. Veale 2015, 81.

134. Veale 2015, 81.

135. Tony Veale, author interview, April 11, 2018.

136. Veale 2015, 80.

137. Tony Veale, author interview, April 11, 2018.

138. Veale 2015, 84.

139. Tony Veale, author interview, April 11, 2018.

140. Veale 2017, 246.

141. Veale 2017, 246.

142. Veale, n.d.

143. Using www.BestofBotWorlds.com.

144. Veale 2017, 249; emphasis in original.

145. Veale 2017, 249.

146. Tony Veale, author interview, April 11, 2018.

147. Tony Veale, author interview, April 11, 2018.

148. Tony Veale, author interview, April 11, 2018.

149. Tony Veale, author interview, April 11, 2018.

150. Tony Veale, author interview, April 11, 2018.

151. Tony Veale, author interview, April 11, 2018.

152. Hannah Davis, author interview, July 27, 2017.

153. Hannah Davis, author interview, July 27, 2017.

154. Mohammad and Turney 2013 and http://www.purl.org/net/NRCemotion
lexicon.

155. Davis and Mohammad 2014. For samples, see https://transprose.bandcamp
.com/album/first-iteration.

156. Davis and Mohammad 2014.

157. Hannah Davis, email to the author, April 10, 2018.

158. Quoted from Mastroianni 2016.

159. See the video in Mastroianni 2016.

160. For some very preliminary results, see Davis 2017.

161. Hannah Davis, author interview, July 27, 2017.

162. Hannah Davis, author interview, July 27, 2017.

163. Simon Colton, author interview, September 2, 2016.

164. Colton, Goodwin, and Veale 2012, 96.

165. Colton, Goodwin, and Veale 2012, 96.

166. Colton, Goodwin, and Veale 2012, 96.

167. Colton, Goodwin, and Veale 2012, 102.

168. Simon Colton, author interview, February 20, 2018.

169. Simon Colton, author interview, February 20, 2018.

170. Simon Colton, author interview, February 20, 2018.

171. Colton, Goodwin, and Veale 2012, 101.

V Staged by Android Lloyd Webber and Friends

1. Catherine Gale, author interview, August 14, 2017.

2. Catherine Gale, author interview, August 14, 2017.

3. Colton took up his current position at Queen Mary University of London in 2018.

4. Gervás et al. 2016.

5. For details, see Collins 2016.

6. See Colton et al. 2016.

7. From *Computer Says Show*, episode 2. This is the second hour of the two-hour documentary on Sky Arts about the making of *Beyond the Fence*.

8. Catherine Gale, author interview, August 14, 2017.

9. Colton et al. 2016.

10. For reviews in full, see Colton et al. 2016.

11. From *Computer Says Show*, episode 2.

12. François Pachet, author interview, January 15, 2018.

13. Bob Sturm and Oded Ben-Tal, author interview, July 19, 2017.

14. Pablo Gervás, author interview, October 9, 2017.

15. Collins 2016, 56.

16. Colton et al. 2016.

17. Catherine Gale, author interview, August 14, 2017.

18. Collins 2016, 54.

19. Collins 2016, 54.

20. Collins 2016, 55.

VI Can Computers Be Creative?

1. Quoted from Knapton 2017.

2. Sir Nigel Shadbolt, author interview, October 18, 2016.

3. Gerfried Stocker, author interview, September 7, 2017.

4. Private exchange with author after the artist's presentation, "My Artificial Muse," at the AI Meetup, London, July 2, 2018.

5. See https://ars.electronica.art/prix/en/about/.

6. Douglas Eck, author interview, February 24, 2017.

7. Douglas Eck, author interview, February 24, 2017.

8. See, for example, Boden 1990; Pease and Colton 2011; and Ritchie 2007.

9. Jason Yosinski, author interview, June 13, 2018.

10. Jason Yosinski, author interview, June 13, 2018.

11. Jason Yosinski, author interview, June 13, 2018.

12. Szegedy et al 2013.

13. See Nguyen, Olsinski, and Clune 2015 and Nguyen et al. 2016.

14. Quoted from Garling 2014.

15. Mark Riedl, author interview, September 29, 2018.

16. Quoted in Voosen 2017.

17. Mark Riedl, author interview, October 13, 2016.

18. Boden 1990, 11.

19. Boden 2016, 69.

344 Notes to Pages 272–279

20. Boden 2016, 70.

21. Boden 2016, 69.

22. See Boden 1990, 7, and Boden 1994, 520. Boden 1994 is actually a precursor to her 1990 book.

23. Boden 1994. This paper is pretty much identical to the one I had the opportunity to critique at the Achievement Project Symposium, held in Kent, December 13–15, 1991. That version was entitled "What Is Creativity?" Alas, the proceedings of this highly relevant conference were never published.

24. Boden 1994, 553.

25. Tony Veale, author interview, September 30, 2016.

26. Colton and Wiggins 2012, 21.

27. Simon Colton, author interview, September 2, 2016.

28. Parrish 2015.

29. Geraint Wiggins, author interview, August 26, 2016.

30. Geraint Wiggins, author interview, August 26, 2016.

31. Geraint Wiggins, author interview, August 26, 2016.

32. Wiggins 2012, 306.

33. Wiggins 2012, 309. There are actually real letters; see part I.

34. Graeme Ritchie, author interview, September 10, 2016.

35. Ritchie 2007.

36. Jordanous 2011.

37. Anna Jordanous, email to the author, June 14, 2018.

38. Anna Jordanous, email to the author, June 14, 2018; Colton 2008, 18; and Jordanous 2011, 103.

39. Tony Veal, email to the author, June 12, 2018.

40. Pablo Gervás, email to the author, June 18, 2018.

41. See Gervás 2011.

42. Anna Jordanous, author interview, September 29, 2017.

43. Jordanous 2011.

44. Jordanous and Keller 2016, 2.

45. Anna Jordanous, author interview, September 1, 2017

46. Jordanous and Keller 2016.

47. Jordanous and Keller 2016, 18.

48. Jordanous 2011.

49. Anna Jordanous, author interview, September 1, 2017.

50. Einstein 1949, 7.

51. See Miller 2000, 2001, 2005, 2009, and 2015.

52. Rosalind Picard, author interview, May 30, 2017.

53. See Picard (1997) 2000, 3.

54. Picard (1997) 2000, ix.

55. Cytowic 1993.

56. Quoted from Lehrer 2009.

57. Picard 2010, 13.

58. Rosalind Picard, author interview, May 17, 2017.

59. Quoted from Higginbotham 2012.

60. As examples: Mark Coeckelbergh (2017) comes to no clear cut conclusion as to whether machines can actually be creative or not. Aaron Hertzmann (2018) argues that technology can do no more than aid art. He writes, "Machines are here to stay, and so is the mystery of creation." Both believe that we will never be able to really understand either human or machine creativity and that machines cannot be regarded as artists. I have argued otherwise in great detail in this book.

61. Moravec 1988, 15.

62. See Miller 1986, ch. 7.

63. See, for example, Sullins 2012.

64. For an opposing view based on the argument that machines are not "out there" and so cannot experience feeling, see Turkle 2018.

65. Poincaré 1908b, 137.

66. Picard (1997) 2000, 128.

67. Asimov 1976.

68. Brian Behlendorf, author interview, August 4, 2016.

69. Dennett 1991, 65.

70. Rosalind Picard, author interview, May 17, 2017.

71. Searle 1980.

72. Searle 2002; see particularly "The Problem of Consciousness," 7–17.

73. See Miller 2009.

74. Dennett 1991, 338.

75. Graziano 2013, 7.

76. Graziano 2013, 8.

77. Graziano 2013, 8.

78. Graziano 2013, 56.

79. Chalmers 1995.

80. Graziano 2013, 6, 7, 13, and 40.

81. Graziano 2013, 218–219.

82. Graziano 2013, 219. I added AlphaGo because it did not yet exist in 2013 when Graziano's book was published.

83. Douglas Hofstadter, author interview, November 8, 2017.

84. Douglas Hofstadter, author interview, November 8, 2017.

85. Douglas Hofstadter, author interview, November 8, 2017.

86. Hofstadter 2009.

87. See Bostrom 2014 and Harari 2015.

88. Pat Langley, author interview, October 30, 2017.

89. See Stanley 2017.

90. Pat Langley, author interview, October 30, 2017.

91. Pat Langley, author interview, October 30, 2017.

92. Lohr 2018. See also Shanahan et. al. 2019.

93. Floreano et al. 2007. For some recent developments, see Metz 2019.

Bibliography

Ackerman, Maya, and Rafael Pèrez y Pèrez. 2017. "A Princess Minuet: A Song Written by Computer Systems." YouTube, July 7. https://www.youtube.com/watch?v=wfIZFMPzClI.

Agüera y Arcas, Blaise. 2016a. "Deep Dream Art and Machine Learning Symposium 2016 Recap." *Medium*, June 1. https://medium.com/artists-and-machine-intelligence/deepdream-art-and-machine-learning-symposium-2016-recap-396d1ecf87e3.

Agüera y Arcas, Blaise. 2016b. "Art in the Age of Machine Intelligence." *Medium*, February 23. https://medium.com/artists-and-machine-intelligence/what-is-ami-ccd936394a83.

Aguilar, Carlos, and Hod Lipson. 2008. "A Robotic System for Interpreting Images into Painted Art Work." In *GA2008, 11th Generative Art Conference*, edited by Celestino Soddu, 372–387.

Ahmed, Murad. 2015. "Lunch with the FT: Demis Hassabis." *Financial Times*, January 30. https://www.ft.com/content/47aa9aa4-a7a5-11e4-be63-00144feab7de.

Akten, Memo. 2015a. "All Watched over by Machines of Loving Grace: Deepdream Edition." http://www.memo.tv/portfolio/all-watched-over-by-machines-of-loving-grace-deepdream-edition/.

Akten, Memo. 2015b. "#Deepdream Is Blowing My Mind." *Medium*, July 9. https://medium.com/@memoakten/deepdream-is-blowing-my-mind-6a2c8669c698.

Akten, Memo. 2017a. "Learning to See: Hello, World." http://www.memo.tv/portfolio/learning-to-see-hello-world/.

Akten, Memo. 2017b. See the video in Akten 2017a.

Alvarez, Luis. 1985. *Alvarez: Adventures of the Physicist*. New York: Basic Books.

artwithMI. 2016. "What Is DeepDream? With Mike Tyka." YouTube, September 12. https://www.youtube.com/watch?v=4P9p8hfHy9Y.

Asimov, Isaac. 1976. *The Bicentennial Man*. New York: Ballantine Books.

Attardo, Salvatore. 2008. "Semantics and Pragmatics of Humor." *Language and Linguistics Compass* 2 (6): 1203–1215. https://onlinelibrary.wiley.com/doi/abs/10.1111/j .1749-818X.2008.00107.x.

Bass, Dina. 2015. "And the New Yorker Cartoon Winner Is … a Computer." *Bloomberg*, August 10. https://www.bloomberg.com/news/articles/2015-08-10/and-the-new -yorker-cartoon-contest-winner-is-a-computer.

Basulto, Dominic. 2015. "Why It Matters that Computers Are Now Able to Judge Human Creativity." *Washington Post*, June 18. https://www.washingtonpost.com/ news/innovations/wp/2015/06/18/why-it-matters-that-computers-are-now-able-to -judge-human-creativity/?utm_term=.b784bb0d6ac3.

Bernardo, Francisco, Michael Zbyszyński, Rebecca Fiebrink, and Mick Grierson. 2017. "Interactive Machine Learning for End-User Innovation." In *Proceedings of the AAAI Symposium Series: Designing the User Experience of Machine Learning Systems*. http:// research.gold.ac.uk/19767/1/BernardoZbyszynskiFiebrinkGrierson_UXML_2017.pdf.

Boden, Margaret A. 1990. *The Creative Mind: Myths and Mechanisms*. 2nd ed. London: Routledge.

Boden, Margaret A. 1994. "Précis of *The Creative Mind: Myths and Mechanisms*." *Behavioral and Brain Sciences* 17 (3): 591–531.

Boden, Margaret A. 2016. *AI: Its Nature and Future*. Oxford: Oxford University Press.

Bostrom, Nick. 2014. *Superintelligence: Paths, Dangers and Strategies*. Oxford: Oxford University Press.

Bretan, Mason. 2015. "'What You Say': A Robot and Human Musical Performance." YouTube, January 14. https://www.youtube.com/watch?v=O-bjTfYILPs.

Bretan, Mason, Gil Weinberg, and Larry Heck. 2016. "A Unit Selection Methodology for Music Generation Using Deep Neural Networks." Arxiv. https://arxiv.org/abs/ 1612.03789.

Brogan, Jacob. 2017. "Out of the Loop." *Slate*, August 9. http://www.slate.com/articles/ technology/future_tense/2017/08/machine_learning_hobbyist_janelle_shane_talks _about_her_wacky_neural_nets.html.

Browne, Malcolm W. 1988. "The Benzen Ring: Dream Analysis." *New York Times*, August 16. https://www.nytimes.com/1988/08/16/science/the-benzene-ring-dream -analysis.html.

Byrnes, Nanette. 2015. "Watson Makes a Salad." *MIT Technology Review* 118 (4): 72–73.

Camerata, Christian. 2018. "The Unintended Effects of Open Office Space." Harvard Business School Newsroom, July 9. https://www.hbs.edu/news/articles/Pages/ bernstein-open-offices.aspx.

Campitelli, Guillermo, Fernand Gobet, and Merim Bilalić. 2014. "Cognitive Processes and the Development of Chess Genius." In *Cambridge Handbook of Expertise and Expert Performance*, edited by K. A. Ericsson, N. Charness, P. Feltovich, and R. R. Hoffman, 350–374. Cambridge: Cambridge University Press.

Catmull, Ed. 2014. *Creativity, Inc: Overcoming the Unseen Forces that Stand in the Way of True Inspiration*. London: Bantum Press.

Chalmers, David. 1995. "Facing up to the Problem of Consciousness." *Journal of Consciousness Studies* 2 (3): 200–219.

Chamberlain, Rebecca, Caitlin R. Mullin, and Johan Wagemans. 2017. "Putting the Art in Artificial: Aesthetic Responses to Computer-Generated Art." *Psychology of Aesthetics, Creativity and the Arts* 12 (2): 177–192. https://www.researchgate.net/profile/Rebecca _Chamberlain/publication/319496343_Putting_the_Art_in_Artificial_Aesthetic _Responses_to_Computer-Generated_Art/links/59b7b0cf0f7e9bd4a7fe6f0d/Putting -the-Art-in-Artificial-Aesthetic-Responses-to-Computer-Generated-Art.pdf.

Chan, Dawn. 2017. "The AI that Has Nothing to Learn from Humans." *Atlantic*, October 20. https://www.theatlantic.com/technology/archive/2017/10/alphago-zero-the-ai -that-taught-itself-go/543450/.

Chipp, Herschel. 1968. *Theories of Modern Art: A Source Book for Artists and Critics*. With contributions by Peter Zelz and Joshua C. Taylor. Berkeley: University of California Press.

Claparéde, E., E. Fehr, and T. Flournoy. 1907. "L'Enquête sur la méthode de travail du mathématician," *L'Enseignement Mathématique* 4:306–312.

Coeckelbergh, Mark. 2017. "Can Machines Create Art?" *Philosophy and Technology* 30 (3): 285–303.

Cohen, Noam. 2008. "He Wrote 200,000 Books (but Computers Did Some of the Work)." *New York Times*, April 14. http://www.nytimes.com/2008/04/14/business/ media/14link.html?_r=2&pagewanted=all.

Collins, Nick. 2016. "A Funny Thing Happened on the Way to the Formula: Algorithmic Composition for Musical Theater." *Computer Music Journal* 40 (3): 41–57. http:// dro.dur.ac.uk/19901/2/19901.pdf?DDD23+tvvd27+dul4eg.

Colton, Simon. 2008. "Creativity versus the Perception of Creativity in Computational Systems." In *Papers from the 2008 AAAI Symposium*, edited by Dan Ventura, Mary L. Maher, and Simon Colton, 14–20. Menlo Park: CA: AAAI Press. http://ccg .doc.gold.ac.uk/ccg_old/papers/colton_aaai08symp.pdf.

Colton, Simon. 2012. "The Painting Fool: Stories from Building an Automated Painter." In *Computers and Creativity*, edited by Jon McCormack and Mark d'Inverno, 3–38. Berlin: Springer-Verlag.

Colton, Simon, Jacob Goodwin, and Tony Veale. 2012. "Full-FACE Poetry Generation." In *Proceedings of the Third International Conference on Computational Creativity
2012*, edited by Mary Lou Maher, Kristian Hammond, Alison Pease, Rafael Pérez y
Pérez, Dan Ventura, and Geraint Wiggins, 95–102. Dublin, Ireland: University College Dublin. http://computationalcreativity.net/iccc2012/wp-content/uploads/2012/
05/095-Colton.pdf.

Colton, Simon, Jakob Haskov, Dan Ventura, Ian Gouldstone, Michael Cook, and
Blanca Pérez-Ferrer. 2015. "The Painting Fool Sees! New Projects with the Automated
Painter." In *Proceedings of the Sixth International Conference on Computational Creativity*, edited by Hannu Toivonen, Simon Colton, Michael Cook, and Dan Ventura,
189–195. Provo, UT: Brigham Young University Press. http://computationalcreativity
.net/iccc2015/proceedings/8_2Colton.pdf.

Colton, Simon, Maria Teresa Llano, Rose Hepworth, John Charnley, Catherine
V. Gale, Archie Baron, François Pachet, et al. 2016. "The *Beyond the Fence* Musical
and *Computer Says Show* Documentary." In *Proceedings of the Seventh International
Conference on Compuational Creativity*, edited by François Pachet, Amilcar Cardoso,
Vincent Corruble, and Fiammetta Ghedini, 311–320. Paris, France: Sony CSL. http://
repository.falmouth.ac.uk/2565/1/colton_iccc2016.pdf.

Colton, Simon, and Geraint A. Wiggins. 2012. "Computational Creativity: The Final
Frontier?" In *Proceedings of the 20th European Conference on Artificial Intelligence*, edited
by Luc De Raedt, Christian Bessiere, Didier Dubois, Patrick Doherty, Paolo Frasconi,
Fredrik Heintz, and Peter Lucas, 21–26. Amsterdam, The Netherlands: IOS Press.
http://ccg.doc.gold.ac.uk/wp-content/uploads/2016/10/colton_ecai12.pdf.Cope,
David. 1999. "Facing the Music: Perspectives on Machine-Composed Music." *Leonardo
Music Journal* 9:79–87.

Cope, David. 2008. *Tinman: A Life Explored*. Bloomington, IN: iUniverse.

Coughlan, Robert. 1954. "Dr. Edward Teller's Magnificent Obsession." *Life*, September 6, 61–74.

Csikszentmihaly, Mihaly. 1975. *Beyond Boredom and Anxiety: Experiencing Flow in
Work and Play*. San Francisco: Jossey-Bass.

Csikszentmihaly, Mihaly. 1988. "Society, Culture, Person: A Systems View of Creativity." In *The Nature of Creativity*, edited by R. J. Sternburg, 325–329. Cambridge:
Cambridge University Press.

Cytowic, Richard. 1993. *The Man Who Tasted Shapes*. London: Abacus/Little Brown.

Davis, Hannah, and Saif M. Mohammad. 2014. "Generating Music from Literature."
In *Proceedings of the 3rd Workshop for Literature*, edited by Anna Feldman, Anna
Kazantseva, and Stan Szpakowicz, 1–10. Gothenburg: Association for Computational
Linguistics. http://aclweb.org/anthology/W14-0901.

Dawn or Doom, Purdue University. 2016. "What Can We Learn from Computers (NOT) Understanding Humor: Julia Taylor Rayz." YouTube, November 3. https://www.youtube.com/watch?v=Vy8WiKvT4gY.

Dennett, Daniel. 1991. *Consciousness Explained*. London: Penguin Books.

Dunn, Ashley L. 2018. "An Architect's Defense of Open Plan Offices." *Fast Company*, August 15. https://www.fastcompany.com/90218754/in-defense-of-open-offices.

Eck, Douglas. 2002. "Meter through Synchrony: Processing Rhythmical Patterns with Relaxation Oscillators." PhD diss., Department of Computer Science, Cognitive Science Program, Indiana University, April. http://citeseerx.ist.psu.edu/viewdoc/download?doi=10.1.1.141.4262&rep=rep1&type=pd.

Eck, Douglas. 2016a. "Critique of First Magenta Music Sample." Google groups, June 2. https://groups.google.com/a/tensorflow.org/forum/#!topic/magenta-discuss/KTFUN_yN84g.

Eck, Douglas. 2016b. "Generating Art & Music—with Douglas Eck." YouTube, June 1. https://www.youtube.com/watch?v=HrilbzptOk4.

Eck, Douglas. 2016c. "Welcome to Magenta!" *Magenta* (blog), June 1. https://magenta.tensorflow.org/blog/2016/06/01/welcome-to-magenta/.

Eck, Douglas. 2017a. "Learning from A.I. Duet." *Magenta* (blog), February 16. https://magenta.tensorflow.org/2017/02/16/ai-duet.

Eck, Douglas. 2017b. "Magenta: Music and Art Generation (TensorFlow Dev Summit 2017)." YouTube, February 15. https://www.youtube.com/watch?v=vM5NaGoynjE.

Eck, Douglas. 2017c. "Project Magenta: Music and Art with Machine Learning (Google I/O '17)." YouTube, May 19. https://www.youtube.com/watch?v=2FAjQ6R_bf0.

Eck, Douglas, and Jasmin Lapalme. 2008. "Learning Musical Structure Directly from Sequences of Music." University of Montreal, Department of Computer Science. http://www.iro.umontreal.ca/~pift6080/H08/documents/papers/lstm_music.pdf.

Eck, Douglas, and Jürgen Schmidhuber. 2002. "Learning the Long-Term Structure of the Blues." In *Proceedings of the International Conference of Artificial Neural Networks*, edited by J. Dorronsoro, 96–103. Berlin: Springer. ftp://ftp.idsia.ch/pub/juergen/2002_icannMusic.pdf.

Einstein, Albert. 1949. "Autobiographical Notes." In *Albert Einstein: Philosopher-Scientist*, edited by P. A. Schilpp, 3–94. La Salle, IL: Open Court Publishing Co.

Einstein, Albert. 1987. *Collected Papers of Albert Einstein: Volume 1*. Edited by John Stachel. Princeton: Princeton University Press.

Einstein, Albert, and Leopold Infeld. 1938. *The Evolution of Physics: The Growth of Ideas from Early Concepts to Relativity and Quanta*. Cambridge: Cambridge University Press.

Eleks. 2016. "Designing Apparel with Neural Style Transfer." Eleks, September 2016. https://labs.eleks.com/2016/09/designing-apparel-neural-style-transfer.html.

Elgammal, Ahmed, Bingchen Liu, Mohamed Elhoseiny, and Marian Mazzone. 2017. "CAN: Creative Adversarial Networks Generating 'Art' by Learning About Styles and Deviating from Style Norms." In *Proceedings of the Eighth International Conference on Computational Creativity*, edited by Ashok Goel, Anna Jordanous, and Alison Pease, 96–103. Atlanta: Georgia Institute of Technology Press. http://computationalcreativity.net/iccc2017/iccc17_proceedings.pdf.

Emerging Technology from the arXiv. 2017. "Machine Creativity Beats Some Modern Art." *MIT Technology Review*, June 30. https://www.technologyreview.com/s/608195/machine-creativity-beats-some-modern-art/.

Engel, Jesse. 2017. "Making a Neural Synthesizer Instrument." *Magenta* (blog), May 18. https://magenta.tensorflow.org/nsynth-instrument.

Engel, Jesse, Cinjon Resnick, Adam Roberts, Sander Dieleman, Mohammad Norouzi, Douglas Eck, and Karen Simonyan. 2017. "Neural Audio Synthesis of Musical Notes with WaveNet Autoencoders." In *Proceedings of the 34th International Conference on Machine Learning*, edited by Doina Precup and Yee Whye Teh, 1068–1077. http://proceedings.mlr.press/v70/engel17a/engel17a.pdf.

Ericsson, Anders K. 2014. "Creative Genius: A Vew from the Expert-Performance Approach." In *The Wiley Handbook of Genius*, edited by Dean Keith Simonton, 321–349. West Sussex, UK: John Wiley and Sons.

Farbood, Mary, and Egon Pasztor. 2007. "Hyperscore (2000–2006)." Last modified January 2, 2007. http://alumni.media.mit.edu/~mary/hyperscore.html.

Farbood, Morwaread Mary. 2011. "Computational Creativity—Morwaread Mary Farbood, New York University." Vimeo, December 2. https://vimeo.com/33012887.

Farbood, Morwaread, Henry Kaufman, and Kevin Jennings. 2007. "Composing with Hyperscore: An Intuitive Interface for Visualizing Musical Structure." In Volume 2007 of the *International Computer Music Association*, 111–117. Ann Arbor: University of Michigan Press. http://hdl.handle.net/2027/spo.bbp2372.2007.133.

Ferreira, Becky. 2016. "Joke-Telling Robots Are the Final Frontier of Artificial Intelligence." *Motherboard*, March 15. https://motherboard.vice.com/en_us/article/z43nke/joke-telling-robots-are-the-final-frontier-of-artificial-intelligence.

Feynman, Richard. 1985. *"Surely You're Joking, Mr. Feynman!" Adventures of a Curious Character*. New York: W. W. Norton.

Fiebrink, Rebecca. 2017. "Machine Learning as Meta-instrument: Human-Machine Partnerships Shaping Expressive Instrumental Creation." In *Musical Instruments in the 21st Century: Identities, Configurations, Practices*, edited by Till Bovermann, Alberto de Campo, Hauke Egermann, Sarah-Indriyati Hardjowirogo, and Stefan Weinzierl, 137–151. Singapore: Springer.

Floreano, Dario, Sara Mitri, Stéphanie Magnenat, and Laurent Keller. 2007. "Evolutionary Conditions for the Emergence of Communication in Robots." *Evolutionary Biology* 17 (6): 514–519.

Fulleylove, Rebecca. 2016. "The Italian Ideas Factory: Fabrica through the Eyes of Its Alumni." *It's Nice That*, April 12. https://www.itsnicethat.com/features/fabrica -research-centre-treviso-alumni-120416.

Garcia, Chris. 2015. "Algorithmic Music—David Cope and EMI." Computer History Museum, April 29. http://www.computerhistory.org/atchm/algorithmic-music-david -cope-and-emi/.

Garling, Caleb. 2014. "'Smart' Software Can Be Tricked into Seeing What Isn't There." *MIT Technology Review*, December 24. http://www.evolvingai.org/files/MIT_Tech _Review_Fooling_paper.pdf.

Gaskin, Sam. 2018. "When Art Created by Artificial Intelligence Sells, Who Gets Paid?" *Artsy*, September 17. https://www.artsy.net/article/artsy-editorial-art-created-artificial -intelligence-sells-paid?utm_source=Cultural+Digital&utm_campaign=ebe744856a -culturaldigital138&utm_medium=email&utm_term=0_f5c318bb03-ebe744856a -115208857.

Gatys, Leon, Alexander S. Ecker, and Matthias Bethge. 2016. "Image Style Transfer Using Convolutional Neural Networks." In *Proceedings of the 2016 IEEE Conference on Computer Vision and Pattern Recognition*, 2414–2423. Las Vegas, NV: IEEE. http:// openaccess.thecvf.com/content_cvpr_2016/papers/Gatys_Image_Style_Transfer _CVPR_2016_paper.pdf.

Georgia Tech Center for Music Technology. 2017. "Deep Shimon." Developed by Mason Bretan. YouTube, May 3. https://www.youtube.com/watch?v=j82nYLOnKtM.

Gervás, Pablo. 2000. "WASP: Evaluation of Different Strategies for the Automatic Generation of Spanish Verse." In *Proceedings of the AISB'00 Symposium on Creative and Cultural Aspects and Applications of AI and Cognitive Science*, 93–100. Birmingham, UK: University of Birmingham Press.

Gervás, Pablo. 2002. "Exploring Quantitative Evaluations of the Creativity of Automatic Poets." In *Workshop on Creative Systems, Approaches to Creativity in Artificial Intelligence and Cognitive Science, 15th European Conference on Artificial Intelligence, 2002*, edited by Frank van Hamelen, 39–46. Amsterdam: ISOS Press. http://nil.fdi.ucm.es/ sites/default/files/GervasECAIws2002.pdf.

Gervás, Pablo. 2011. "Dynamic Inspiring Sets for Sustained Novelty in Poetry Generation." In *Proceedings of the Second International Conference on Computational Creativity*, edited by Dan Ventura, Pablo Gervás, D. Fox Harrell, Mary Lou Maher, Alison

Pease, and Geraint Wiggins, 111–116. Mexico City: Division de Ciencias de la Comunicacion y Diseno, Universidad Autonoma Metropolitana, Unidad Cuajimalpa.

Gervás, Pablo, Raquel Hervá, Carlos León, and Catherine V. Gale. 2016. "Annotating Musical Theatre Plots on Narrativeative Structure and Emotional Content." In *Seventh International Workshop on Computational Models*, edited by Ben Miller, Antonio Lieto, Stephan G. Ware, and Mark A. Finlayson, 1–16. Leibniz: Dagstuhl.

Ghedini, Fiammetta, François Pachet, and Pierre Roy. 2015. "Creating Music and Texts in Flow Machines." In *Multdisciplinary Contributions to the Science of Creating Thinking (Creativity in the Twenty-First Century)*, edited by Geovanni Emanuele Corazza and Sergio Agnoli, 325–343. Berlin: Springer.

Ghiselin, Brewster, ed. 1952. *The Creative Process: A Symposium*. New York: New American Library.

Gibney, Elizabeth. 2017. "Self-Taught AI Is Best Yet at Strategy Game Go." *Nature*, October 18. https://www.nature.com/news/self-taught-ai-is-best-yet-at-strategy-game-go-1.22858.

Glass, Philip. 2015. *Words without Music*. London: Faber and Faber Ltd.

Gonthier, George. 2005. "A Computer-Checked Proof of the Four Colour Theorem." http://www2.tcs.ifi.lmu.de/~abel/lehre/WS07-08/CAFR/4colproof.pdf.

Goodfellow, Ian, Jean Pouget-Abadie, Mehdi Mirza, Bing Xu, David Warde-Farley, Sherji Ozair, Aaron Courville, and Yoshua Bongio. 2014. "Generative Adversarial Nets." In *Advances in Neural Information Processing Systems 27 (NIPS 2014)*, edited by Z. Ghahramani, M. Welling, C. Cortes, N. D. Lawrence, and K. Q. Weinberger. https://papers.nips.cc/paper/5423-generative-adversarial-nets.pdf.

Goodwin, Ross. 2016a. "Adventures in Narrated Reality." *Medium*, March 18. https://medium.com/artists-and-machine-intelligence/adventures-in-narrated-reality-6516ff395ba3.

Goodwin, Ross. 2016b. "Adventures in Narrated Reality, Part II." *Medium*, June 9. https://medium.com/artists-and-machine-intelligence/adventures-in-narrated-reality-part-ii-dc585af054cb.

Goodwin, Ross. 2018. *1 the Road*. With an introduction by Kenric McDowell. Paris: Jean Boîte Editions.

Graziano, Michael S. A. 2013. *Consciousness and the Social Brain*. Oxford: Oxford University Press.

Ha, David, and Douglas Eck. 2017. "A Neural Representation of Sketch Drawings." https://arxiv.org/pdf/1704.03477.pdf.

Hadamard, Jacques. 1954. *An Essay on the Psychology of Invention in the Mathematical Field*. New York: Dover. First published 1945.

Harari, Yuval Noah. 2015. *Homo Deus: A Brief History of Tomorrow*. London: Vintage.

Harmon, Sarah. 2015. "FIGURE8: A Novel System for Generating and Evaluating Figurative Language." In *Proceedings of the Sixth International Conference on Computational Creativity*, edited by Hannu Toivanen, Simon Colton and Dan Ventura, 71–77. Provo, UT: Brigham Young University Press.

Hegarty, John. 2014. *Hagarty on Creativity: There Are No Rules*. London: Thames and Hudson.

Helmholtz, Hermann von. (1891) 1971. *Selected Writings of Hermann von Helmholtz*. Wesleyan, CT: Wesleyan University Press.

Hertzmann, Aaron. 2018. "Can Computers Create Art?" *The Machine as Artist (for the 21st Century)* 7 (2). https://doi.org/10.3390/arts7020018.

Hesse, Christopher. 2017. "Image-to-Image Demo: Interactive Image Translation with pix2pix-tensorflow." Affinelayer.com, February 19. https://affinelayer.com/pixsrv/.

Heyman, Stephan. 2015. "How Computing Can Help Art Historians." *New York Times*, July 15. https://www.nytimes.com/2015/07/16/arts/international/how-computing-can-help-art-historians.html.

Higginbotham, Adam. 2012. "Welcome to Rosalind Picard's Touchy-Feely World of Emphatic Tech." *Wired*, November 27. https://www.wired.co.uk/article/emotion-machines.

Highfield, Roger, and Paul Carter. 1993. *The Private Lives of Albert Einstein*. London: Faber and Faber.

Hildescheimer, Wolfgang. 1983. *Mozart*. New York: Vintage Books.

Hochreiter, Sepp, and Jürgen Schmidhuber. 1997. "Long Short-Term Memory." *Neural Computation* 9 (8): 1735–1780.

Hofstadter, Douglas. 1979. *Gödel, Escher, Bach: An Eternal Golden Braid*. New York: Basic Books.

Hofstadter, Douglas. 2009. "Essay in the Style of Douglas Hofstadter." *AI Magazine* 30 (3): 82–88.

Holmes, Edward, 1845. *The Life of Mozart: Including His Correspondence*. London: Chapman and Hall.

Holmes, Kevin. 2011. "Meet 'Paul' and 'Pete,' the Sketching Robots." *Vice*, June 21. https://creators.vice.com/en_uk/article/78wmve/meet-paul-and-pete-the-sketching-robots-2.

Horng, Eric. 2010. "Northwestern Prof Defends Federally Funded Humor Grant." ABC News, September 2. http://abc7chicago.com/archive/7647039/.

Huang, Cheng-Zhi Anna, Tim Cooijmans, Adam Roberts, Aaron Courville, and Douglas Eck. 2017. "Counterpoint by Convolution." In *ISMIR Proceedings 2017*, edited by Xiao Hu, Sally Jo Cunningham, Doug Turnbull and Zhiyao Duan, 211–218. Suzhou, China: International Society for Music Information Retrieval. https://ismir2017.smcnus.org/wp-content/uploads/2017/10/187_Paper.pdf.

Huang, Cheng-Zhi Anna, Ian Simon, and Monica Dinculescu. 2018. "Music Transformer: Generating Music with Long-Term Structure." *Magenta* (blog), December 13. https://magenta.tensorflow.org/music-transformer.

Huang, Cheng-Zhi Anna, Ashish Vaswani, Jakob Uszkoreit, Noam Shazeer, Ian Simon, Curtis Hawthorne, Andrew M. Dai, Matthew D. Hoffman, Monica Dinculescu, and Douglas Eck. 2019. "Music Transformer: Generating Music with Long-Term Structure." https://openreview.net/pdf?id=rJe4ShAcF7. Published as a conference paper at ICLR 2019.

Isaacson, Walter. 2011. *Steve Jobs*. London: Little, Brown.

Isaacson, Walter. 2014. *The Innovators*. New York: Simon and Schuster.

Isola, Phillip, Jun-Yan Zhu, Tinghui Zhou, and Alexei A. Efros. 2017. "Image-to-Image Translation with Conditional Adversarial Networks." In *Proceedings of the 2017 Conference on Computer Vision and Pattern Recognition*, edited by Xiao Hu, Sally Jo Cunningham, Doug Turnbull, and Zhiyao Duan, 5967–5976. https://arxiv.org/pdf/1611.07004.pdf.

Jennings, Ken. 2011. "My Puny Human Brain." *Slate*, February 16. http://www.slate.com/articles/arts/culturebox/2011/02/my_puny_human_brain.html.

John-Steiner, Vera. 2000. *Creative Collaboration*. Oxford: Oxford University Press.

Jordanous, Anna. 2011. "Evaluating Evaluation: Assessing Progress in Computational Research." In *Proceedings of the Second International Conference on Computational Creativity*, edited by Dan Ventura, Pablo Gervás, D. Fox Harrell, Mary Lou Maher, Alison Pease, and Geraint Wiggins, 102–107. Mexico City: Division de Ciencias de la Comunicacion y Diseno, Universidad Autonoma Metropolitana, Unidad Cuajimalpa.

Jordanous, Anna, and Bill Keller. 2016. "Modelling Creativity: Identifying Components through a Corpus-Based Approach." *PLoS ONE*, 11 (10): 1–27.

Kasparov, Garry. 1996. "The Day that I Sensed a New Kind of Intelligence." *Time*, March 25. http://content.time.com/time/subscriber/article/0,33009,984305-1,00.html.

Kasparov, Garry. 2010. "The Chess Master and the Computer." *New York Review of Books*, February 11. http://www.nybooks.com/articles/2010/02/11/the-chess-master-and-the-computer/.

Kasparov, Garry. 2018. "Chess, a *Drosophila* of Reasoning." *Science* 362 (6419): 1087. http://science.sciencemag.org/content/362/6419/1087.

Kennedy Center. 2016. "MacArthur Foundation: Jason Moran, George Lewis—Millenium Stage." YouTube, October 2. https://www.youtube.com/watch?v=Mn3M2JLQOts.

Klingemann, Mario. 2017a. "Alternative Face." YouTube, February 4. https://www.youtube.com/watch?v=af_9LXhcebY.

Klingemann, Mario. 2017b. "Machimaginarium." Vimeo, May 16. https://vimeo.com/217699101.

Knapton, Sarah. 2017. "AlphaGo Zero: Google DeepMind Supercomputer Learns 3,000 Years of Human Intelligence in 40 Days." *Telegraph*, October 18. https://www.telegraph.co.uk/science/2017/10/18/alphago-zero-google-deepmind-supercomputer-learns-3000-years/.

Knight, Will. 2017. "35 Innovators Under 35, Inventors: Ian Goodfellow." *MIT Technology Review*. https://www.technologyreview.com/lists/innovators-under-35/2017/inventor/ian-goodfellow/.

Kobie, Nicole. 2017. "Can an AI Make You Laugh Out Loud?" *Alphr*, September 8. http://www.alphr.com/artificial-intelligence/1006967/can-an-ai-make-you-laugh-out-loud.

Kogan, Gene. 2015. "Experiments with Style Transfer." http://genekogan.com/works/style-transfer/.

Kogan, Gene. 2018. "Pix2Pix." http://ml4a.github.io/guides/Pix2Pix/.

Kuenzli, Rudolf E., and Francis M. Naumann, eds. 1989. *Marcel Duchamp, Artist of the Century*. Cambridge, MA: MIT Press.

Kurzweil, Ray. (2005) 2016. *The Singularity Is Near: When Humans Transcend Biology*. London: Gerald Duckworth and Co.

La Grange, Henry-Louis de, and Günther Weiss. 1995. *Gustav Mahler: Letters to His Wife*. In collaboration with Knud Martner. Berlin: Wolf Jobst Siedler Verlag GmbH.

Langley, Pat, Herbert Simon, Gary L. Bradshaw, and Jan M. Zytkow. 1987. *Scientific Discovery: Computational Explorations of the Creative Processes*. Cambridge, MA: MIT Press.

Lawson, Mark. 2009. "This Artificially Intelligent Music May Speak to Our Minds, but Not Our Souls." *Guardian*, October 22. https://www.theguardian.com/commentisfree/2009/oct/22/music-computer-compose-copy.

Lee, M. H. 2017. "Go Players Excited about 'More Humanlike' AlphaGoZero." Korea Bizwire, October 19. http://koreabizwire.com/go-players-excited-about-more-humanlike-alphago-zero/98282.

Lehrdahl, Fred, and Ray Jackendoff. 1982. *A Generative Theory of Atonal Music*. Cambridge, MA: MIT Press.

Lehrer, Jonah. 2009. "When Senses Intersect." *Scientific American*, May 12. https://www.scientificamerican.com/article/when-senses-intersect/.

Lewis, George. 2000. "Too Many Notes: Computers, Complexity and Culture in Voyager." *Leonardo Music Journal* 10:33–39.

Lohr, Steve. 2016. "IBM Is Counting on Its Bet on Watson and Paying Big Money for It." *New York Times*, October 17. https://www.nytimes.com/2016/10/17/technology/ibm-is-counting-on-its-bet-on-watson-and-paying-big-money-for-it.html.

Lohr, Steve. 2018. "Is There a Smarter Path to Artificial Intelligence? Some Experts Hope So." *New York Times*, June 20. https://www.nytimes.com/2018/06/20/technology/deep-learning-artificial-intelligence.html.

Luan, Fujun, Sylvain Paris, Eli Shechtman, and Kavita Bala. 2017. "Deep Photo Style Transfer." In *Proceedings of the 2017 Conference on Computer Vision and Pattern Recognition*, edited by Xiao Hu, Sally Jo Cunningham, Doug Turnbull and Zhiyao Duan, 6997–7005. http://openaccess.thecvf.com/content_cvpr_2017/papers/Luan_Deep_Photo_Style_CVPR_2017_paper.pdf.

Luman, Douglas. 2015. "Book Review: #!" *Found Poetry Review*, August 4. http://www.foundpoetryreview.com/blog/book-review-nick-montfort/.

Mandler, George, 1994. "Hypermnesia, Incubation, and Mind-Popping: On Remembering without Really Trying," In *Attention and Performance XV*, edited by C. Umilta and M. Moskovitch, 1–33. Cambridge, MA: MIT Press.

Marshall, Alex. 2018. "A Robot Walks into a Bar. But Can It Do Comedy?" *New York Times*, August 8. https://www.nytimes.com/2018/08/08/arts/ai-comedy-artificial-intelligence-piotr-mirowski.html.

Mastroianni, Brian 2016. "Orchestra Music Created with the Help of Artificial Intelligence."In *CBS News*, September 27. https://www.cbsnews.com/news/orchestra-music-symphonologie-by-artificial-intelligence-human-composers/.

Mateas, M., and Nick Montfort. 2005. "A Box, Darkly: Obfuscation, Weird Languages, and Code Aesthetics." In *Proceedings of the 2005 Digital Arts and Culture Conference*, 144–153. Copenhagen: University of Copenhagen.

McCarthy, John, Marvin L. Minsky, Nathaniel Rochester, and Claude E. Shannon. (1955) 2006. "A Proposal for the Dartmouth Summer Research Project on Artificial Intelligence: August 31, 1955." *AI Magazine* 27 (4): 12–14.

McDonald, Kyle. 2015. "Comparing Artificial Artists." *Medium*, September 1. https://medium.com/@kcimc/comparing-artificial-artists-7d889428fce4.

McDowell, Kenric. 2016. "Music, Art & Machine Intelligence 2016 Conference Proceedings." *Medium*, June 27. https://medium.com/artists-and-machine-intelligence/music-art-machine-intelligence-2016-conference-proceedings-ea376a4e2576.

Merill, Brad. 2014. "It's Happening: Robots May Be the Creative Artists of the Future." MakeUseOf, December 17. https://www.makeuseof.com/tag/happening-robots-may-creative-artists-future/.

Metz, Cade. 2016a. "Google's Artificial Brain Is Pumping out Trippy—and Pricey—Art." *Wired*, February 29. https://www.wired.com/2016/02/googles-artificial-intelligence-gets-first-art-show/.

Metz, Cade. 2016b. "This Is the Cutting Edge of Deep Learning Research." Interview with Yann Lecun. https://www.forbes.com/sites/quora/2016/08/05/this-is-the-cutting-edge-of-deep-learning-research/#37e931e951c8.

Metz, Cade. 2019. "DeepMind Can Now Beat Us at Multiplayer Games, Too," May 30. https://www.nytimes.com/2019/05/30/science/deep-mind-artificial-intelligence.html.

Metz, Rachel. 2017. "Why Google's AI Can Write Beautiful Songs but Still Can't Tell a Joke." *MIT Technology Review*, September 7. https://www.technologyreview.com/s/608777/why-googles-ai-can-write-beautiful-songs-but-still-cant-tell-a-joke/.

Miller, Arthur I. (1981) 1998. *Albert Einstein's Special Theory of Relativity: Emergence (1905) and Early Interpretation (1905–1911)*. Berlin: Springer-Verlag.

Miller, Arthur I. 1986. *Imagery in Scientific Thought: Creating 20th-Century Physics*. Cambridge, MA: MIT Press.

Miller, Arthur I. 1992. "Scientific Creativity: A Comparative Study of Henri Poincaré and Albert Einstein." *Creativity Research Journal* 5 (4): 385–414.

Miller, Arthur I. 1994. "Why Did Poincaré Not Formulate Special Relativity in 1905?" In *Henri Poincaré: Science and Philosophy, International Congress, Nancy, France*, edited by John-Luis Greffe, Gerhard Heinzmann, and Kuno Lorenz, 69–101. Berlin: Akademie Verlag.

Miller, Arthur I. 2000. *Insights of Genius: Imagery and Creativity in Science and Art*. Cambridge, MA: MIT Press.

Miller, Arthur I. 2001. *Einstein, Picasso: Space, Time and the Beauty that Causes Havok*. New York: Basic Books.

Miller, Arthur I. 2002. "Erotica, Aesthetics and Schrödinger's Wave Equation." In *It Must be Beautiful: Great Equations of Modern Science*, edited by Graham Farmelo, 80–101. London: Granta Books.

Miller, Arthur I. 2005. *Empire of the Stars: Friendship, Obsession and Betrayal in the Quest for Black Holes*. London: Abacus.

Miller, Arthur I. 2009. *137: Jung, Pauli and the Pursuit of a Scientific Obsession*. New York: Norton.

Miller, Arthur I. 2012. "Henri Poincaré: The Unlikely Link between Einstein and Picasso." *Guardian*, July 17. https://www.theguardian.com/science/blog/2012/jul/17/henri-poincare-einstein-picasso.

Miller, Arthur I. 2014. *Colliding Worlds: How Cutting-Edge Science Is Redefining Contemporary Art*. New York: W. W. Norton.

Miller, Arthur I. 2015. "Creativity: How Cutting-Edge Science Is Redefining Contemporary Art." Latitude Podcast #1, Latitude Festival, October 28, with Marius Kwimt. https://www.latitudefestival.com/news/listen-latitude-podcast-1.

Miranda, Eduardo. 2014a. "Biocomputer Music." Vimeo, November 10. https://vimeo.com/111409050.

Miranda, Eduardo. 2014b. *Thinking Music: The Inner Workings of a Composer's Mind*. Plymouth, England: University of Plymouth Press.

Miranda, Eduardo, Andrew Adamatzky, and Jeff Jones. 2011. "Sounds Synthesis with Slime Mould of Physarum Polycephalum." *Journal of Bionic Engineering* 8 (2): 107–113.

Mohammad, Saif M., and Peter D. Turney. 2013. "Crowdsourcing a Word-Emotion Association Lexicon." *Computational Intelligence* 29 (3): 436–465.

Montfort, Nick, and Rafael Pérez y Pérez. 2008. "Integrating a Plot Generator and an Automatic Narrator to Create and Tell Stories." In *Proceedings of the International Joint Workshop on Computational Creativity*, edited by Pablo Gervás, Rafael Pérez y Pérez, and Tony Veale, 61–70. Technical Report IT/2008/2 Departamento de Ingeniería del Software e Inteligencia Artificial Universidad Complutense de Madrid. http://computationalcreativity.net/ijwcc08/ijwcc08proceedings.pdf.

Montfort, Nick, Rafael Pérez y Pérez, D. Fox Harrell, and Andrew Campana. 2013. "Slant: A Blackboard System to Generate Plot, Figuration, and Narrative Discourse Aspects of Stories." In *Proceedings of the Fourth International Conference on Computational Creativity*, edited by Mary Lou Maher, Tony Veale, Rob Saunders, and Oliver Brown, 168–175. Sydney, Australia: University of Sydney Press.

Montfort, Nick. 2014. *#!*. Denver, CO: Counterpath.

Montfort, Nick. 2017. *The Truelist*. Denver, CO: Counterpath.

Moravec, Hans. 1988. *Mind Children: The Future of Robot and Human Intelligence*. Cambridge MA: Harvard University Press.

Mordvintsev, Alexander, Mike Tyka, and Christopher Olah. 2015. "Inceptionism: Going Deeper into Neural Networks." *Google AI Blog*, June 17. https://research.googleblog.com/2015/06/inceptionism-going-deeper-into-neural.html.

MusicTechFest. 2015. "MTF London: Rebecca Fiebrink." YouTube, May 12. https://www.youtube.com/watch?v=yc5CL5EoPqg.

Nazim, Sarah. 2018. "'Hello World' Is the First Mainstream Music Album Composed with AI." RX Music, January 15. https://rxmusic.com/editorial/hello-world-is-the -first-mainstream-music-album-composed-with-ai/.

Newell, Allen, and Herbert A. Simon. 1972. *Human Problem Solving*. Upper Saddle River, NJ: Prentice Hall.

Newitz, Annalee. 2016. "Movie Written by AI Algorithm Turns Out to Be Hilarious and Intense." *Ars Technica*, June 9. https://arstechnica.com/gaming/2016/06/an-ai -wrote-this-movie-and-its-strangely-moving/.

Nguyen, Anh, Jason Yosinski, and Jeff Clune. 2015. "Deep Neural Networks Are Easily Fooled: High Confidence Predictions for Unrecognizable Images." In *2015 Conference on Computer Vision and Pattern Recognition*, 427–436. https://www.computer.org/ csdl/proceedings-article/cvpr/2015/07298640/12OmNzvz6IH.

Nguyen, Anh, Alexey Dosovitskiy, Jason Yosinski, Thomas Brox, and Jeff Clune. 2016. "Synthesizing the Preferred Inputs for Neurons in Neural Networks via Deep Generator Networks." In *Proceedings of the Neural Information Processing Systems (NIPS 2016)*, edited by D. D. Lee, M. Sugiyama, U. V. Luxburg, I. Guyon, and R. Garnett, 1–9. http://papers.nips.cc/paper/6519-synthesizing-the-preferred-inpits-for-neurons -in-neural-networks-via-deep-generator-networks.pdf.

Noll, A. Michael. 1970. "Art Ex Machina." *IEEE Journal* 8 (4): 10–14.

Noll, A. Michael. n.d. "Early Years at Bell Labs (1961–1971)." Unpublished. Courtesy of A. Michael Noll.

Nugent, Ciara. 2018. "The Painter behind These Artworks Is an AI Program. Do They Still Count as Art?" *Time*, August 20. http://time.com/5357221/obvious-artificial -intelligence-art/.

Olewitz, Chloe. 2016. "A Japanese AI Program Just Wrote a Short Novel, and It Almost Won a Literary Prize." *Digital Trends*, March 23. https://www.digitaltrends .com/cool-tech/japanese-ai-writes-novel-passes-first-round-nationanl-literary-prize/.

Oore, Sageev. 2016. "Human Learning What WaveNet Learned from Humans." *Magenta* (blog), September 23. https://magenta.tensorflow.org/2016/09/23/learning -music-from-learned-music.

O'Toole, Garson. 2013. "Good Artists Copy; Great Artists Steal." Quote Investigator. https://quoteinvestigator.com/2013/03/06/artists-steal/#note-5574-11.

Pachet, François. 2003. "The Continuator: Musical Interaction with Style." *Journal of New Music Research* 32 (3): 333–341.

Pachet, François. 2011. "Markov Constraints: Steerable Generation of Markov Sequences." *Constraints* 16:148–172. https://link.springer.com/content/pdf/10.1007/ s10601-010-9101-4.pdf.

Pachet, François. 2015. "Flow-Machines: CP Techniques to Model Style in Music and Text." Association for Constraint Programming. https://www.a4cp.org/node/1066.

Papadopoulos, A., Pierre Roy, and François Pachet. 2016. "Assisted Lead Sheet Composition Using FlowComposer." In *Proceedings of the 22nd International Conference on Principles and Practice of Constraint Programming—CP, Toulouse, France, September 2016*, edited by Michael Rueher, 769–785. Berlin: Springer.

Parrish, Allison. 2015. "Exploring (Semantic) Space with (Literal) Robots." Open Transcripts, June 3. http://opentranscripts.org/transcript/semantic-space-literal-robots/.

Parrish, Allison. 2018a. *Articulations*. New York: Counterpath Press.

Parrish, Allison. 2018b. "Articulations: A Fragment Fragment Fragment." *Adjacent*, June 15. https://itp.nyu.edu/adjacent/issue-3/articulations-a-fragment-fragment-fragment/.

Patch, Nick. 2016. "Algorithm and Blues: Putting a Google Written Song to the Test." https://www.thestar.com/entertainment/music/2016/08/14/algorithm-and-blues-putting-a-google-written-song-to-the-test.html.

Pathak, Deepak, Philipp Krähenbühl, Jeff Donahue, Trevor Darrell, and Alexei A. Efros. 2016. "Context Encoders: Feature Learning by Inpainting." In *2016 IEEE Conference on Computer Vision and Pattern Recognition*, 2636–2544. Las Vegas, Nevada: IEEE. https://www.cv-foundation.org/openaccess/content_cvpr_2016/papers/Pathak_Context_Encoders_Feature_CVPR_2016_paper.pdf.

Pease, Alison, and Simon Colton. 2011. "Computational Creativity Theory: Inspirations behind the FACE and the IDEA Models." In *Proceedings of the Second International Conference on Computational Creativity*, edited by Dan Ventura, Pablo Gervás. D. Fox, Mary Lou Maher, Alison Pease and Geraint Wiggins, 72–77. Mexico City: Division de Ciencias de la Comunicacion y Diseno, Universidad Autonoma Metropolitana, Unidad Cuajimalpa https://pdfs.semanticscholar.org/04b7/27fb2aa0e10eabc89890700dbf5b9ea30028.pdf.

Pérez y Pérez, Rafael. 2017. *MEXICA: 20 Years–20 Stories (20 AÑOS–20 HISTORIAS)*. Denver, CO: Counterpath Press.

Perloff, Marjorie. 2010. *Unoriginal Genius: Poetry by Other Means in the New Century*. Chicago: University of Chicago Press.

Picard, Rosalind. (1997) 2000. *Affective Computing*. Cambridge, MA: MIT Press.

Picard, Rosalind. 2010. "Affective Computer: From Laughter to IEEE." *IEEE Transactions on Affective Computing* 1 (1): 11–17.

Poincaré, Henri. 1908a. "L'invention mathématique" [Mathematical discovery]. In *La science et méthode* [Science and Method], 43–63. Paris: Flammarion.

Poincaré, Henri. 1908b. "Les définitions mathématiques et l'enseignement" [Mathematical definitions and education]. In *La science et méthode* [Science and Method], 123–151. Paris: Flammarion.

Preston, Elizabeth. 2015. "How Machines Write Poetry." *Motherboard*, December 15. https://motherboard.vice.com/en_us/article/ezpdb7/how-machines-write-poetry.

Radford, Alex, Luke Metz, and Soumith Chintala. 2016. "Unsupervised Representation Learning with Deep Convolutional Generative Adversarial Networks." https://arxiv.org/pdf/1511.06434.pdf.

Rea, Naomi. 2018. "AI-Generated Art Just Got Its First Mainstream Gallery Show. See It Here—and Get Ready." Artnet News, August 29. https://news.artnet.com/exhibitions/ai-generated-art-gallery-show-1339445.

Ridler, Anna. 2017. "The House of Usher." Vimeo, May 16. https://vimeo.com/217670143.

Ritchie, Graeme. 2007. "Some Empirical Criteria for Attributing Creativity to a Computer Program." *Minds and Machines* 17 (1): 67–99.

Ritchie, Graeme. 2009. "Can Computers Create Humor?" *AI Magazine* 30 (3): 71–80.

Roberts, Sioban. 2015. *Genius at Play: The Curious Mind of John Horton Conway*. London: Bloomsbury Publishing Plc.

Robinson, Ken. 2015. "Creativity Is in Everything: Especially Teaching." KQED News, MindShift, April 22. https://www.kqed.org/mindshift/40217/sir-ken-robinson-creativity-is-in-everything-especially-teaching.

Rumelhart, David E., James L. McClelland, and the PDP Research Group. 1986. *Parallel Distributed Processing: Explorations in the Microstructure of Cognition, Volume 1: Foundations*. Cambridge, MA: MIT Press.

Safi, Michael. 2016. "Like a Beautiful Painting: Image of New Year's Mayhem in Manchester Goes Viral." *Guardian*, January 2. https://www.theguardian.com/uk-news/2016/jan/03/like-a-beautiful-painting-image-of-new-years-mayhem-in-manchester-goes-viral.

Sample, Ian. 2017. "'It's Able to Create Knowledge Itself': Google Unveils AI That Learns on Its Own." *Guardian*, October 18. https://www.theguardian.com/science/2017/oct/18/its-able-to-create-knowledge-itself-google-unveils-ai-learns-all-on-its-own.

Sbai, Othman, Mohamed Elhoseiny, Antoine Bordes, Yann LeCun, and Camille Couprie. 2018. "DesIGN: Design Inspiration from Generative Networks." https://research.fb.com/wp-content/uploads/2018/04/design-design-inspiration-from-generative-networks.pdf.

Schering, Arnold. 1912. *Bach-Jahrbuch, 1912*. Leipzig: Breitkopf and Härtel.

Schneider, Tim, and Naomi Rea. 2018. "Has Artificial Intelligence Given Us the Next Great Art Movement? Experts Say Slow Down, the 'Field Is in Its Infancy.'" Artnet News, September 25. https://news.artnet.com/art-world/ai-art-comes-to-market-is-it-worth-the-hype-1352011.

Searle, John. 1980. "Minds, Brains and Programs." *Behavioral and Brain Sciences* 3 (3): 417–424.

Searle, John. 2002. *Consciousness and Language.* Cambridge: Cambridge University Press.

Shahaf, Dafna, Eric Horvitz, and Robert Mankoff. 2015. "Inside Jokes: Identifying Humorous Cartoon Captions." In *Proceedings of the 21st ACM SIGKDD International Conference on Knowledge Discovery and Data Mining*, 1065–1074. Sydney, NSW, Australia: ACM. https://www.microsoft.com/en-us/research/wp-content/uploads/2016/11/phumor.pdf.

Shanahan, Murray. 2010. *Embodiment and the Inner Life: Cognition and Consciousness in the Space of Possible Minds.* Oxford: Oxford University Press.

Shanahan, Murray, Antonia Creswell, David Barrett, Kyriacos Nikiforou, Christos Kaplanis, and Marta Garnelo. 2019. "An Explicitly Relational Neural Network Architecture," May 24. https://arxiv.org/pdf/1905.10307v1.pdf.

Simon, Herbert. 1988. "Creativity and Motivation: A Response to Csikszentmihalyi." *New Ideas in Psychology* 6:177–181.

Simon, Ian, and Sageev Oore. 2017. "Performance RNN: Generating Music with Expressive Timing and Dynamics." *Magenta* (blog), June 29. https://magenta.tensorflow.org/performance-rnn.

Simonton, Dean. 2017. "Big-C versus Little-c Creativity: Definitions, Implications, and Inherent Educational Contradictions." In *Creative Contradictions in Education, Creativity Theory and Action in Education 1*, edited by R. A. Beghetto and B. Sriraman, 3–19. Basel, Switzerland: Springer International Publishing. https://static1.squarespace.com/static/52d6f16be4b0770a479dfb9c/t/580e30a13e00be470f93e7c4/1477324962037/CreativeContradictions+%28sample+chapter+_+Chp+1%29.pdf.

Simonton, Dean. 2018. *The Genius Checklist: Nine Paradoxical Tips on How You Can Become a Creative Genius.* Cambridge, MA: MIT Press.

Singh, Divya, Margareta Ackerman, and Rafael Pérez y Pérez. 2017. "A Ballad of Mexicas: Automated Lyrical Writing." In *Proceedings of the Eighth International Congress on Computational Creativity*, edited by Ashok Goel, Anna Jordanous, and Alison Pease, 229–236. Atlanta: Georgia Institute of Technology Press. http://computationalcreativity.net/iccc2017/iccc17_proceedings.pdf.

Smith, David. 2013. "Scroogled: Google Poaches Top Microsoft Engineer Blaise Agüera y Arcas." *International Business Times*, December 16. http://www.ibtimes.com/scroogled-google-poaches-top-microsoft-engineer-blaise-aguera-y-arcas-1510816.

Solovine, Maurice. 1956. *Albert Einstein: Lettres à Maurice Solovine.* Paris: Gauthier-Villars.

Stanley, Kenneth O. 2017. "Neuroevolution: A Different Kind of Deep Learning." *O'Reilly*, July 13. https://www.oreilly.com/ideas/neuroevolution-a-different-kind-of-deep-learning.

Sterling, Bruce. 2016. "Tech Art: Welcome to Magenta." *Wired*, June 2. https://www .wired.com/beyond-the-beyond/2016/06/tech-art-welcome-magenta/.

Stock, Oliviero, and Carlo Strapparava. 2003. "Getting Serious about the Development of Computational Humor." In *Proceedings of the Eighteenth International Joint Conference on Artificial Intelligence*, edited by Georg Gottlob and Toby Walsh, 59–64. Burlington, MA: Morgan Kaufmann.

Stock, Oliviero, and Carlo Strapparava. 2006. "Laughing with HAHAcronym, a Computational Humor System." In *AAAI'06 Proceedings of the 21st National Conference on Artificial Intelligence*, edited by Anthony Cohen, 1675–1678. Cambridge, MA: AAAI Press. https://www.aaai.org/Papers/AAAI/2006/AAAI06-278.pdf.

Stocker, Gerfried, Christine Schöpf, and Hannes Leopoldseder, eds. 2017. *AI: Artificial Intelligence: The Other I.* Berlin: Hatje Cantz Verlag MBH.

Sturm, Bob L. 2017. "The Drunken Pint, a folk-rnn Original." *High Noon GMT* (blog), February 18. https://highnoongmt.wordpress.com/2017/02/18/the-drunken-pint-a -folk-rnn-original/.

Sturm, Bob L., and Oded Ben-Tal. 2017. "Taking the Models Back to Music Practice: Evaluating Generative Transcription Models Built Using Deep Learning." *Journal of Creative Music Systems* 2 (1): 1–29. https://www.researchgate.net/publication/ 319905403_Taking_the_Models_back_to_Music_Practice_Evaluating_Generative _Transcription_Models_built_using_Deep_Learning.

Sturm, Bob L., Oded Ben-Tal, Úna Monaghan, Nick Collins, Dorien Herremans, Elaine Chew, Gaëtan Hadjeres, Emmanuel Deruty, and François Pachet. 2018. "Machine Learning Research That Matters for Music Creation: A Case Study." *Journal of New Music Research* 48 (1): 36–55. Lancaster: Routledge/Taylor & Francis Online. https://www.tandfonline.com/doi/abs/10.1080/09298215.2018.1515233.

Sturm, Bob L., João Felipe Santos, Oded Ben-Tal, and Iryna Korshunova. 2016. "Music Transcription Modelling and Composition Using Deep Learning." In *Proceedings of the 1st Conference on Computer Simulation of Musical Creativity*, University of Huddersfield, UK, June 17–19. https://drive.google.com/file/d/0B1OooSxEtl0FcTBiOGdvSTBmWnc/ view.

Sullins, John P. 2012. "Robots, Love, and Sex: The Ethics of Building a Love Machine." *IEEE Transactions on Affective Computing* 3 (4): 398–409.

Swafford, Jan. 2014. *Beethoven: Anguish and Triumph.* London: Faber and Faber.

Szegedy, Christian, Wojciech Zaremba, Ilya Sutskever, Joan Bruna, Dumitru Erhan, Ian Goodfellow, and Rob Fergus. 2013. "Intriguing Properties of Neural Networks." Last revised February 19, 2014. https://arxiv.org/pdf/1312.6199.pdf.

Taylor, Julia M., and Lawrence J. Mazlack. 2004. "Computationally Recognizing Wordplay in Jokes." In *Proceedings of the Annual Meeting of the Cognitive Science Society*, vol. 26, edited by Kenneth Forbus, Deirdre Gentner, and Terry Regier, 1315–1320. Mahwah, NJ: Lawrence Erlbaum Associates Inc. https://escholarship.org/uc/item/0v54b9jk.

Tech Events. 2015. "EmTech MIT 2015 Robots among Us: Seeking Creative Machines." YouTube, November 10. https://www.youtube.com/watch?v=7w8x0tU-2i8.

Thiel, Peter. 2014. *Zero to One: Notes on Startups or How to Build the Future.* London: Penguin Random House.

Thoutt, Zack. 2017. "What Are Creative Adversarial Networks (CANs)?" *Hackernoon* (blog), September 25. https://hackernoon.com/what-are-creative-adversarial -networks-cans-bb81d09aa235.

Toulouse, Édouard. 1910. *Henri Poincaré.* Paris: Flammarion.

Tresset, Patrick, and Oliver Deussen. 2014. "Artistically Skilled Embodied Agents." In *Proceedings of the 50th Annual Convention of the AISB.* http://doc.gold.ac.uk/aisb50/ AISB50-S04/AISB50-S4-Tresset-paper.pdf.

Turkle, Shirley. 2018. "There Will Never Be an Age of Artificial Intimacy." *New York Times,* August 11. https://www.nytimes.com/2018/08/11/opinion/there-will-never -be-an-age-of-artificial-intimacy.html.

Ulanoff, Lance. 2014. "Need to Write 5 Million Stories a Week? Robot Reporters to the Rescue." Mashable, July 1. https://mashable.com/2014/07/01/robot-reporters -add-data-to-the-five-ws/#6YRZPuRcagq7.

Vance, Ashlee. 2015. *Elon Musk: How the Billionaire CEO of SpaceX and Tesla Is Shaping Our Future.* London: Virgin Books.

van den Oord, Aäron, Sandor Dieleman, and Heiga Zen. 2016. "WaveNet: A Generative Model for Raw Audio." DeepMind.com, September 8. https://deepmind.com/ blog/wavenet-generative-model-raw-audio/.

van den Oord, Aäron, Sander Dieleman, Heiga Zen, Karen Simonyan, Oriol Vinyals, Alex Graves, Nal Kalchbrenner, Andrew Senior, and Koray Kavukcuogln. 2016. "WaveNet: A Generative Model for Raw Video." https://arxiv.org/pdf/1609.03499.pdf.

Vargas, Jose Antonio. 2010. "The Face of Facebook: Mark Zuckerberg Opens Up." *New Yorker,* September 20. https://www.newyorker.com/magazine/2010/09/20/the -face-of-facebook.

Veale, Tony. 2015. "Game of Tropes: Exploring the Placebo Effect in Computational Creativity." In *Proceedings of the Sixth International Conference on Computational Creativity,* edited by Hannu Tolvonen, Simon Colton, Michael Cook and Dan Ventura, 78–85. Provo, UT: Brigham University Press.

Veale, Tony. 2017. "Déjà Vu All Over Again: On the Creative Value of Familiar Elements in the Telling of Original Tales." In *Proceedings of ICCC 2017, the 8th*

International Conference on Computational Creativity, edited by Ashok Goel, Anna Jordanous, and Alison Pease, 245–252. Atlanta: Georgia Institute of Technology. http://computationalcreativity.net/iccc2017/iccc17_proceedings.pdf.

Veale, Tony. n.d. "ScealextricSimulator." www.BestofBotWorlds.com.

Voosen, Paul. 2017. "How AI Detectives Are Cracking Open the Black Box of Deep Learning." *Science*, July 6. http://www.sciencemag.org/news/2017/07/how-ai-detectives-are-cracking-open-black-box-deep-learning.

Wallas, Graham. 1926. *The Art of Thought.* London: Jonathan Cape.

Walshe, Jennifer. 2014. "Aisteach: The Avant-Garde Archive of Ireland." http://www.aisteach.org/.

Weinberg, Gil. 2015. "Professor Gil Weinberg: 'Robotic Musicianship at Georgia Tech.'" Talks at Google. YouTube, March 25. https://www.youtube.com/watch?v=v5eUo2R_Lrc.

Weisberg, Robert W. 2006. "Modes of Expertise in Creative Thinking: Evidence from Case Studies." In *Cambridge Handbook of Expertise and Expert Performance*, edited by K. A. Ericsson, N. Charness, P. Feltovich, and R. R. Hoffman, 761–787. Cambridge: Cambridge University Press.

Weizenbaum, Joseph. 1976. *Computer Power and Human Reason, From Judgment to Calculation.* New York: W. H. Freeman.

Wiggins, Geraint. 2012. "The Mind's Chorus: Creativity before Consciousness." *Cognitive Computation* 4 (September): 306–319.

Wilson, Chris. 2010. "I'll Be Bach: A Computer Programme Is Writing Great, Original Works of Classical Music. Will Human Composers Soon Be Obsolete?" *Slate*, May 19. http://www.slate.com/articles/arts/music_box/2010/05/ill_be_bach.html.

Wotiz, J. H., and Susanna F. Rudofsky. 1954. "Kekulé's Dreams: Fact or Fiction." *Chemistry in Britain* 20:720–723.

Zhu, Jun-Yan. 2017. "CycleGAN." GitHub. https://github.com/junyanz/CycleGAN.

Zhu, Jun-Yan, Taesung Park, Phillip Isola, and Alexei Efros. 2017. "Unpaired Image-to-Image Translation Using Cycle-Consistent Adversarial Networks." In *Proceedings of the 2017 IEEE International Conference on Computer Vision*, 2242–2251. http://openaccess.thecvf.com/content_ICCV_2017/papers/Zhu_Unpaired_Image-To-Image_Translation_ICCV_2017_paper.pdf.

Index